1992

Homer's Ancient Readers

*

MAGIE CLASSICAL PUBLICATIONS

Homer's Ancient Readers

THE HERMENEUTICS OF GREEK EPIC'S EARLIEST EXEGETES

*

edited by

ROBERT LAMBERTON
AND
JOHN J. KEANEY

PRINCETON UNIVERSITY PRESS

PRINCETON, NEW JERSEY

Library of Congress Cataloging-in-Publication Data

Homer's ancient readers : the hermeneutics of Greek epics earliest
exegetes / edited by Robert Lamberton and John J. Keaney.
p. cm. — (Magie classical publications)
Papers delivered in somewhat different form at a conference held
at Princeton University, Oct. 6–7, 1989.
Includes bibliographical references and index.
1. Homer—Appreciation—Greece—Congresses. 2. Homer—Criticism
and interpretation—History—Congresses. 3. Epic poetry, Greek—
History and criticism—Theory, etc.—Congresses. 4. Authors and
readers—Greece—History—Congresses. I. Lamberton, Robert.
II. Keaney, John J. III. Series.
PA4037.H775 1992
ISBN 0-691-06934-4
883'.01—dc20 91-26215 CIP

Publication of this book has been supported by a grant from the
David Magie '97 Publication Fund of the Department of Classics
of Princeton University

This book has been composed in Linotron Bembo

The jacket illustration and emblem, *Reading Sphinx*, was drawn
by Richard Anderson from photographs of a plaster cast of a
carnelian scarab, once in the collection of the art historian Paul
Arndt but now impossible to locate. The scarab is said to have
come from Greece, though it is not Attic, and has been dated on
the basis of comparanda to ca. 460 B.C. The juxtaposition of the
fabulous creature with the written text constitutes a unique
ancient representation of the enigmatic reader.

∗ Contents ∗

* Introduction *

ROBERT LAMBERTON

THE HISTORY of the influence of Homer has been studied in a variety of ways, but the history of the meaning of the text, of its interaction with perhaps a hundred generations of readers, has yet to be written.[1] The seven papers in this collection all contribute in one way or another to the project of that second history.

This is not to say that this project is without precedents. Some of the questions addressed here are not unfamiliar in the realm of the history of classical scholarship. There are, however, several points of difference between the way they are treated here and the way they have been treated in the past, notably by Rudolf Pfeiffer.[2] The philological tradition Pfeiffer traced, and in which he situated himself, is based on a methodology that is in part explicit and in part implicit and largely unexamined. Its approach to the problem of meaning is deeply reductionist, as practical scientific inquiry tends to be. The meaning of a text is, for this tradition, largely a matter of the meanings of words and the syntax of sentences. The first category of information is dealt with by lexicographers, the second by grammarians. Once the reader knows the meanings of the words and understands the syntax of the sentence, that sentence has yielded its meaning. This is not to say that the philological tradition has denied the

[1] For the ancient reception of Homer, even general discussion of the influence of the epics is lacking, though admittedly the task would be so enormous that it would require writing a history of Greek and Latin literature from the perspective of Homeric influence. Among studies of specific periods, tremendously valuable is Jan Fredrik Kindstrand, *Homer in der zweiten Sophistik*. The history of the modern reception of Homer was surveyed by Georg Finsler, *Homer in der Neuzeit von Dante bis Goethe*, and numerous more limited studies have refined and improved his general picture. Exemplary among these are the two studies by Noémi Hepp, "Homère en France au xviᵉ siècle" and *Homère en France au xviiᵉ siècle*, and Kirsti Simonsuuri's *Homer's Original Genius: Eighteenth-Century Notions of the Early Greek Epic*. Several studies that have emphasized the diversity of the readings of Homer that come down to us. Howard Clarke (*Homer's Readers: A Historical Introduction to the Iliad and Odyssey*) surveys critical evaluation of the two poems from antiquity to the twentieth century. A few studies, notably George deF. Lord's *Homeric Renaissance*, explore the influence of specific readings—in this case, the influence of the allegorists on Chapman. In an ancient context, an interesting study of the interaction of interpretation and creation is to be found in Robin R. Schlunk, *The Homeric Scholia and the Aeneid*.

[2] Rudolph Pfeiffer, *History of Classical Scholarship From the Beginnings to the End of the Hellenistic Age* and *History of Classical Scholarship From 1300 to 1850*.

existence of any larger contexts relevant to the understanding of texts. Once the text has been read on the level already described, it can be situated in a historical context (consisting largely of other texts, perhaps supplemented by archaeological information), and it can throw light on the thought of its author and on the history and values of his or her culture.

There is certainly nothing intrinsically mistaken about this approach. With its long and august history, it can credibly be traced back in some of its aspects to the philological inquiries of Aristotle. But it is easily confused with something that it emphatically is *not*, that is, a straightforward systematization—an elevation to the level of a science—of the acts of ordinary readers. In fact, the philological tradition has chosen largely to ignore the real and acute problems of reading and interpretation that all readers confront every day. The vast majority of readers are dealing with texts in their own mother tongues, the vocabulary and syntax of which are burned into their nervous systems at a very deep level. They ask questions of texts that are very rarely the questions raised by the philological tradition. They pose problems of meaning in ways that differ fundamentally from those posed by philologists.

Each of the papers in this collection sets out to engage this problem, which the mainstream of scholarship has skirted. How did ancient readers deal with the *Iliad* and *Odyssey*, the authoritative texts standing at the beginning of Greek tradition? What demands did they make on them? To what questions did they expect them to be able to yield answers? These lines of inquiry promise to throw light on two separate but related issues. First, they clarify the position of the *Iliad* and *Odyssey* in the intellectual world of antiquity—a first chapter, so to speak, in a history of the meaning of those poems that remains to be completed. Second, these essays throw light on the nature of reading itself and as such constitute a chapter in the history of reading.

Only a small category of readers record their efforts, and not all of these do so in the form of explicit essays in interpretation or explicit claims about the meaning of texts. There is a much larger class of "readings" of Homer that reach us in the indirect form of rewritings, adaptations, and other modes of recycling Homeric material into new art. Indeed, this process starts so early in the case of Homer that we are at a loss to draw clear lines of demarcation between the "Homeric" and the "Posthomeric"—the better term might be "Homeristic." Compositions such as the *Hymns*, the minor epics, and even the iambic *Margites* must have attached themselves to the name of the poet very early. Not only Homeric myth and Homeric diction, but the very Homeric poetic identity, for all its recalcitrant anonymity—the Homeric persona—was available for appropriation at such an early date that it would be presumptuous to imagine that we know the text of any Homeric poem in a stage that predates that of the earliest imitators and adaptors. The complexity of the interaction of archaic Greek poetic traditions is extraordinary,[3] but what is most certain is that the *Iliad* and the *Odyssey* and their satellites constitute a pervasive presence throughout those traditions, constantly interacting with new poetic developments, constantly reread and adapted to new contexts. And of course the process continues beyond the archaic period, by way of those famous "chops (τεμάχη) from Homer's banquets" that Aeschylus[4] served up on the Athenian stage, down through Apollonius Rhodius, Virgil, and beyond.

I mention this here, simply to indicate why the present collection of essays is of necessity limited to the discussion of the relatively manageable category of recoverable interpretive efforts of an explicit nature. The history of the interpretive rewriting and adaptation of the Homeric epics is roughly coextensive with the history of Greek and then Latin literature and does not stop there. No essay is found here on Pindar,[5] on the dramatists, on Apollonius Rhodius or Virgil, not because the contribution of those readers of Homer was unimportant in the evolution of the understanding of the epics, but because it was of a different nature from the contributions of interpreters who offered their acts of interpretation as ends in themselves (ends subordinated, of course, to the larger goal of the understanding of Homer) and not as a function of the creation of new works of literature.

There are in fact surprisingly few readings of Homer preserved from antiquity. If we compare, for instance, Judaic tradition with Hellenic, the difference is immediately apparent—on the one hand, an entire literature of exegesis and commentary on authoritative archaic texts; on the other, what we might call a reticence about interpretation. As Charles Segal's introductory paper makes clear, however, a concern with the nature of audience response—the "reading" of the listeners that the poems project as audience for heroic song—is to be traced to the epics themselves. The

---

[3] The analysis of the phenomenon has taken numerous forms, ranging from the statistical (Richard Janko, *Homer, Hesiod, and the Hymns*) to the evocation of patterns of intertextual influence and competition (Piero Pucci, *Hesiod and the Language of Poetry* and *Odysseus Polutropos: Intertextual Readings in the Odyssey and Iliad*).

[4] By his own account, according to Athenaeus 8 347e.

[5] Gregory Nagy has recently brought new sophistication to the study of Pindar's appropriation of Homer in *Pindar's Homer*.

history of the interpretation of the poems begins within the poems, and these earliest monuments in European literature have been interacting with ideas about their meaning for millennia.

Nevertheless, among the Greeks, the interpretation of literary texts remained a subliterary activity until a relatively late date, or so the preserved body of texts would lead us to believe. The small number of exceptions, such as the Derveni papyrus,[6] and the discussion of the meaning of a poem of Simonides in Plato's *Protagoras* (343–48), provide sufficient indication, however, that the interrogation of poetic texts and the formulation of competing claims about their meaning were very much a part of the intellectual life of the Greeks of the classical period. That passage in the *Protagoras* along with one in the *Republic* in which Socrates rejects the educational use of the Homeric poems "whether they're allegorical or not" (οὔτ᾽ ἐν ὑπονοίαις πεποιημένας, οὔτε ἄνευ ὑπονοιῶν 378d) have generally been cited as the basis for a claim that Plato was hostile to interpretation in general and to allegorical interpretation in particular.[7]

Plato's position in the larger history of the interpretation of the *Iliad* and *Odyssey* remains problematic in spite of his overall hostility to the interpretation of poetry.[8] In one of its aspects, that hostility is perhaps inevitable, given the very nature of the Socratic enterprise as Plato presents it. The same passage in the *Protagoras* mentioned above (343–48) is the *locus classicus*.[9] There we are presented with a Socrates who rejects the discussion of the meaning of poetic texts on the basis that there is no elenchus, no viable procedure of testing and refutation, of individuals' claims about such questions. The corollary to this observation is that the interrogation of poetic texts is not a promising path to the truth, so that poetry joins etymology and the other discredited areas of inquiry set aside one after another in Socrates' epistemological quest. The cost of this inevitable rejection is relatively easy for Socrates to bear—clearly one of the many paradoxes Plato weaves into the portrait of his teacher. It would have seemed a very high price to most of his contemporaries.

[6] This fourth-century papyrus recovered from a Macedonian tomb in 1962, containing eighteen lines of Orphic hexameter poetry in a matrix of largely allegorical interpretation, is still not adequately published. See S. G. Kapsomenos, "The Orphic Papyrus Roll of Thessalonica," along with the unauthorized anonymous publication "Der orphische Papyrus von Derveni," and comment in M. L. West, *The Orphic Poems*, 68–113.

[7] See the important articles of J. Tate, "Plato and Allegorical Interpretation" and "On the History of Allegorism."

[8] This matter is evoked very briefly below, 35–36 and 115, and treated at greater length by Paul Vicaire, *Platon, critique littéraire*, esp. 81–103, where the texts relevant to the question "comment Platon jugeait Homère" are assembled.

[9] See my *Homer the Theologian*, 300.

Although it is manifestly not part of his program to offer a reading of Homer, Plato is the first author in whom we find an examination of the paradox of reading, coupled with a detailed critique of the epic tradition that extends from the level of an ontological esthetics, by way of theology, to pedagogy. Needless to say, the *Iliad* and *Odyssey* are found wanting on all levels, and it is left to the subsequent generation—that is, to Aristotle—to redefine the terms on which the esthetic object, and specifically the poetic text, may be recovered as a worthy object of philosophical inquiry.

Thus the contribution of Nicholas Richardson to this volume, "Aristotle's Reading of Homer and its Background," has by its very nature a vast, perhaps an impossibly vast, task to perform. It must bridge the gap between the audiences projected in the poems themselves and readers of the third quarter of the fourth century. But although Aristotelian tradition itself claimed that the first critic of Homer was his rival Sagaris, succeeded after Homer's death by Xenophanes of Colophon,[10] and the less extravagant tradition that reached Porphyry made Theagenes of Rhegium, whom we can date around 525, the "first to write on Homer,"[11] Aristotle remains the earliest author to devote to the explication of Homer a book of which we possess significant fragments. Because this book of *Homeric Questions* secured for Aristotle his place at the head of the tradition of Homer's readers, as here defined, a look at just what it seems to have contained will be useful.[12] We may also pose at this point the question of the continuity that has been claimed between the Homeric researches of Aristotle and those of the scholars of the Museum in Alexandria, which began a generation or two after his death.[13]

---

[10] Diogenes Laertius 2.46 = Aristotle fr. 75 (Rose), one of the mysterious bits of information assigned to the "third book" of the *Poetics*, but placed by Rose, quite reasonably, with the other fragments of the dialogue Περὶ ποιητῶν. The Sagaris of the mss. is conventionally emended to Syagros, but there seems little to choose between them.

[11] Porphyry, *Quaest. Hom. Il.* (Schrader), 241, 10–11.

[12] The title is variously reported as Ὁμηρικὰ ἀπορήματα, προβλήματα, and ζητήματα, but this confusion of virtual synonyms is frequent in titles of this pattern. The fragments were collected by Valentinus Rose (*Aristotelis qui ferebantur librorum fragmenta*, nos. 142–79). Rose considered the book a Peripatetic compilation (*Aristoteles pseudepigraphus*, 149) and as with other works in the Aristotelian canon, we should not assume that the collection of "Aristotelian" ἀπορήματα was closed at his death. The forty fragments Rose published in *Aristoteles pseudepigraphus* included three (Nos. 20a [145], 30a [156], and 38 [165]) that he chose not to republish in the *Fragmenta*. These are referred to below by reference to *Aristoteles pseudepigraphus*.

[13] The idea of Aristotle as the founder of κριτική and γραμματική is as old as Dio Chrysostom (36.1). For the modern scholars who have embraced this view and asserted the continuity between Aristotle's work on Homer and that of the Alexandrians, see R. Pfeiffer,

The thirty-seven fragments assembled by V. Rose, almost entirely from the scholia, and attributed to the *Homeric Questions* of Aristotle, support the evidence of the title that the book consisted of solutions to a series of difficulties, rather then a continuous analytic essay. The problems are identified as "unreasonable things," "paradoxes," or things "one might be surprised at."[14] Sometimes the scholiast simply tells us that "Aristotle asked" or "was puzzled" at a given problem, and however the difficulty itself may be formulated, we are most frequently told that Aristotle "solved" the problem in a given way.[15] To take a typical example, "Aristotle asks" how Polyphemus came to be born a Cyclops, given that his father was a god and his mother a sea nymph, and "it is solved" from the nature of myth: Comparanda are mustered to show that Boreas fathered horses in myth and Pegasus was born to Poseidon and Medusa (fr. 172). This same pattern of appeal to the mythic as a realm in its own right with its own rules, often at odds with those of the real world, can be found in a crucially important Aristarchan scholion as well, where it clearly serves as an alternative to allegorical explanation of the myth in question.[16] We see already that there is reason to believe that certain fundamental strategies that we find in the Alexandrian tradition of commentary on Homer are solidly Aristotelian.

Aristotle's "reading," then, was composed of a series—perhaps quite a large one—of cruxes requiring solutions. As we shall see, this piecemeal approach characterizes the critical stance of most of the ancient readers of Homer of whom we have any record. Though this approach to the problem of meaning in the epics was clearly the one that prevailed through most of Aristotle's interpretive book, there is nevertheless evidence in our limited sample to indicate that it did not exhaust the range of Aristotle's inquiries.[17] First of all, though the precedent for the Alexandrians' side-

---

History of Classical Scholarship From the Beginnings, 67. Pfeiffer notably rejected this idea and emphasized the originality of the Alexandrian enterprise (88–104).

[14] ἄλογον, fr. 147; ἄτοπον, frs. 146, 152, cf. 159; παράδοξον, fr. 167; θαυμάσαι δ᾽ ἄν τις, fr. 144. In one case, the need for explanation appears to derive from the more conventional appeal to appropriateness: ἀπρεπές, fr. 143, and (rejected) fr. 38 [= 165] from *Aristoteles pseudepigraphus*.

[15] ζητεῖ Ἀριστοτέλης, fr. 172; ἀπόρησεν ὁ Ἀριστοτέλης, frs. 145, 159; λύων or λύει in frs. 149, 152, 160, 161, 164, 166, 170–74. On the subject generally, see A. Gudeman, "Λύσεις."

[16] Schol. D E 385. See below, 70.

[17] Rather surprisingly, Rose's fragments give little indication of attention to specific lexical problems in the *Homeric Questions*, but a fragment from Eustathius that Rose rejected (fr. 20a = 145 in *Aristoteles pseudepigraphus*) claims that Aristotle said regarding the epithet

stepping of the allegorical reading of myth can be found here, it is nevertheless unavoidable that several of the "solutions" attributed to Aristotle are allegorical solutions—that is, they take the form of claims that, although Homer's text superficially says one thing, it is in fact "saying something else."[18] This sort of explanation of problematic passages was certainly not new in Aristotle's time—indeed, it was probably the mainstay of pedagogic explication of Homer in the fifth century[19]—but the interesting thing is that we find it enshrined here in Aristotle's collection of interpretive "solutions."

The most striking instance relates to the oxen of Helios (fr. 175), which scholiasts on the passage report was read "as a physical allegory" (φυσικῶς) by Aristotle. The seven flocks of fifty cattle belonging to the sun were the mythical representation of the 350 (actually 354) solar days of the lunar year. When Eustathius elaborates on this reading, he simply observes that "they say Aristotle read these herds allegorically as the 350 days in the twelve lunar months."[20] This sounds more like the author of the pseudo-Aristotelian treatise "On the Cosmos" than the authentic Aristotle (though this particular bit of lore is not to be found in that work).[21]

κέρᾳ ἀγλαέ (Il. 11.385), κέρᾳ ἀγλαὸν ἀντὶ τοῦ αἰδοίῳ σεμνυνόμενον, going on to observe that Aristotle probably was thinking of the scorpion-tongued Archilochus who used "soft horn" ἀπαλὸν κέρας for "penis" (αἰδοῖον). That there is a metonymy here is certain. "Horn" can mean (according to Hesychius) either "hair," "bow," or "penis." The latter is by far the most attractive meaning in context, and there is no real reason to doubt that the contribution might have been Aristotle's (rather than that of Aristophanes of Byzantium, to whom Rose arbitrarily reassigned it). If it belongs here, it shows at least an early Peripatetic concern with lexical problems of a sort that extend beyond primary senses of words to metaphorical extensions of those primary meanings—a matter well enough attested in the authentic works of Aristotle.

[18] This standard etymology of the verb ἀλληγορέω and its noun ἀλληγορία reminds us that the phenomenon in question is first and foremost a trope of rhetoric, and that the interpretation of allegory, like the interpretation of speech that is ironic or sarcastic, is primarily the articulation of an authorial intention that is veiled and obliquely expressed and therefore deliberately problematic. This is a deliberately generous definition of "allegorical reading," and several attempts at finer distinctions will be found in this collection, notably in A. A. Long's contribution.

[19] See Plato, Rep. 2.378d, and Konrad Müller, "Allegorische Dichtererklärung," col. 17.

[20] ἰστέον δὲ ὅτι τὰς ἀγέλας ταύτας καὶ μάλιστα τὰς τῶν βοῶν φασὶ τὸν Ἀριστοτέλην ἀλληγορεῖν εἰς τὰς κατὰ δωδεκάδα τῶν σεληνιακῶν μηνῶν ἡμέρας. . . . Eustathius 1717 (Aristotle fr. 175, Rose).

[21] There is no doubt that we receive as "Aristotelian" interpretive material from other sources. One of the fragments from Eustathius that Rose rejected—in all probability correctly—attributes to Aristotle a very Stoic-sounding allegory about the nourishment of the

But even if this egregious bit of physical allegory with its strongly Stoic flavor might be an intrusion into the fragmented corpus of Aristotelian readings of Homer, three of the other fragments also relate "solutions" we would call allegorical. Each in fact points to an area where allegorical reading was to predominate in the later tradition. The first relates to the "marvel" (τέρας) revealed to the Greeks at Aulis, and what troubled Aristotle here, we are told, is the fact that although the unremarkable devouring of the nestlings by the snake was duly interpreted as prophetic by Calchas, the truly remarkable transformation of the snake into stone is left without comment. Aristotle provides the missing interpretation: The lithification of the snake represented the "slowness and toughness of the war" (fr. 145).[22] The context demands that this element be a sign, a σημεῖον, and the interpretation offered supplies a glaring omission. In another instance, the description of a supernatural object turns out to be characterized by an unexpected metonymy. Homer speaks of the head of Medusa as residing in Hades (Od. 11.634), but he has already located it in its traditional place on Athena's aegis (Il. 5.741). Aristotle's solution (fr. 153): "She never had the actual head of the Gorgon on her shield, . . . but rather the capacity to stun that emanated from the Gorgon and affected those who looked upon her."[23]

The final Aristotelian allegory is of particular interest, because it turns on a matter of theology, precisely the area in which the allegorical reading of the revered archaic poems had the richest future before it. Aristotle seems to have offered a series of alternative solutions to the problem that Helios in Homer is said at one point to "see and hear all things" (Il. 3.277) but then in the Odyssey, in the episode of the oxen of the sun, requires nymphs to herd and look after his flocks (fr. 149).[24] One solution, accord-

---

gods (= the celestial bodies) by "exhalations" (fr. 30a = 156 in Aristoteles pseudepigraphus, from Eustathius ad Od. 12.62).

[22] The interpretive effort is more complex and interesting than this brief paraphrase indicates, and Aristotle, as often, seems to have been concerned to pry into the motives and the latent dynamics of the interaction of characters. What he interrogates here is Calchas's silence, his failure to interpret what so obviously needs interpretation. Is it that he sees, as others must have, that the lithification of the snake represents the fact that the expedition— or much of it—will never return, will be ἄνοστος? But the brief version boils down to what is evoked above: ἡ δὲ τοῦ δράκοντος ἀπολίθωσις κατὰ μὲν Ἀροστοτέλην τὴν βραδυτῆτα ἐδήλου καὶ τὸ σκληρὸν τοῦ πολέμου (Schol. B 305, from Aristotle fr. 145 [Rose]).

[23] φησὶ δ'Ἀριστοτέλης ὅτι μήποτε ἐν τῇ ἀσπίδι οὐκ αὐτὴν εἶχε τὴν κεφαλὴν τῆς Γόργονος, . . . ἀλλὰ τὸ ἐκ τῆς Γόργονος γιγνόμενον τοῖς ἐνορῶσι πάθος καταπληκτικόν. Schol. B E 741 (= Aristotle fr. 153, Rose).

[24] This particular fragment evokes the genre of "Problems" familiar from Plutarch's

---

ing to Aristotle, is to say "that that which reports—i.e., Lampetia—is to Helios as sight is to a human being."[25] The Homeric theological panoply, far from innocent by Aristotle's time, had endured generations of attacks and defenses, generally allegorical. Nevertheless, this striking claim—that the nymphs who serve Helios are to be read as metaphors for whatever quality it is (analogous to one of our senses) that allows that deity universal perception—is a treatment of that theology that looks forward to developments associated with later Platonism.

But beyond all the "solutions," allegorical and otherwise, Aristotle's *Homeric Questions* seem to have included something else. Aristotle probably did not produce an edition of Homer,[26] but he did sometimes propose alternate readings. When a problem was resolved in this way, the scholiast who reports the only surviving example indicates, this was not a "solution," but something else, a "rewriting" (καὶ λῦσαι μὲν οὐ βεβούληται, μεταγράφει δέ, fr. 171). Specifically, the Homeric epithet αὐδήεσσα (which must mean something like "having the power of speech" but does in fact still pose problems of interpretation) bothered him in several of its applications—for Circe and Calypso, he preferred his own coinage αὐλήεσσα intended to indicate that they lived alone, and for Ino οὐδήεσσα, or "earth-dwelling." His reasoning, as reflected in the scholion, would hardly impress a modern textual critic, and no Aristotelian conjectures or corrections are known to have found favor and entered the received text. It is nevertheless very likely that many such "rewritings" from unknown sources did in fact enter the text. Already, before the work of the Alexandrians, the *Iliad* and *Odyssey* had long been interacting in such ways with scholarly readers' ideas about their meaning, so that the text itself had become inseparable from the history of its meaning.

Aristotle has occupied us at length here because, little though we know of his Homeric labors, the tiny bits preserved give a clear indication both of the sorts of problems that occupied Homeric interpreters in his time and the sorts of solutions they offered. There is a remarkable continuity, both in questions and solutions, from the classical period down to the end of the tradition, and the baggage of interpretive material that the text of

---

Greek and Roman Questions, where a series of solutions is supplied but the author normally offers no final choice among them. It is certainly possible that some of Aristotle's "solutions" took this rather disappointing, inconclusive form.

[25] λύων δ' Ἀριστοτέλης φησί, ὅτι . . . , ἢ ὅτι τῷ ἡλίῳ ἦν τὸ ἐξαγγεῖλαν ἡ Λαμπετία ὥσπερ τῷ ἀνθρώπῳ ἡ ὄψις. . . . Schol. B Γ 277 (= Aristotle fr. 149, Rose).

[26] So R. Pfeiffer (*History of Classical Scholarship From the Beginnings*, 71) believed, almost certainly correctly.

the epics accumulated seems to have grown continuously, such that the periodic compilations produced by scholars such as Aristotle, Porphyry, and Proclus represent attempts not so much to change the history of the interpretation of Homer as to assemble and organize that history.

It is clear, however, that with the rise of the Stoa the status of interpretation changed. The preserved fragments of Zeno and Chrysippus demonstrate that the founders of the Stoa frequently took positions on the meaning of myths, texts, and artifacts. It has long been an article of faith in the orthodoxy of classical scholarship that the Stoics were systematic allegorists of texts and that the rise of allegorism to philosophical (and philological) respectability is to be laid at their door.[27] Several of the papers here assembled lay the groundwork for the reassessment of this bit of received wisdom and throw new light on the status and scope of interpretive activities in the Stoa.

That their adversaries and detractors accused the Stoics of willful misreading and distortion of the meaning of early poetry cannot be disputed. Plato had adopted an adversarial position with regard to the "Homeric encyclopedia" and the Ionian philosophical tradition before him had been actively hostile (with the possible exception of the Pythagoreans). Aristotle certainly did not privilege Homeric accounts of things, except as a function of the age and attendant respectability of those accounts. But Stoics cited the poets often and took at least some utterances of Homer and Hesiod as having truth value.

This use of poetry seems, in fact, to have been a salient characteristic of the Stoa from the start, just the sort of characteristic that appealed, for instance, to Cicero and offered him an opportunity to dramatize vividly just how Stoics were different from other thinkers. He does this to considerable effect in his dialogue *On The Nature of the Gods*, where the Epicurean Velleius leads the attack, accusing Zeno in his own book of similar title of having twisted the meaning of the fables (*fabellae*) of Orpheus, Musaeus, Hesiod, and Homer, "so that even the most ancient poets, who had no idea of these things, would seem to be Stoics" (*De nat. deor.* 1.41).[28] After the Stoic position has been stated by Lucilius Balbus in Book 2, with generous use of etymological analysis of divine names, of citations of poetry, and explanations of the gods of myth as natural forces and phenomena, Cotta, representing the position of the Academy, again attacks the Stoa on now familiar grounds. "The castration of Ouranos by

[27] See R. Pfeiffer, *History of Classical Scholarship From the Beginnings*, 237–38.
[28] This passage is discussed below by A. A. Long, 49–50.

his son and the binding of Kronos by his—you defend these and similar things so that those who fabricated them end up seeming not only not to have been madmen, but even to have been philosophers."[29]

The theme is repeated and elaborated by Plutarch and Galen. Plutarch characterizes the Stoic Cleanthes' manipulation of poetic expressions to turn Zeus into an exhalation as "a game" (παιδιά, De aud. po. 31e),[30] and for Chrysippus's similar claims about poetic epithets, the last major figure of the early Stoa earns the epithet "sticky" (γλίσχρος), perhaps to be expanded to "petty-minded" or "implausible."[31] Chrysippus does not play games, like his predecessor, but "formulates far-fetched accounts carrying no credibility" (εὑρεσιλογῶν ἀπιθάνως). The accusation of willful misreading is only one part of Galen's continuing tirade against Chrysippus. The latter is repeatedly ridiculed for taking seriously popular and nonspecialist opinions and trying to make them into serious science or philosophy[32]—he might have found the truth, had he avoided numerous pitfalls including "the evidence of poets, along with women [!], and other people who know nothing."[33] Best of all, he should have read Plato for a true perspective on myths and not wasted his time "interpreting their allegories" (ἐξηγούμενον αὐτῶν τὰς ὑπονοίας).[34]

Much of what is of value in the Stoa has had to be recovered from the midst of this polyphonic hostile tirade, and the past generation of scholarship on the Stoa has made great advances in doing so. However, for the simple reason that interpretation of the sort called allegorical in antiquity

---

[29] "Exsectum a filio Caelum, vinctum itidem a filio Saturnum, haec et alia generis eiusdem ita defenditis ut ii qui ista finxerunt non modo non insani sed etiam fuisse sapientes videantur." De nat. deor. 3.62.

[30] A. A. Long, below, 62, n. 48, suggests "childishness" or "irony" as possible translations here.

[31] Cf. Plato Cratylus 414c, Republic 488a. Paul Shorey in the Loeb Republic declared the word "untranslatable and often misunderstood." It is fairly commonly used, however, of strained and implausible interpreters.

[32] De plac. Hipp. et Plat. 2.2; vol. 5, 213–14 Kühn.

[33] De plac. Hipp. et Plat. 3.8; vol. 5, 357–58 Kühn: ποιητῶν μαρτυρίας ἅμα γυναιξὶ καὶ τοῖς ἄλλοις ἰδιώταις.

[34] David Armstrong, in his thoughtful and helpful comments on the manuscript for these papers, supplies another vivid example from the Epicurean Diogenianus (second century CE?), who attacks Chrysippus for citing Homer in a misleading way and sums up, "And it is quite in keeping for the poet, who does not promise to tell us the truth about the nature of things, but imitates the experiences and characters and opinions of all sorts of people, to say things that are contradictory, but it is not in keeping for the philosopher either to say contradictory things or for this very reason to use a poet as evidence" (Diogenianus, quoted in Eusebius Preparatio evangelica 6.8.7).

has seemed to most students of the intellectual world of Greece and Rome to have no possible redeeming interest, this is one area where the received opinion regarding the activities of the Stoics has until now gone largely unchallenged. There were enough odd Stoic ideas and arguments that seemed capable of being recovered and redeemed as serious philosophy, without venturing into the morass of the seemingly indefensible hermeneutics that was clearly one of the points their adversaries had always loved most to mock.

With A. A. Long's article in this collection, complemented by James I. Porter's reassessment of Crates of Mallos, a new direction has been suggested in the understanding of the interpretive activities of the Stoics. Careful attention to just what sorts of interpretive moves are actually documented for the Stoa leads Long to question whether in fact the parodic picture we get from some passages in Cicero and from Plutarch and Galen is not more diatribe than description. That Stoics found meaning in phenomena, including the names and epithets of the gods, the objects of cult, myths, and sometimes the poetic texts that embodied those myths, seems clear, but in fact the same could be said of intellectually respectable people in many cultures. What Long calls in question is whether they were, in fact, allegorists of poetic *texts*, either in the sense some of their critics seem to have claimed or in any sense at all.

During the first half of the third century BCE, the systematic scientific and antiquarian study of the text of Homer (along with other archaic and classical Greek poetry) was begun in Alexandria in the library of the Museum created by Ptolemy I. Our picture of the philosophical allegiances of the scholarly world of Hellenistic Greece has been influenced by the persistent ancient criticism of the Stoa for misuse of ancient poetry. Along with any reassessment of the relationship of the Stoa to early poetry must go a corresponding reassessment of the intellectual environment of those earliest textual critics.

The scholia of our medieval manuscripts of the *Iliad* and *Odyssey*, along with other evidence, make it clear that, parallel with the work of the scholars of Alexandria, there was another major center of textual criticism at Pergamum. The work of the Alexandrian Homer scholars culminates in that of Aristarchus in the mid-second century, roughly contemporary with the arrival of Crates of Mallos in Pergamum. As Rudolf Pfeiffer put it, "And then the Stoics came"—the Stoics who "were necessarily allegorists in their interpretation of poetry."[35] This is the picture

---

[35] R. Pfeiffer, *History of Classical Scholarship From the Beginnings*, 235, 237.

that has prevailed—a school of textual critics in Alexandria embarked on a fundamentally new and innovative attempt to recover the past in its own terms, a school that in some of its activities followed the intellectual lead of Aristotle and the Peripatos,[36] and in Pergamum a competing school, dominated by the Stoa and hence inevitably committed to the by no means new activity of allegorical interpretation. The allegorists, needless to say, were interested in recovering the past not in its own but in *their* own terms. This picture, as James Porter's essay below suggests, suffers from serious defects. He assembles the evidence we actually possess for Crates' activities and paints the picture of a decidedly eccentric thinker, one who defies classification into any major school—and who, as Porter points out, is not even called a Stoic in the surviving literature before the tenth-century lexicon known as the *Suda*.

What emerges from these two innovative studies is a picture of the early Stoics as readers of Homer who approached the poems in a manner not unlike that of Strabo (who was himself in some sense a Stoic).[37] Strabo's descriptions of the use of the epics as research materials is both sympathetic and revealing. He emphasizes the difficulty of sorting out the conflicting and contradictory strands of the theological material in particular and insists (echoing Polybius) that to make proper use of the *Odyssey* narrative as geographical evidence one must carefully assess the constituent parts, always bearing in mind that along with "information (ἱστορία), whose goal is truth," poetry is composed of "rhetoric of presentation (διάθεσις), whose goal is vivid effect," and of "fable (μῦθος), whose goal is pleasure and amazement." The *Odyssey*, then, for the geographer, is like a mine. The good ore of truth is to be found there, but a great deal is present as well that is a function of the poetry itself and has nothing to do with the truth. Still, the obscure lode of information is there. "To fabricate the whole thing would be neither credible nor Homeric."[38]

To believe that there are veins of truth to be recovered from the text of Homer—whether in the form of geographical data, or of divine epithets and names, or of specific myths of obscure signification—is quite a dif-

---

[36] As noted above, Pfeiffer laid emphasis on the originality of the Alexandrians and their self-conscious reaction against Aristotelian poetics, but in some principles of interpretation there is clearly continuity between the *Homeric Questions* of Aristotle and the work of Zenodotus and Aristarchus.

[37] There are several relevant passages, including Strabo 1.2.17, quoting Polybius at length on the relationship of the narrative of the wanderings of Odysseus to actual geography, and 10.3.23 on theology, discussed in my *Homer the Theologian*, 26–27, and 122.

[38] τὸ δὲ πάντα πλάττειν οὐ πιθανόν, οὐδ᾽ Ὁμηρικόν. Strabo 1.2.17.

ferent thing from elevating the poet to the position of a visionary sage whose every utterance is privileged. Although extraordinary claims could be made for the wisdom of Homer from an early date (as Plato's *Ion* clearly shows), and although the Stoa must in some sense have acted as mediator, the program of systematic interrogation of the Homeric poems alongside other privileged sources of philosophical or theological truth emerges into the philosophical mainstream only in the second century CE.[39]

From that time, when in "Pythagorean" or dogmatic Platonist circles the *Iliad* and *Odyssey* were associated both with the myths of the Platonic dialogues and with the wisdom of Pythagoras as well as such "alien wisdom" as could be gleaned from the Brahmans, Jews, Magi, and Egyptians,[40] a new attitude toward Homer emerged that was to last as long as there were polytheist Greek thinkers. In the reading of the epics developed among the later Platonists, each episode bristles with a proliferation of levels of reference, all contributing to the cumulative force of, first, the poem as a whole, and second, the greater myth beyond the epics, the Troy tale itself. For readers such as Porphyry in the third century and Proclus in the fifth, the true subject of the *Iliad* and *Odyssey* was the fate of souls and the structure of the universe. The first poem recounted the descent of souls into this world of strife, represented in the screen of the fiction by the metaphor of war, a descent triggered by the powerful attraction of the beauty of the cosmos (Helen). The second related the difficult return of one of those souls, plunged into the sea of matter and embroiled with the deities presiding over it, until he at last would achieve the state of "dryness" promised by Teiresias and finally free himself of all memory of the material universe.

There is no doubt that this reading had competitors and adversaries, but to judge by the pattern of the citations of Homer in the preserved literature—the philosophical literature in particular—of late antiquity, it or something like it was remarkably widespread. It is, in fact, for all its oddness, the one ancient reading of the poem that reaches us largely intact and well documented, and it exercised a powerful attraction even in the Latin Middle Ages, when the *Iliad* and *Odyssey* as such were unknown.

[39] I have studied this phase of ancient Homer interpretation in *Homer the Theologian*, and it would be inappropriate to recapitulate that study at length here. In my contribution to this volume, I have concentrated on the nature of the Neoplatonists' debts to their predecessors and on what seems to be their original contribution to the reading of Homer.

[40] This reflects the program of Numenius's book *On the Good*. See *Homer the Theologian*, 60, and below, 122.

It would be impossible to claim that we have in this book covered everything that is known of the ancient interpretive reading of Homer. There are countless critical assessments that reach us, often carrying some implied burden of interpretation. But there are in fact no other surviving ancient readings that we can document even as well as those presented here. We might piece together some "other Homers"—for instance, "Homer the Educator," a composite figure who could be reassembled from all those authors who shaped their reading of the epics around the postulate that the principal goal of the poet was educational. Plutarch would be a primary source here, and the abundant evidence for his understanding of Homer would form a substantial basis for reconstructing such a reading. Moreover, the existence of a large interpretive community committed to this perspective might be demonstrated. There are very few dissenting voices to the proposition that Homer's goals were educational, beyond the obscure Epicurean Philodemus, who seems to say, "Homer was conversant with reality, but whether it was for the sake of education, I wonder."[41]

There are likewise critics who praise Homer and describe Homer at great length, and from the best of these—and certainly 'Longinus' would be the first to come to mind—a reading might be extrapolated. But wonderful and rich as 'Longinus's' appreciation of the esthetic qualities and imaginative scope of the text is, it does not in itself constitute an interpretive reading, nor is it committed to any specific position on the meaning of the text, as such. Nor, despite all the comment on Homer from Roman poets and critics, do we find in that area any serious assault on the problem of interpreting the poems. The sole exception might be Macrobius, again working in the tradition of the later Platonists, in whose *Saturnalia* the extensive discussion of Virgil ("your Mantuan Homer"[42]) includes a good deal of interpretive material relating to Homer. But everything here fits into the larger category of Neoplatonist reading, with little that is distinctively Roman beyond its cultural perspective, most conspicuous in the approach to Homer as background and precedent to Virgil.

The final papers below, those of Robert Browning and Anthony Grafton, take us beyond the area specifically designated in the title of the vol-

---

[41] This depends on Christian Jensen's text of fr. 2 of the fifth book of Philodemus's *On Poems*: ὁ τοίνυν Ὅμηρος ἐπέγνωκε τὰ πράγματα, εἰ δὲ ὡς ἐπὶ παιδείαν ζητῶ. Christian Jensen, *Philodemus über die Gedichte, fünftes Buch*, 7. His translation was "Homer nun hat sich mit der Wirklichkeit vertraut gemacht, ob aber zum Zweck der Erziehung, ist mir zweifelhaft. . . ."

[42] "Homerus vester Mantuanus," *Saturnalia* 1.16.43.

ume. Rather than Homer's ancient readers themselves, these studies treat the influence, first in Byzantium and then in the Latin West during the Renaissance, of the various traditions of reading Homer. Not surprisingly, the two situations are radically different. In the Greek East, the picture is largely one of continuity. A great deal has been written about the absorption of Homer into Christian education—this is, in fact, another area where a composite "reading" might be reconstructed.[43] Stripped of theological authority, the epics proved quite adaptable to appropriation by subtle hermeneutic thinkers such as Basil the Great, whose own religious tradition was characterized by a great deal of sophistication in the use of texts, scriptural and otherwise. Thus, after a period of tension, Homer had regained his pedagogical preeminence, to retain it where and whenever Greek was taught in the context of Christian Hellenism. Browning offers a fascinating account of what happened next, as new interpreters worked to make the text accessible to new groups of readers in the changing Byzantine empire.

What Grafton gives us in closing is a privileged look into the reception by the Renaissance humanists of the decidedly odd claims about the meaning of the text of Homer that they found in ancient sources and in the scholia. The earliest editions of Homer, like the manuscripts on which they were based, were encumbered with introductory essays of an interpretive nature, ranging from the richly imaginative essay on the cave of the Nymphs in *Odyssey* 13 by the Neoplatonist Porphyry to the ponderous encomium that went under the name of Plutarch and the title *On the Life and Poetry of Homer*. The tendency since the latter part of the eighteenth century has been to pare all of that material away and to attempt to see Homer face-to-face, without reading through all of the dubious interpretive material supplied by millennia of scholarly tradition, but such paring was, of course, out of the question for the first humanists. Grafton vividly evokes their encounter with the text and its interpreters, in part through Guillaume Budé's unpublished marginalia to his copy of the 1488 *editio princeps* of Homer, now in the Firestone Library of Princeton University.

This collection of essays as a whole constitutes both a survey of a relatively neglected area of scholarship and an appeal for more and more serious attention to the earliest chapters in the history of the reception of

---

[43] It would not be difficult, in any case, to paint a more subtly nuanced picture than that offered by Hugo Rahner in the chapter tellingly entitled "Der heilige Homer" in his *Griechische Mythen in christlicher Deutung*.

Homer. It is in a sense no surprise that those chapters are the most neglected, because to Medievalists and to Modernists it has long been evident that the poems, translated into new cultural contexts, both transformed those contexts and were transformed by them. What these papers
taken together demonstrate is that this is a process that began very early
in the history of the poems, and that the pattern of interaction of text and
interpretation that was already set by the Hellenistic period has had a pervasive importance for all subsequent perception of the meaning of the
Iliad, the *Odyssey*, and the Troy tale.

. . . . .

The papers assembled here were delivered in somewhat different form at
a conference entitled *Homer's Ancient Readers* held at Princeton University, Oct. 6–7, 1989. The conference was conceived as a comprehensive
survey of all the ancient readings of the *Iliad* and *Odyssey* for which we
have any substantial evidence, as well as an overview of the influence of
those readings, first in the Byzantine East and then among the humanists
of the Renaissance in the West. The thoughtful and suggestive responses
to individual sessions contributed by Georgia Nugent and Richard Martin, as well as a number of penetrating questions from the floor, both
enriched the sessions and in many instances proved useful to the participants as they revised their papers for publication. The remarks of David
Armstrong and an anonymous reviewer whose advice was sought by the
Magie Publications Committee were likewise of tremendous value in the
process of revising and editing the resultant volume. The project was formulated from the start to produce a volume of essays constituting a systematic introduction, mapping this neglected area of classical scholarship.

All of the papers have been revised, and those covering the most problematic area (the Stoa) and the least explored area (the influence of the
ancient interpreters on the Renaissance humanists) have been expanded.
Thus, although the coverage of the history of ancient Homer interpretation is uneven, that unevenness itself reflects something of the state of
research in the field. Footnotes have been revised around a uniform system of reference, but each contributor has his own style and approach to
his material, and no attempt has been made to reduce those styles to a
single, uniform voice. Finally, although we have attempted to give each
other all the room possible to develop our own arguments, avoiding fla-
grant contradiction, it is nevertheless true that the contributors would
inevitably find themselves in disagreement among themselves with regard to some issues regarding the nature, value, and intellectual respect-

ability of "uncanny" modes of reading, ancient and modern. We hope, however, that this honest tension enriches the book rather than fragmenting it.

We all owe a debt of gratitude to those at Princeton University Press who have contributed to the project: to Joanna Hitchcock, who first took it in hand and got the ball rolling; to her assistant Valerie Jablow, who was long the kingpin of the operation while editors and contributors were scattered around the globe; and to Marta Steele, whose judicious copyediting has removed inconsistencies and added a great deal of polish to the volume.

Both the conference and the present volume were made possible by the generous support of the Magie Publication Fund of the Department of Classics of Princeton University; Princeton's Program in the History, Archaeology, and Religions of the Ancient World; its Program in Hellenic Studies; and the Andrew W. Mellon Foundation. I would like to express my personal thanks for the support of the J. D. Brown Dean's Fund and the Program in Hellenic Studies during the editing process.

✳ *Abbreviations* ✳

NOTE: Names of ancient authors and works are generally spelled out, but abbreviations are sometimes used. If not made clear in context, these can be deciphered with the help of the lists of abbreviations in LSJ and OLD (below).

ANRW   *Aufstieg und Niedergang der römischen Welt.* Wolfgang Haase and Hildegard Temporini, eds. Berlin: De Gruyter, 1972–cont.

CAG   *Commentaria in Aristotelem Graeca.* 22 vols. + 3. Berlin: Prussian Academy of Letters, 1883–1903.

CPF   *Corpus dei papiri filosofici greci e latini.* Francesco Adorno et al., eds. Florence: Olschki, 1989–cont.

D-K   *Die Fragmente der Vorsokratiker,* griechisch und deutsch von Hermann Diels. Walther Kranz, ed. 12th ed. Berlin: Weidmann, 1966–1967.

Loeb   The Loeb Classical Library, Cambridge, Mass., and London: Harvard Univ. Press and Heinemann.

LSJ   *A Greek-English Lexicon,* compiled by Henry George Liddell and Robert Scott, revised and augmented throughout by Sir Henry Stuart Jones. 9th ed., with supplement. Oxford: Oxford Univ. Press, 1968.

OLD   *Oxford Latin Dictionary.* A. Sonter et al., eds. Oxford: Oxford Univ. Press, 1968–1982.

PMG   D. L. Page, *Poetae Melici Graeci.* Oxford: Oxford Univ. Press, 1962.

P-W   *Paulys Realencyclopädie der classischen Altertumswissenschaft,* revision begun by Georg Wissowa. . . . Stuttgart, later Munich: J. B. Metzler, succeeded by Alfred Druckenmüller, 1894–1980.

SVF   *Stoicorum Veterum Fragmenta.* H. von Arnim, ed. 4 vols., 1902. Rpt. Stuttgart: Teubner, 1964.

Homer's Ancient Readers

✳

CHAPTER ONE

Bard and Audience in Homer*

CHARLES SEGAL

T HE ATTEMPT to make Homer know everything, from farming to fighting, is like trying to make the sacred olive bough known as the εἰρε- σιώνη hold apples and pears and other things too heavy for it. Such is the comparison of Hipparchus, quoted by Strabo in defending Homer against Eratosthenes' attacks on his poems as merely frivolous, fanciful entertainment (ψυχαγωγία, Strabo 1.2.3). One sort of knowledge, however, the ancient readers almost unanimously grant Homer: knowledge about words and song, the arts of speech and persuasion, or what Strabo calls ῥητορικὴ φρόνησις, "rhetorical skill," best exemplified by Odysseus in the *Iliad* (especially books 2, 3, and 9: see Strabo 1.2.5). Homer shows the same knowledge of the other side of making songs and speeches—not just their creation but also their reception. This essay is a study, then, not of Homer's readers but of Homer's hearers—of what he thinks, or might think, of his audiences, actual and possible.

The Homeric poems repeatedly depict ancient audiences listening to singers. The gods banqueting on Olympus are entertained by Apollo and the Muses (*Il.* 1.602f.); grape pickers lighten their toil by joining the young boy who sings the "Linus song" in the vineyard (*Il.* 18.561–72). In the former passage "banquet," Apollo's "lovely lyre," and "Muses" with their "beautiful voice" are joined together in a coordinate construction as simultaneous attributes of divine happiness (1.601–04):

> ὣς τότε μὲν πρόπαν ἦμαρ ἐς ἠέλιον καταδύντα
> δαίνυντ᾽, οὐδέ τι θυμὸς ἐδεύετο δαιτὸς ἐΐσης
> οὐ μὲν φόρμιγγος περικαλλέος, ἣν ἔχ᾽ Ἀπόλλων,

* This study was completed during a Fellowship at the Center for Advanced Study in the Behavioral Sciences, Stanford, California. I am grateful for financial support at the Center, which was provided by the National Endowment for the Humanities (#RA-20037-88) and the Andrew W. Mellon Foundation. I have adapted a few pages, revised and recast, from my essay "Poetry, Performance, and Society in Early Greek Literature," *Lexis: Poetica. retorica e comunicazione nella tradizione classica*, vol. 2, no. 1 (1988) 123–44. I thank the editor, Professor Vittorio Citti, and the publisher, Piovan Editore, for permission to make use of this material.

Μουσάων θ᾽, αἳ ἄειδον ἀμειβόμεναι ὀπὶ καλῇ.

Thus they feasted the entire day to the setting of the sun, nor did their spirit lack the equal share in the *feasting*, nor the very lovely *lyre* that Apollo held, nor the *Muses*, who sang in responsion with their *beautiful voices*.

Like the Muses who inspire him, the poet of early Greece is a singer. His aim is to produce songs performed at more or less public occasions, ranging from a large panhellenic festival, such as those at Delos or Mycale, to an affair of state such as Hieron's inauguration of his newly founded city of Aetnaea (commemorated in Pindar, *Pythian* 1), to local family gatherings, feasts, and symposia in the houses of the rich. While the Hellenistic Callimachus holds his writing tablet on his knees and doubtless a pen (or stylus) in his hand (Callimachus *Aetia* 1.21f. Pfeiffer), the Homeric poet holds a lyre.

Our first detailed account of song in Homer, and therefore in Western literature, depicts a scene of group festivity in the open air. On the shield of Achilles girls and boys dance together, a lad plays a clear-sounding lyre in their midst, and the dancers sing as they follow the tune and "skip with their feet" (*Il.* 18.567–72). There is also dancing accompanied by flute and lyre at a wedding feast, doubtless also outdoors because women are watching from the forecourt. Later a large crowd watches a dance "like that at broad Cnossus" (18.591), and two whirling acrobats "lead off the singing" (18.604f.).

As such passages indicate, poetry is envisaged as part of a performance, as the living voice of song (what John Herington calls "the song culture").[1] Whether secular or ritual, whether public or private, poetry belongs to a social occasion. The spectators who "stand about" admiring or enjoying themselves on the shield of Achilles are an inconspicuous but essential element of the scene (18.496, 603).

All the more significant, therefore, is the private context of song, as Achilles, in his tent, sings the "glorious deeds of heroes," the κλέα ἀνδρῶν (*Il.* 9.185–91). He is playing on a lyre with a silver bridge that he took when he destroyed Eetion's city—a reminder of his own κλέος and prowess as a warrior. More important, he is singing only for himself, "giving pleasure to his heart" (φρένα τερπόμενον, 9.186; τῇ ὅ γε

---

[1] C. J. Herington, *Poetry into Drama*, part 1, passim. On the importance of song in the world of the Homeric poems, see Wolfgang Schadewaldt, "Die Gestalt des homerischen Sängers," in *Von Homers Welt und Werk*, 54–86, especially 62–65, 67f.

θυμὸν ἔτερπεν, 9.189). Note what Homer does *not* say: Patroclus is not listening or paying attention to the song; he is only "waiting for Achilles to leave off singing" (δέγμενος Αἰακίδην, ὁπότε λήξειεν ἀείδων, 9.191). We are not to confuse the singing of this great warrior with that of a bard; he gives pleasure only to himself, not to others (note φρένα τερπόμενον, in the middle voice, 9.186). The hero of the *Odyssey* is very different, as we shall see.

Private song figures at the opposite end of the social scale too, though with more pathos, in the description of the two shepherds on Achilles' shield. Innocently they "take joy in their pipes," τερπόμενοι σύριγξι (18.525ff.), remote ancestors of Theocritus's Daphnis and Milton's Lycidas, save that in this violent world they "did not foresee the ambush," whose members carry off the cattle and "kill the herdsmen besides" (18.529).

Alcinous's palace in *Odyssey* 8 is the setting for Homer's fullest account of bardic performance; and the scene has the richness, ease, and splendor that one would expect in this happy, comfort-loving land of the Phaeacians. The palace and court gradually fill with the king's followers, young and old (8.57f.). Alcinous makes an elaborate sacrifice for the coming feast: twelve sheep, eight boars, two oxen. The meat is prepared, and "they fashioned the lovely banquet" (τετύκοντό τε δαῖτ᾿ ἐρατεινήν, 8.61). As the crowning touch, the herald leads in the bard, the blind Demodocus. A silver-studded stool is set for him in the midst of the banqueters; his lyre is carefully hung within reach, above his head; and bread, meat, and wine are placed before him (8.65–70). This bard, like Phemius on Ithaca, is no wandering minstrel to be classed with the "craftsmen" (δημιοεργοί) who come and go from the palace (17.383–85).[2] He is a permanent fixture in the royal establishment and has a respected place and regular duties there.

Later, in book 13, Odysseus has finished his long tale in the palace of Alcinous, and a charmed silence descends over the hall. The king, who has already congratulated the speaker on his grace as a raconteur (11.367f.), urges his guests to add more gifts (13.7–9): "To each one of you I speak enjoining this, you who always drink the aged bright wine in my halls and hear the bard" (αἴθοπα οἶνον/αἰεὶ πίνετ᾿ ἐμοῖσιν, ἀκουάζεσθε δ᾿ ἀοιδοῦ). The implication is that the bard is a prized ac-

---

[2] On this passage see W. Schadewaldt, *Von Homers Welt und Werk*, 69, 70; George Walsh, *The Varieties of Enchantment: Early Greek Views of the Nature and Function of Poetry*, 15f.; more recently, Francesco Bertolini, "Odisseo aedo, Omero carpentiere: *Odissea* 17.384–85," with further bibliography.

coutrement of a rich and generous house. Hearing him is like drinking the good wine of his patron, a privilege that puts the guests under an obligation.

The Demodocus scene probably reflects the ideal rather than the actual, and the wish fulfillment may be as much for the poet as for his audience. Nevertheless, the basic situation may not be beyond the possibilities of an eighth-century aristocrat. As the princes of the Italian Renaissance collected sculptures or paintings to display their culture, affluence, and power and adorned their palaces with memorials of great people of the past in the form of busts, frescoes, and statues, so the nobles of the Greek renaissance, twenty-two hundred years earlier, may well have adorned their houses with poets who could monumentalize in song the great deeds of the past and thereby provide models of heroic excellence and grandeur. At this period material culture in Greece is still relatively modest; and a resident bard, for a long or short term, probably represents an inexpensive investment.

The luxuries of the time are social and (fortunately for posterity) artistic. A good bard enhances a good feast. It is tempting, of course, to think that Homer actually sang at or after banquets (though perhaps not "for small earnings and good cheer," in Richard Bentley's notorious formulation); and bards like him may well have sung at the courts of nobles and princes. If, as Anthony Snodgrass argues, great scarcity and poverty lay in the not-so-distant past, his audience would appreciate images of a time when there was always an extra ox or hog to be sacrificed and the wine flowed endlessly.[3] Through such regal settings as those in which Demodocus sings, Homer can transport his eighth-century audience into the wealth and abundance of the heroic age.

One of the *Odyssey*'s most insistent messages is that eating properly and listening properly go closely together.[4] Only the rude, cannibalistic Cyclops asks his guest for a story before feeding him. The hospitable Eumaeus, who admiringly compares his disguised guest's narrative ability to that of a professional bard (17.518–21), feeds him two dinners (14.80–120 and 414–45). The best audience in the poem, the Phaeacians, permits the after-dinner tale to go on for the length of four books (9–12)

[3] On the economic duress of the tenth and ninth centuries BC in Greece, see Anthony Snodgrass, *Archaic Greece: The Age of Experiment*, 15ff. See also his *The Dark Age of Greece*, 413f.

[4] See, for instance, Douglas Stewart, *The Disguised Guest*, 68f.; Suzanne Saïd, "Les crimes des prétendants, la maison d'Ulysse et les festins de l'Odyssée," especially 13; William G. Thalmann, *Conventions of Form and Thought in Early Greek Epic Poetry*, 158ff.

as Odysseus tells his story with the skill of a bard (cf. 11.363–69).[5] When Eumaeus describes to Penelope the disguised beggar's "charm" with words, he begins with a wish that the suitors would be quiet so that Penelope too might feel the spell of his guest's tales, which he enjoyed for three nights and three days on his farm (17.513–21). Those noisy suitors, however, are the most disrespectful audience we see, and they eventually get arrows from the bowstring instead of music from the lyre, as Athena/ Mentes had hinted and as Telemachus had warned at the first feast of the poem (1.225–29, 253–59).

The close relation between song and feasting is crystallized into the formulaic phrase ἀναθήματα δαιτός, song as "the accompaniment of the feasting." With intentional irony, the formula's first occurrence in the *Odyssey* describes an occasion when that "accompaniment" is reluctant: Phemius sings "by necessity" to Telemachus's unwelcome guests, the suitors who arrogantly appropriate the good things of the palace, bard included (see *Od.* 1.154). The only other occurrence of the phrase in the Homeric corpus comes after Odysseus has accomplished the trial of the bow and is about to make the singing of the bowstring into an "accompaniment of the feasting"—a feast that is the suitors' last meal (21.430).[6]

But, to return from the bow to the lyre, even "good" audiences do not sit in the rapt silence of the Phaeacian nobles around Odysseus (11.333f.). Menelaus, for example, whose tastes incline slightly toward the grosser side, has acrobats to entertain his guests. This detail may be as much a commentary on Menelaus as a reflection on the taste of Homeric audiences. Despite the importance of music and singing, there is good reason to think that when an ἀοιδός sings people are expected to listen to what he says and not just enjoy a catchy tune. Thus, when Demodocus performs among the Phaeacians, he plays to accompany choral dancing only once, whereas in his three other appearances his words are obviously the primary focus of interest.

But things in Homer, and especially in the *Odyssey*, are always a little more complicated than they seem. Consider the most frivolous and risqué story in the epic corpus, Demodocus's song of the adultery of Ares and Aphrodite, the beautiful gods who are caught in bed by the cunning

---

[5] The relevance of this scene to Homeric conceptions of bardic performance has often been noted: See W. Schadewaldt, *Von Homers Welt und Werk*, 81; G. Walsh, *The Varieties of Enchantment*, 7ff.; D. Stewart, *The Disguised Guest*, 157.

[6] On the repetition see S. Saïd, "Les crimes des prétendants," 25. In *Od.* 8.99 Homer uses the similar expression ἥ δαιτὶ συνήορός ἐστι θαλείη of the lyre (φόρμιγξ), which he does not repeat elsewhere.

net of Hephaestus. This song offers the delight or τέρψις that is ideally suited to the rather brittle hedonism of the Phaeacians. Such was essentially the judgment of Plutarch, some two millennia ago, in his delightful essay "How a Young Man Should Listen to Poetry." But this piece of apparently frothy entertainment proves, in fact, to be the model for Odysseus's own story: The grimy, hardworking little man of soot and sweat defeats the big, gorgeous hunk—a prefiguration of Odysseus combating the Cyclops but also perhaps a hint of that antiaristocratic sentiment that seems to creep in here and there.[7] But there is contrast as well as parallelism. The woman whom Odysseus will win back is not the goddess of love nor the embodiment of sex appeal like Helen, but the soul of domestic virtue, patience, and prudence. And Homer gives us a further surprise: The trickery practiced around the bed will be not the husband's but the wife's (the test of the living olive tree). This singing, then, exemplifies the multiple functions of the poet in his society: pure entertainment at one level, concern with the central values and conflicts in the world of the poem at another.

This is a revealing scene for differences in audience response.[8] Both Odysseus and the Phaeacians "took pleasure in hearing" the song of Aphrodite's adultery (8.367–69). Yet it is not this tale of the gods but rather the song about the sufferings of the Achaeans that wins from Odysseus the most extravagant praise that a bard receives in Homer (8.474–83). Odysseus not only honors Demodocus with a choice cut of meat but also suggests that he has been taught by the Muse and even by Apollo himself (8.487f.; contrast 8.44 and 63, where Demodocus's skill derives only from "a god" or "the Muse"). What Odysseus prizes is the ability to evoke not the carefree realm of the remote Olympians but the human woe that stirs the heart, told, he says, "as if you were present yourself or heard from someone else [who was]" (8.491).[9] So the Muses

[7] For the thematic relevance of the song of Ares and Aphrodite to the poem, see most recently S. Douglas Olson, "*Odyssey* 8: Guile, Force and the Subversive Poetics of Desire," especially 137, 141, with further bibliography; also Rick M. Newton, "Odysseus and Hephaestus in the *Odyssey*," especially 14–16. For the question of antiaristocratic sentiment in the poem see, e.g., S. G. Farron, "The Odyssey as an Anti-Aristocratic Statement," 59–101; for a less extreme and more balanced view, see Kurt Raaflaub, "Die Anfänge des politischen Denkens bei den Griechen," 208–11; also Ian Morris, "The Use and Abuse of Homer," 123ff.

[8] For some of these differences, see G. Walsh, *The Varieties of Enchantment*, 4ff., 6ff.; also W. G. Thalmann, *Conventions of Form and Thought*, 160ff.; Hélène Monsacré, *Les Larmes d'Achille*, 151ff.

[9] On this valuing of the bard's vivid "presence" at the event as a poet of truth, see

themselves, in the poet's invocation to the Catalogue of Ships in the *Iliad*, "are present and know everything," whereas we mortals have only hearsay (*Il.* 2.485f.).

The differences in response between the Greek warrior and the hedonistic Phaeacians are already encoded into Demodocus's tale of Ares and Aphrodite in the contrasts among the divine spectators of the lovers' embarrassment. The female divinities stay away (8.324), while Hermes makes a locker-room joke to Apollo. This releases the tension among the other (male) gods in "laughter unquenchable," like Hephaestus's clumsy wine service in the *Iliad* that breaks the tension of this first feast on Olympus (*Il.* 1.597–600). But even this male response is divided: Poseidon is not amused and remains concerned, serious, and legalistic (8.344–58). This narrative of Olympian frivolity becomes itself a spectacle of audience response within a performance, like the wedding song on the shield of Achilles (cf. 8.321 and 325 and *Il.* 18.495–97), with a major division in the mood of the spectators.

Odysseus goes on to request a third song of Demodocus, the story of the wooden horse and the capture of Troy. Again he weeps, and again Alcinous observes him. This time, however, Alcinous does not hold his peace (as he had in the case of the first song, 8.93ff.) but delivers a long speech that ends with some generalizations on mortal suffering and the request for Odysseus's identity. The gods, he says, "have spun out doom for men so that there may be song for those to come" (ἵνα ἦσι καὶ ἐσ-σομένοισιν ἀοιδή, 8.580). Helen makes a very similar reflection in her scene with Paris, but the differences are important. She speaks in the first person, and her concern is about men; Alcinous's is about song. The gods have set upon *us* an evil doom, she says, "so that *we* may be a subject of song for men to come" (ὡς καὶ ὀπίσσω/ἀνθρώποισι πελώμεθ᾽ ἀοίδιμοι ἐσσομένοισι, *Il.* 6.357f.). The distance that Alcinous thus implies between the pleasurable effect (τέρψις) of song on its hearers and the pain of its subject matter becomes even clearer as he goes on to ask whether Odysseus has lost a kinsman or dear companion in the war (8.581–86). He thus acknowledges that an audience could feel a personal involvement in the subject of song, but he still does not envisage the possibility that the specific involvement of Odysseus's response lay in exactly the opposite direction, effacing the distance between the subject and its audience.

W. Schadewaldt, *Von Homers Welt und Werk*, 82; more recently Mario Puelma, "Der Dichter und die Wahrheit in der griechischen Poetik von Homer bis Aristoteles," 68ff., with further bibliography.

Such is the effect of the simile that compares Odysseus's weeping at the story of the fall of Troy in Demodocus's song to that of a woman in a captured city as she is led off to slavery—a city very much like the Troy of Demodocus's song (8.523ff.).

Everything about this scene, then, articulates two very different modes of response: the aesthetic distance of Alcinous that can treat poetry (fiction) as a source of pure pleasure (τέρψις) and the intense, painful involvement of Odysseus as he participates, through memory, in the sufferings of war that are the subject matter of the song. The simile of the weeping captive woman further suggests the possibility that this identification with the subject matter of the song applies not just to the memory of an actual participant like Odysseus, but also to vicarious participation by anyone, for the simile evokes a response of pity for the victims of any war, not just the Trojan war of which Demodocus has just sung. With the exception of the extraordinary scene between Priam and Achilles in *Iliad* 24, there is little in the heroic code that would encourage Odysseus to identify with his conquered enemy, especially one of the opposite sex.

Through these contrasting responses, Homer reveals the paradox (of which Hesiod too is aware) between the pleasure that mimetic art affords its audience and the pain in its contents. For the hedonistic Phaeacians, war itself is absorbed into ἀοιδή, song (8.580); for Odysseus the sufferings of war, even in song, are still sufferings and bring tears. The simile that compares him to a captive woman, however, creates a deliberate slippage between the two positions and at least raises the possibility that the division may not always be so sharp. Menelaus, like Alcinous, regards weeping as an undesirable response to an after-dinner song, the reverse of the τέρψις (pleasure) that song should bring or enhance (4.193–95 and cf. 220–26; 8.538–43). Menelaus's court, however, having been touched directly by the sufferings of the narrator as Alcinous's court has not, joins in the weeping (4.183–88).

A further detail complicates the contrast between Odysseus and the Phaeacians. In the long speech in which Alcinous makes his formal request for Odysseus's identity and asks the reasons for his weeping, he tells of a prophecy that Poseidon will one day destroy one of his ships as it returns from escorting a passenger to his homeland (8.564–69). Characteristically, he dismisses the prophecy as something that the god may or may not accomplish (8.570f.). Alcinous's lack of concern, as we learn later, is mistaken, for the angry god does fulfill the prophecy (13.170–83). In fact we see the Phaeacians for the last time gathering in fear about

10

Poseidon's altar as they attempt to appease his wrath (13.183–87). These events have some bearing on poet and audience, for in Demodocus's second song, about Ares and Aphrodite, it was Poseidon who resolved the embarrassment. His solemn pledge assuages Hephaestus's anger and secures Ares' release (8.344–58). This is a Poseidon suited to Phaeacian aestheticism. He intervenes to keep the violation of marriage in the realm of play, without the consequences, for example, that it has on Ithaca. Odysseus's Poseidon, however, is not a god who soothes anger or intervenes in the name of peace. This wrathful, dangerous Poseidon, beyond the frame of Phaeacian song, is the god that Alcinous now begins to know, if only as a remote possibility (8.570f.; cf. 13.125–64).

From the point of view of "real" life, of course, the tales of Odysseus at Troy and of Ares and Aphrodite on Olympus are equally "mythical," and so are both Poseidons too. But for a moment Homer allows the two modes of "mythical" narration to cross over into each other. The Phaeacian king relates a kind of story (albeit in the future rather than the past) that thematically resembles Odysseus's life story in its divine blocking figure as the central antagonist. This story, moreover, will be fulfilled as "fact" in book 13. Homer thus brings together story as pleasurable entertainment (Demodocus's Poseidon) and story as emotionally involving exemplar of human suffering (the Poseidon who punishes the Phaeacians in book 13) that could also apply to "us" the listener. Such too is the involvement of Odysseus conveyed through the simile of the weeping captive woman. This scene, as we suggested above, juxtaposes the bard's inspired performance, as song, of a specific event in the past (the fall of Troy) with a hearer's emotional response to a situation that could happen in "reality," at any time.

This kind of narrative self-consciousness, typical of the *Odyssey*, forces the hearer to become aware of the work's construction of its fictionality or mythicality and thus of the disjunction between different levels of "reality." It is analogous to the self-consciousness about plot construction that emerges in the retrospective narrative of the Second Nekyia. There the slain suitor Amphimedon tells a version of Odysseus's success that includes the conscious collusion of Odysseus and Penelope in setting up the contest of the bow. "Odysseus in his multifaceted craftiness ($\pi o \lambda v$-$\kappa \varepsilon \rho \delta \varepsilon i \eta \sigma \iota v$)," Amphimedon says, "*ordered* his wife to set up for the suitors the bow and the hoary iron (of the axes)"; and this event, he adds, proved to be "the beginning of the slaughter" (24.167–69). Odysseus, of course, gave no such orders; but Homer thus shows his audience an alternative dénouement, a version that he might have used but chose not to.

11

The "multifaceted craftiness" is in this case as much the poet's as his hero's.[10] This bard has the same kind of flexibility to reshape his tale as his chief character has to reshape his life narrative.

Homer shows his control of the narrative in another way at one of the poem's major transitions, the shift from Telemachus back to Odysseus at the beginning of book 5. In book 1, when Athena formally introduces Odysseus by winning Zeus's sympathy for his sufferings, Zeus replies, "My child, what is this saying that has escaped the barrier of your teeth? How then would I forget ($\lambda\alpha\theta o\acute{\iota}\mu\eta\nu$) divine Odysseus, who surpasses mortals in intelligence . . . ?" (1.64–66) In the corresponding scene in book 5, Zeus repeats his formulaic first line (5.22 = 1.64) but omits the second line about "forgetting Odysseus." Instead, Athena, as in book 1, initiates the mention of Odysseus, absent from the narrative now for four books, by "making mention" of him and his many sufferings ($\lambda\acute{\epsilon}\gamma\epsilon~\kappa\acute{\eta}\delta\epsilon\alpha$ $\pi\acute{o}\lambda\lambda$' $O\delta\upsilon\sigma\widehat{\eta}o\varsigma/\mu\nu\eta\sigma\alpha\mu\acute{\epsilon}\nu\eta$, 5.5f.). She then continues with the complaint that "no one remembers divine Odysseus among the people over whom he ruled ($\dot{\omega}\varsigma~o\breve{\upsilon}~\tau\iota\varsigma~\mu\acute{\epsilon}\mu\nu\eta\tau\alpha\iota~O\delta\upsilon\sigma\widehat{\eta}o\varsigma~\theta\epsilon\acute{\iota}o\iota o/\lambda\alpha\widehat{\omega}\nu~o\breve{\iota}\sigma\iota\nu$ $\breve{\alpha}\nu\alpha\sigma\sigma\epsilon$, 5.11f.). She is here recalling Zeus's verse about "forgetting divine Odysseus" in book 1 (1.65) but has put "memory" in place of "forgetting" ($\mu\acute{\epsilon}\mu\nu\eta\tau\alpha\iota$, 5.11; $\lambda\alpha\theta o\acute{\iota}\mu\eta\nu$, 1.65). This change comes just at the point when many of the people ($\lambda\alpha o\acute{\iota}$) in the audience may well be asking themselves whether their bard has "forgotten divine Odysseus"; and he reassures them by "reminding / relating" and "remembering" that he has forgotten neither the main hero nor his own plot line. Indeed, he brings back the "memory" of his hero with a foretaste of his most spectacular and also most disastrous triumph in the repeated $\mu\acute{\eta}~\tau\iota\varsigma$ . . . $o\breve{\upsilon}$ $\tau\iota\varsigma$ of 5.8 and 11, a reference to Odysseus's "guile" ($\mu\widehat{\eta}\tau\iota\varsigma$) of giving his name as Nobody ($o\breve{\upsilon}~\tau\iota\varsigma$) to deceive the Cyclops in book 9. Because both "relating" and "remembering" are characteristic activities of the oral bard, Homer is here delicately signaling to his audience that he anticipates their possible malaise at the postponement of the main narrative and also asserting his own overall command of the story's direction that should alleviate that concern.

It is a commonplace of classical criticism that whereas the *Odyssey* loves to talk about poetry and song, the *Iliad* is very reticent.[11] True, the *Iliad* shows very few bards in action. Yet Achilles can take up his lyre in the

---

[10] On this episode see most recently Simon Goldhill, "Reading Differences: The *Odyssey* and Juxtaposition," 6f.; he stresses how Homer here plays with his audience's expectations.

[11] See, for instance, D. Stewart, *The Disguised Guest*, 148ff.

privacy of his tent to sing of the "glorious deeds of heroes," the κλέα ἀνδρῶν, a phrase that could describe the events of the *Iliad*. In fact the very withdrawal that by its enforced leisure makes this song possible is now shaping the story of Achilles that will have a conspicuous place, thanks to the bard of the *Iliad*, among these κλέα ἀνδρῶν.[12] This paradox is in turn part of the deeper paradox that Achilles' rejection of the heroic code in the ninth book leads to the deeper, more powerful, and more thoughtful formulation of that code that is the *Iliad*. The paradoxes of Achilles' song of heroes thus reflect his simultaneous rejection and affirmation of the heroic world. More generally, they anticipate the paradoxical relations between distance and involvement, pleasure and participation in the bardic narrative of war, killing, and suffering—paradoxes that the *Odyssey* explores more directly and in greater detail.

More explicitly than Achilles, Helen, as we have observed, reflects on the future of the war as a subject of song for men to come (6.357f.). And parallel to this explicit verbal reflection on her future fame in song is her weaving the present conflict on a tapestry in book 3, the age-old women's way of telling stories in the wordless medium of their world (3.125–28): "Iris found Helen in her chamber, and she was weaving a great work of the loom, double-folded, deep red, and upon it she wove the many struggles of the horse-taming Trojans and the bronze-armored Achaeans."

The poem presents another woman whose life is also bound to the events of the war and who, like Helen, climbs to the wall to take a long view. But whereas Helen's weaving in her chamber in book 3 contains the "many struggles of the horse-taming Trojans and bronze-armored Achaeans," Andromache's weaving is only of "many-colored flowers" (22.441f.).[13] Andromache cannot make an artwork of the war raging around her. The two kinds of weaving enable Homer to objectify his literary self-consciousness. He can thus crystallize his own narrative reflexivity into clear, external actions, just as in the *Odyssey* he can suggest different modes of responding to song in the different responses of Odysseus and the Phaeacians.

The differences between Helen and Andromache also raise the issue of narrative perspective or point of view. Helen's distanced weaving of the

---

[12] See Françoise Frontisi-Ducroux, *La Cithare d'Achille*, 53.

[13] For the contrasts between the two scenes, see my essay "Andromache's *Anagnorisis*: Formulaic Artistry in *Iliad* 22.437–76," 40f. It is among these differences that Andromache is inside the house, fully engrossed in the domestic tasks of her wifely role, including the preparations for her weary husband's return, whereas Helen is out on the wall, being admired for her beauty by the elders of Troy.

battle scenes comes to an end when the goddess Iris calls her from her quiet chamber to the scene of action, the walls of Troy from which we see, with her, the Greek army and its leaders (*Il* 3.121–233). Whereas Helen thinks of her absent brothers, "far away in lovely Lacedaemon" (3.234–44), Andromache's view from the wall is not of distant events, nor are her thoughts for those far away; she takes in the present scene only, the death of Hector that completes her tragedy. Although the *Iliad* rarely takes advantage of this kind of distancing of events through the aesthetic frame in the way that the *Odyssey* does, it has its own kind of literary self-consciousness.

Or consider the famous scene between Glaucus and Diomedes in book 6. At this moment of intense fighting, the action surprisingly comes to a halt. The telling of tales replaces fighting. Without breaking the illusion, Homer momentarily lets the act of narration step into the foreground, as if he is gently reminding us that we are *listening* to a story of battle, not fighting one.[14] But the content of this narrative also makes us appreciate the specific nature of Homer's song. The Lycian Glaucus tells the story of his ancestor, Bellerophon, a story of illicit love and palace intrigue, secret signs, fire-breathing monsters, and flying horses. Does Homer want us to perceive this as a typical Near Eastern tale, one of those many bizarre tales that the Greeks had been eagerly absorbing from their eastern neighbors for at least the past century? To push the point, does Homer also mean us to appreciate the contrast with the more sober, more austere story of human conflict to which he has held himself in the severe masterpiece that is the *Iliad*?[15] Whether or not the *Iliad* was composed with the aid of writing, it is certainly not the naive or primitive voice of *Volk*, nature, or the pure warrior spirit, in the way that eighteenth and nineteenth century critics from Vico and F. A. Wolf to Ruskin and even Gilbert Murray could claim.

In the *Odyssey*, to be sure, the contrast between aesthetic distance and emotional involvement is not displaced from poetry into weaving or into the kind of contrast that exists between Helen and Andromache in the *Iliad* but is developed with much stronger and more explicit focus on po-

[14] On the scene see F. Frontisi-Ducroux, *La Cithare d'Achille*, 37.

[15] Although the probably orientalizing motifs of the Chimaera and the Lycian setting point to Near Eastern connections, Homer has also removed the fabulous detail of the flying horse (Pegasus) and has Bellerophon kill the Chimaera only by "obeying the portents of the gods" (*Il.* 6.183). In the background too, of course, is folktale, which has likewise been transformed into the very different register of epic narrative: See Francesco Bertolini, "Dal folclore all' epica: esempi di trasformazione e adattamento," especially 138–40.

etry per se. Or, to put it differently, the *Odyssey* has a language of *overt* poetic reflexivity that the *Iliad* lacks. It even takes a playful delight in making a display of its own inventiveness.[16] It is not perhaps accidental that the *Odyssey* is the first poem of Western literature to tell the myth of Proteus. Teiresias's prophecy that Odysseus must take off again after his return to Ithaca, or the effort with which Zeus and Athena have to hold him back from further fighting are the hallmark of a poet who can keep his many-turning hero and his own many-turning story going interminably, with ever-new adventures and ever-continuing battles.

In contrast to the fluency and eagerness of Demodocus's singing among the Phaeacians, the first mention of song or singing in the poem depicts a bard who sings "by necessity" (ἀνάγκῃ, 1.154). On this occasion, our introduction to the palace on Ithaca, Telemachus confides to the stranger (Athena in disguise) that the suitors think only of "the lyre and singing, because they are eating another man's substance without payment" (1.159f.; cf. 151f.). The sequence of ideas suggests that the suitors may like poetry well enough, but they like it particularly when it accompanies a good meal, that is, as Telemachus says in line 152, when it is ἀναθήματα δαιτός, an accompaniment of the feasting. We soon learn the title of Phemius's song: "The Grim Return of the Achaeans"; but this is the only song in the palace whose actual subject is specified (1.325f.). Otherwise, very little is said of what the bard sings on Ithaca, nor are the suitors ever shown as reacting to or caring about the quality or the material of the songs they hear.

Characteristically, this first song brings a "pleasure" or τέρψις that sharply divides its hearers. As in the case of Demodocus's song of "Odysseus and the Wooden Horse," one member of the audience weeps while the rest "take pleasure." The teenager, rather careless of mother's feelings, approves of the bard's recital of what is newest in fashion. Penelope, looking back to the past and the losses of which this song reminds her, withdraws after her ineffectual protest and weeps with her maids upstairs (1.360–64).

Despite her departure, her appearance has created a disturbance that Telemachus, in his first assertion of budding manly authority, has to quiet (1.368–71): "Suitors of my mother, you who practice insult most violent (ὑπέρβιον ὕβριν ἔχοντες), now let us take joy in the feasting, and let there be no shouting, since it is a lovely thing (καλόν) to listen to a bard

---

[16] See, for instance, D. Stewart, *The Disguised Guest*, 146–95; S. Goldhill, "Reading Differences," passim.

such as is this one, godlike in his voice." The strange collocations reveal how anomalous singing is in this setting: insult and feasting, violence and pleasure, shouting and a godlike voice. In fact, this scene shows the suitors at their best; they never again behave even this well. After Telemachus's call for orderly listening, the first of the suitors to speak is the most shameless, Antinous, and he complains of Telemachus's "lofty address and bold speaking" (ὑψαγόρην τ᾽ ἔμεναι καὶ θαρσαλέως ἀγορεύειν, 385), while the others bite their lips. At the suitors' last feast, he meets his end in silence, with Odysseus's first arrow in his throat, kicking away the table and scattering the food on the ground (22.15–21).

Phemius's song of the "Grim Return of the Achaeans" is the only song to which the suitors listen "in silence." Otherwise, song is for them only "the accompaniment to the feasting," a kind of Mycenaean muzak, to deaden the clatter of the cups. The bard is merely the physical background to their eating and drinking, as Telemachus perhaps implies when he describes the suitors to his father in book 16 and lists the bard along with the herald and the two carvers of meat (16.252ff.). The suitors would just as soon throw the javelin, the discus, or for that matter the odd ox hoof or footstool. Their idea of real fun is to see the two beggars slug it out. At their last banquet, there is no mention of song or bard at all. But instead of a bard, they have the prophet Theoclymenus, with his ominous vision of darkness and bloody meats (20.345–57). The suitors' last song is performed by Odysseus himself as he finally throws off his rags, handles the great bow as a bard handles the lyre, makes it sing like a swallow, and then with triumphant irony shouts that it is time "for singing and the lyre, accompaniments of the feasting"—with the irony in the formula that I mentioned above.

The *Odyssey*'s first scene of bardic performance gets special prominence from the suspense created by postponing the song of Phemius for nearly two hundred lines after his introduction. He enters with his lovely lyre and beautiful song in 1.153–55; but we have to wait until the end of the interview between Telemachus and Athena/Mentes (1.158–324) for the song (1.325, τοῖσι δ᾽ ἀοιδὸς ἄειδε, takes up ἦ τοι ὁ φορμίζων ἀνεβάλλετο καλὸν ἀείδειν, 1.155). And, as we have observed, this song then becomes the focus of a three-way conflict between Telemachus, Penelope, and the suitors (1.336ff.).

Demodocus's entrance receives an even fuller description than does Phemius's. Homer tells us no less than six times that this bard's skill has a divine origin,[17] with the culminating praise that it comes from "either

---

[17] *Od.* 8.44f., 63f., 73, 480f., 488, 498.

the Muse, daughter of Zeus, or [from] Apollo" (8.488). Here too there is
a steady progression of honors for the poet, from the initial epithet "divine bard" (8.43, repeated at the end by Alcinous, 8.539) to Odysseus's
honorific speech and gift of meat when he asks for the "Song of the
Wooden Horse" (8.474–91). Homer even suggests an etymological play
on Demodocus's name as "honored among the people" (Δημόδοκον
λαοῖσι τετιμένον, 8.472). And he also introduces a number of unique
personal details: the Muses' gift of song in compensation for blindness
(8.63f., the reverse of their punishment of Thamyris in *Il.* 2.594–600), the
combination of singing tales of gods and heroes and serving as an accom-
panist for the dance (8.256ff.); Odysseus's reflection that bards receive
honor and reverence from all men because of the Muse's love and teaching (8.479–81); and Alcinous's generalization that "the gods weave doom
for mortals so that there may be song for men of the future" (8.579f.).

The Phaeacians fully appreciate their bard, but their score in audience
attentiveness may even be a little too high, for when Arete and then Alcinous compliment Odysseus on his bardlike skill, they urge him to delay
his return and thus present him with a delicate problem out of which he
tactfully maneuvers (11.335–61).[18] He finds a better balance in audience
response among the eager, attentive listeners who constitute his true
friends on Ithaca, especially Eumaeus and Penelope. The trusty swineherd Eumaeus would gladly while away the long night with the tales of
his guest, listening to the woes that he has endured (14.191–98). Later
Eumaeus praises this guest to Penelope, telling how he "enchanted" him
with his tales like a bard (17.513–22), unknowingly repeating the terms
of the Phaeacian praise of Odysseus in book 11: silence, "enchantment,"
and bardlike skill. But the respectful silence that is reality on Scheria is
only a wish among the noisy suitors on Ithaca (cf. 17.513 and 11.333).
"Wine is the mirror of a man," the lyric poet Alcaeus wrote some hundred years after Homer. But in the *Odyssey*, song, or how one listens to
song, is also such a mirror.

These scenes of telling one's life story show us another appeal of bardic
song, and one that runs throughout all of archaic and classical Greek culture. For Eumaeus the telling of tales—and, by implication, the singing
of songs—is a sharing of the woes of life that bind together all men as
"miserable mortals," δειλοῖσι βροτοῖσι. Hence the two men, Odysseus the beggar and the swineherd Eumaeus, exchange their experiences

---

[18] For an interesting analysis of this tension from the point of view of the oral performer,
see William F. Wyatt, Jr., "The Intermezzo of Odyssey 11 and the Poets Homer and Odysseus," especially 240–47.

of κήδεα, "griefs," with sympathy on both sides (cf. 14.185). Eumaeus's comment is characteristic (14.361ff.): "Wretched among strangers, much did you stir my heart telling each of these things that you suffered and all your wanderings." Alcinous's reflection on seeing Odysseus weep over Demodocus's song of Troy is the complement to this affective view of song (8.579f.): "The gods have spun out doom for men so that there may be song for those of the future." The Phaeacian king, characteristically, looks at the song (ἀοιδή) from the outside, as an aesthetic object, rather than at the sufferings that make up its contents. In the next book Odysseus, hearing Eumaeus's tale, echoes Eumaeus's sympathy: "Alas, how, small as you were, swineherd Eumaeus, were you tossed far from your native land and your parents" (15.381f.). This is the kind of involvement that a good story creates. Men weep over such tales, as Odysseus did over Demodocus's song of Troy; and this emotional response of tears, though concealed out of politeness to the host, is not regarded as remarkable or shameful.

There is a direct line between this function of song as a celebration of human solidarity in the face of suffering and the development of Attic drama, which in so many other respects owes much to Homer. Drama, among other things, creates the community of the theater as a community of shared grief and compassion. We may think of plays like Euripides' *Andromache, Suppliants, Hecuba,* or *Trojan Women.* Here, for example, is the chorus's closing song in the *Hippolytus* (1462–66):

> κοινὸν τόδ᾽ ἄχος πᾶσι πολίταις
> ἦλθεν ἀέλπτως.
> πολλῶν δακρύων ἔσται πίτυλος·
> τῶν γὰρ μεγάλων ἀξιοπενθεῖς
> φῆμαι μᾶλλον κατέχουσιν.

This woe came without expectation as common to all the citizens. There will be an oar-beat of many tears; for the tales of the great that are worthy of grieving do more prevail.

Through the experience of this "common woe" in the tragic spectacle, the individual spectator participates in the "community" of suffering mortality and thereby experiences the brotherhood and the solace of grief contained in the poetic tradition.[19] The epic equivalent is the ever-present generality of the δειλοὶ βροτοί in the background of the poems, the

---

[19] On this feature of tragedy, see my "Theater, Ritual, and Commemoration in Euripides' *Hippolytus,*" especially 62ff.

suffering, ephemeral mortals whose "wretchedness" of all times and places is reflected in the innumerable victims, named and unnamed, of war and its aftermath. If we leap ahead about a thousand years, we see this community of shared suffering established as a regular topos of consolation literature. Plutarch, writing, not speaking, to a friend who has lost a son, begins his *Consolatio ad Apollonium* thus: "I had long since been sharing in your pain and your grief, Apollonius, when I heard of your dearest son's departure from life . . ." (101e–f). And he concludes:

> Resume, therefore, the spirit of a brave-hearted and high-minded man and set free from all this wretchedness both yourself and the mother of the youth, and your relatives and friends, as you may do by pursuing a more tranquil form of life, which will be most gratifying both to your son and to all of us who are concerned for you, as rightly we should be (καὶ πᾶσιν ἡμῖν τοῖς κηδομένοις σου κατὰ τὸ προσῆκον, 121f–122a).

It is as if the letter effects the consolation itself by including Apollonius within the community of "all" the kin and friends who share in his suffering.

In terms of audience response, the most sympathetic and attentive audience that we see in Homer is the longed-for wife to whom Odysseus tells the tale of his wandering in book 23 (248–341). Even more than the Phaeacians's response, Penelope's fascinated and involved hearing provides a clue to what might be the bard's ideal audience: There is a quiet, attentive, personally engaged, and patient listening, with "joy in the hearing." There is no postprandial or postcoital dozing; she stays awake "until he had related everything" (23.306–09). Here, as in the meeting of (disguised) husband and wife in book 19, we may also catch a glimpse of the privileged circumstances in which a bard might try out new songs or improve old ones: a quiet setting; a single, well disposed auditor; all the time he needs; and the opportunity to sing of something he loves. If Homer did in fact at some point dictate the "monumental composition" he finally achieved, might he have done it in an atmosphere of friendly calm analogous to that between Odysseus and Eumaeus or Odysseus and Penelope?

Making songs and telling tales, however, are always integral parts of the plot of the poem; and so is this scene between husband and wife. Their joy in listening and telling recreates and exemplifies that mutual trust and concern that belong to the ideal of ὁμοφροσύνη (likemindedness) that Odysseus singles out as the greatest happiness in marriage at

19

the point when he has overcome the biggest obstacles to his return (23.301–09; cf. 6.181–85).[20] Indeed, Penelope enacts this special involvement in the teller's story when she insists that, before they bed down for the full account of his wanderings (23.306ff.), Odysseus recount the prophecy of Teiresias, even though this is a tale that will definitely not give "joy to the heart" (23.256–67).

This telling gives a momentary flash of an anti-*Odyssey*: a tale received without the "pleasure" that aesthetic distance makes possible. It is a narrative of a long voyage to the "towns" of strange men (ἐπεὶ μάλα πολλὰ βροτῶν ἐπὶ ἄστε᾽ ἄνωγεν/ἐλθεῖν, 23.267f.; cf. 1.1–4). Like Odysseus hearing Demodocus's song of Troy, it is also a tale that its audience (i.e., Penelope) hears with intimate personal concern and therefore without "joy" or "pleasure" in the woes about to be rehearsed (23.265–68):

> αὐτὰρ ἐγὼ μυθήσομαι οὐδ᾽ ἐπικεύσω.
> οὐ μέν τοι θυμὸς κεχαρήσεται· οὐδὲ γὰρ αὐτὸς
> χαίρω, ἐπεὶ μάλα πολλὰ βροτῶν ἐπὶ ἄστε᾽ ἄνωγεν
> ἐλθεῖν.

Well, I will tell you the tale and not conceal it. Yet your spirit will take no joy in it; for I myself have no joy, since (Teiresias) ordered me to go to very many towns of men.

This reluctant exchange of personal fortunes between husband and wife also recreates a somewhat analogous situation between a differently reunited couple, Helen and Menelaus in book 4. But their exchange of life stories contains implicit accusation, distrust, and guilt; and their talk of the past brings them no delight or forgetfulness of woes (4.235–89).[21] To resolve their conflict and bring them peace in their household, they need the Circe-like drug that Helen puts in the wine (4.220–32), something external to the tales themselves. Odysseus's telling, by contrast, has a magic spell of its own, its κηληθμός or θέλξις (cf. 11.334, 17.514, 521).

The poets obviously had a practical interest in suggesting that the bard's presence at a banquet sets a seal of approval on the host's good behavior and upright character. From the *Odyssey* to the *Oresteia*, the harmonious banquet-song gets a deeper meaning, perhaps most program-

---

[20] For a good discussion of ὁμοφροσύνη in the poem, see Norman Austin, *Archery at the Dark of the Moon: Poetic Problems in Homer's Odyssey*, 181, 188f., 203f.

[21] See W. G. Thalmann, *Conventions of Form and Thought*, 166; also Anne Bergren, "Helen's 'Good Drug': *Odyssey* IV 1–305," especially 205ff.; S. Goldhill, "Reading Differences," 21–24.

matically in Pindar. One need only think of his *Pythian* 1, the richest elaboration of the situation of the performance itself as a microcosm of the social and political order (1–6):

> Χρυσέα φόρμιγξ, Ἀπόλλωνος καὶ ἰοπλοκάμων
> σύνδικον Μοισᾶν κτέανον· τᾶς ἀκούει
> μὲν βάσις ἀγλαΐας ἀρχά,
> πείθονται δ᾽ ἀοιδοὶ σάμασιν
> ἀγησιχόρων ὁπόταν προοιμίων
> ἀμβολὰς τεύχῃς ἐλελιζομένα.
> καὶ τὸν αἰχματὰν κεραυνὸν σβεννύεις
> αἰενάου πυρός.

Golden Lyre, jointly shared possession of Apollo and the violet-tressed Muses: This the dance-step, beginning of radiance, hears; and the singers obey the signals whenever you, quivering in song, fashion the preludes of hymns that lead the choruses. And you quench the spear-pointed lightning of (Zeus's) ever-flowing fire.

Through Apollo and the Muses, Pindar lifts the power of the joyfully resounding instrument at the festive performance from earth to the heavens, where it embodies both the order of art and the moral order of the gods working among mortals.

Homer is far from the more abstractive mental operations of using metaphor to separate poetry from the actual conditions of performance. Unlike Pindar, he never treats song as a symbol of something other than itself. Such a step may go along with the movement toward an increasingly literate culture that Pindar's poetry indirectly begins to reflect.[22] Yet the *Odyssey*'s self-consciousness about poetry at the least hints at the poet's moral authority. This emerges at its clearest in the comparison of Odysseus to a bard stringing his lyre at the moment when he bends his great bow and makes it sing like a swallow for the shot that restores order, kingship, and marriage on Ithaca (21.406f., 411). And, as we have noted, how an audience in this poem listens to a bard or a bard-like narrator is a touchstone of its moral character.

Yet if the poet of the *Odyssey* is explicit about the analogy between bard and hero, the poet of the *Iliad* is not so very far away. Although the *Iliad* does not take the final step of assimilating bard and hero, it too ennobles art by presenting the best of the Achaeans in a bardic role, singing the κλέα ἀνδρῶν in the solitude of his tent. Hesiod suggests that poetry, by

---

[22] See my *Pindar's Mythmaking*, 153ff.

evoking the memory of past events, brings a pleasurable forgetting of sorrows (*Theogony* 54f., 98–103).[23] Are we to see this therapeutic function of poetry put into practice by Homer's Achilles? In the *Odyssey* song and narratives of the past belong to pleasure, not grief, and tears are not the appropriate response to an after-dinner story or song.

Giving pleasure, τέρψις, to his audience is obviously the Homeric bard's first concern, but it is not his only one. By the very fact of creating a tearful response of sadness, as we have seen, the *Odyssey*-poet also calls attention to the paradoxical pleasure that its tales of woe create.[24] In a culture where knowledge of the past is preserved largely through oral transmission, the bard also preserves the memory of earlier generations and the names of those who would otherwise be "invisible" in Hades, ἄφαντοι or ἄϊστοι. What is alive is what is heard on the lips of men, i.e., what the bards preserve in song.[25] Hence Homer can count on his audience's interest in the catalogue of the Achaean princes and the cities they rule (*Il.* 2.494–759). The generations of men are as fleeting as the seasonal growth of leaves, but Homer can give the generations of the Lycian Glaucus a more than seasonal life by incorporating them into his song (*Il.* 6.145–211).

In the *Odyssey* the first threat to the hero's return is the destruction of memory: The Lotos Eaters, the first people to be encountered beyond the familiar limits of Troy and the heroic world, would keep Odysseus and his men stranded in never-never land through the amnesiac drug that would make them "forget their return" (νόστου λαθέσθαι, *Od.* 9.97). The loss of the memory of his homeland in Circe's bed will deprive him of his humanness just as surely as her drugs deprive his comrades of their human form. The other side of that loss of human identity is to be forgotten in the homeland that waits for him, to be carried off to some unknown place "without fame (ἀκλειῶς), unseen, unknown," leaving no trace in the "hearing" of men (*Od.* 1.241f.; cf. 4.727f.).

---

[23] This paradoxical connection of the memory of the Muse's song and the forgetfulness it brings has often been noted. For recent discussion and bibliography see G. Walsh, *The Varieties of Enchantment*, 22f.; W. G. Thalmann, *Conventions of Form and Thought*, 136; F. Bertolini, "Odisseo aedo, Omero carpentiere," 155f.

[24] See *Od.* 1.340–55, 4.183–95, 8.536–43, and 572–78; also above, note 8.

[25] See Eric A. Havelock, *Preface to Plato*, passim, especially chap. 4; also his *The Literate Revolution in Greece and Its Cultural Consequences*, 122ff. This "presentness" of what oral communication keeps alive in the "hearing" of men in a preliterate society produces what anthropologists refer to as the homoeostasis of oral cultures. See I. Morris, "The Use and Abuse of Homer," 87, with the references there cited; and Walter J. Ong, *Orality and Literacy*, 46ff.

The Sirens' song holds a subtle form of this self-obliteration. It is a deadly alternative to being remembered among the living generations who define and continue one's human identity. Although their song of Troy promises both "knowledge" and "pleasure" (12.188), these effects are entirely detached from a human community. Sitting in the watery waste somewhere between Circe's island and the Clashing Rocks, these singers are surrounded not by a living, eager audience of men and women in a palace or a place of assembly but by the skin and bones of rotting corpses (12.45f.), the horrid truth behind the "flowery meadow" of their island (12.159), and the sweet seduction of their voice (12.44).[26] This decay and putrefaction are the complete antithesis of the "nonperishable glory" (κλέος ἄφθιτον) conferred by song, just as the remoteness of their voice from any human society and the solitariness of Odysseus's listening are the negation of the communal context where life-giving memory has a place.

By keeping alive the memory of noble deeds, the bard also preserves and promulgates the values embodied in heroic action. Tyrtaeus's use of Homeric battle scenes to celebrate the rather un-Homeric solidarity of the Spartan hoplite formation is a familiar example.[27] The bard's function as the vocal embodiment of the communal values exemplified in his songs is perhaps what leads Agamemnon to the step of putting his bard in charge of watching over Clytaemnestra during his long absence at Troy.[28] The task in fact proves to be beyond the abilities of this anonymous singer, who clearly should have stuck to what he knew best (cf. *Od.* 3.267–71). Is this bard's anonymity in fact a mark of his failure?[29]

Because the Greeks, at least to the end of the fifth century B.C., envisage poetry as part of a performance and as the living voice of song, they pay special attention to its vocal dimension. Its physical qualities recur again and again in metaphors of sweetness, flowing, abundance, or

[26] On the Sirens see G. Walsh, *The Varieties of Enchantment*, 14f.; my "*Kleos* and Its Ironies in the *Odyssey*," 38–43; Piero Pucci, "The Song of the Sirens," and *Odysseus Polutropos: Intertextual Readings in the Odyssey and the Iliad*, 209–13; J.-P. Vernant, "Figures féminines de la mort en Grèce," 143f.; also my "Ritual and Commemoration in Early Greek Poetry and Tragedy," 332; W. Schadewaldt, *Von Homers Welt und Werk*, 82 aptly describes the Sirens as "dämonische Gegenbilder der Musen."

[27] See, for example, Tyrtaeus 8.31–33 and *Il.* 13.130–33.

[28] See Stephen Scully, "The Bard as the Custodian of Homeric Society: *Odyssey* 3.263–72," 274ff.; also Jesper Svenbro, *La Parole et le marbre*, 31ff.

[29] S. Scully, "The Bard as the Custodian of Homeric Society," 74, takes a different view of this bard's anonymity as "generic, that is, characteristic of the singer's craft and appropriate to his art."

strength. Invoking the Muse in the proem to the Catalogue of Ships, Homer speaks enviously of a "voice unbroken" and "a heart of bronze"— reminders of the physical effort that sustained recitation demands of the oral poet.

A voice that "flows tirelessly sweet from the mouth" is the magical possession of Hesiod's Muses as they sing to Zeus on Olympus. In the space of five lines, Hesiod uses three different words for the poet's "voice," each time with a different epithet: ἀκάματος αὐδή, ὄπα λειριόεσσαν, ἄμβροτον ὄσσαν. Each time too the voice participates in an active, energetic movement: It "flows," "spreads forth," or "is sent forth."[30] Nestor, the repository of traditional wisdom codified into tales and legends, has a voice that "flows sweeter than honey" (Il. 1.249). The elders of Troy, past their prime but still good speakers (ἀγορηταὶ ἐσθλοί), have a clear, sharp voice, like the cicadas singing in trees (Il. 3.150–52). In thinking of the performance of this poetry, then, we need to keep in mind not just its quality of orality but what Paul Zumthor calls its vocality—the beauty, strength, and resonance of the voice that sang it (cf. Il. 2.489f.).[31]

This attention to the materiality and tangibility, almost the visibility, of the voice, extends to other features of the performance. The poet fills his scenes describing bards with concrete things, much as the painter of ripe geometric vases fills his surface with ornaments, animals, or designs. The moment of the song's beginning is adorned with rich objects that hold good cheer, comfort, and beauty (Od. 8.65–70):

> τῷ δ᾽ ἄρα Ποντόνοος θῆκε θρόνον ἀργυρόηλον
> μέσσῳ δαιτυμόνων, πρὸς κίονα μακρὸν ἐρείσας.
> κὰδ᾽ δ᾽ ἐκ πασσαλόφι κρέμασεν φόρμιγγα λίγειαν
> αὐτοῦ ὑπὲρ κεφαλῆς καὶ ἐπέφραδε χερσὶν ἑλέσθαι
> κῆρυξ· πὰρ δ᾽ ἐτίθει κάνεον καλήν τε τράπεζαν,
> πὰρ δὲ δέπας οἴνοιο, πιεῖν ὅτε θυμὸς ἀνώγοι.

In the midst of the feasters Pontonoos placed for him (Demodocus) a silver-studded seat, and set it against a tall pillar. And the herald took down from its peg the clear-singing lyre above his head, and showed him how to take it into his hands. And beside him he set a basket of food and a lovely table and a cup of wine to drink, as his heart bade him.

---

[30] On this passage see F. Bertolini, "Odisseo aedo, Omero carpentiere," 156, with note 45; 163.

[31] See Paul Zumthor, La Poésie et la voix dans la civilisation médiévale, 9–36, especially 11f.

When the song is done, the herald again "hung the clear-singing lyre from its peg and took the hand of Demodocus and led him forth from the hall" (8.105–07). This handing back and forth of the lyre is repeated three times in Demodocus's second song (8.254f., 257, 261f.).

The pattern had already been established, although far more briefly, at the first appearance of a bard, Phemius's singing among the suitors on Ithaca (1.153). The details are omitted from Demodocus's third and last song, perhaps because Homer wants to give special emphasis to Odysseus's response, which takes the form of a signal mark of honor: having the herald put a cut of meat into the singer's hands (8.471–83). Close repetition of the formulas introducing Demodocus early in the book helps show both the continuity with the previous honor and the new, even more distinctive token of respect.[32] In terms of the formulaic structure of the theme "respect for the bard," the chine of roast pork (whatever its effects on Demodocus's digestion and clarity of voice) replaces the lyre. Even here, however, the lyre is not forgotten, for at the end, when King Alcinous notices Odysseus weeping, he orders, "Let Demodocus stay his clear-singing lyre" (8.537).

If we glance ahead some two and half centuries to Pindar, we can at once appreciate this delight that Homer takes in the sensory pleasures that make song "the accompaniment of the feasting." Where Homer is literal, Pindar makes metaphors. Demodocus gets real wine; Pindar, in the radiant poem of *Olympian* 7, for Diagoras of Rhodes, makes the wine that foams in its golden cup into a symbol of the gift of the song that he is offering to the victor.

Another scene of the *Odyssey* may contain an authentic kernel of physical detail about the performance, in this case the performer's attachment to his instrument as an especially precious possession. In book 22, after Odysseus has dispatched the suitors, the bard Phemius makes his appearance. He crawls out of his hiding place and takes refuge at the altar of Zeus in order to ask for mercy (22.330ff.). He enters the narrative here in the characteristically bardic pose of his first appearance, "holding in his hands the clear-singing lyre."[33] When he decides to approach Odysseus and clasp his knees in supplication, he "first places the smooth lyre on the ground, in between the mixing bowl and the silver-studded stool" (22.340f.). These details are gratuitous. Are they perhaps an indirect re-

---

[32] Cf. κῆρυξ δ᾽ ἐγγύθεν ἦλθεν ἄγων ἐρίηρον ἀοιδόν, 8.471 = 8.62; μέσσῳ δαιτυμόνων, πρὸς κίονα μακρὸν ἐρείσας, 8.473 = 8.66; also 8.484f. = 8.71f.; and line 482 closely resembles 68.

[33] *Od.* 22.332; cf. 1.153; note too that 22.331 = 1.154; cf. also 8.67f. and 8.105f., of Demodocus.

145,820

25

flection of the singer's professionalism? The singer would protect his instrument as a modern violinist might his Stradivarius. We may recall too Achilles' lyre, precious booty from Eetion's city (*Il.* 9.188).

Homer chooses this setting of bloody corpses and overturned tables for what is probably his fullest account of poetic inspiration. "You will feel grief if you kill a poet," Phemius tells Odysseus, for I am a poet who "sings for gods and men. I am αὐτοδίδακτος, and a god breathed into my breast songs of every sort."

> αὐτῷ τοι μετόπισθ᾽ ἄχος ἔσσεται, εἴ κεν ἀοιδὸν
> πέφνῃς, ὅς τε θεοῖσι καὶ ἀνθρώποισιν ἀείδω.
> αὐτοδίδακτος δ᾽ εἰμί, θεὸς δέ μοι ἐν φρεσὶν οἴμας
> παντοίας ἐνέφυσεν (22.345–48).

For all of the abject situation in which he finds himself, the bard manages to assert his privileged position. His songs are "for gods and men," and his inspiration comes from a god. When he calls himself αὐτοδίδακτος, he may mean that he "has learned the songs from himself," i.e., that he is not just repeating what he has acquired from a specific human teacher or model.[34] Yet the word does not exclude divine aid. In fact, his next sentence makes it clear that the poet regards the sources of his inspiration as mysterious and therefore divine. In that contact with divinity lies his claim to a special value for himself. Inspired by "a god," he also sings "for men and gods"—*hominum divumque voluptas*, one might say, with Lucretius.[35] By choosing this unlikely occasion to reflect on the poet's divine inspiration, Homer sets his special value into even higher relief.

When Phemius combines his point about being self-taught, αὐτοδίδακτος, with the inspiration of a god, he defines his ability to make songs as not just a personal quality or a mark of genius. The ancient poet views his art as coming *both* from his own power *and* from a god. He may sing, like Phemius among the suitors, "by necessity," ἀνάγκῃ (1.154 = 22.331); but he also sings, as does Demodocus, "in whatever way his θυμός, his impulse, bids him" (8.45 ὅππῃ θυμὸς ἐποτρύνῃσιν ἀείδειν). In a variation on this expression, he sings "when the Muse has impelled him to sing the famed deeds of heroes" (8.73, also of Demodocus: Μοῦσ᾽ ἄρ᾽

---

[34] The passage continues to be much discussed: see W. Schadewaldt, *Von Homers Welt und Werk*, 78f.; G. Walsh, *The Varieties of Enchantment*, 11–13; W. G. Thalmann, *Conventions of Form and Thought*, 126f.; M. Puelma, "Die Dichter und die Wahrheit," 69, with note 7; Walter Pötscher, "Das Selbstverständnis des Dichters in der homerischen Poesie," 12.

[35] W. Schadewaldt, *Von Homers Welt und Werk*, 67, plausibly suggests that the reference is to festivals in honor of the gods and purely secular occasions like banquets.

26

ἀοιδὸν ἀνῆκεν ἀειδέμεναι κλέα ἀνδρῶν). The bard needs the Muse, or the god, to keep him in touch with the memory of remote events, to provide inspiration, or to complete his limited knowledge (as in the invocation of the Muses in the Catalogue of Ships, *Il.* 2.485f.). At the same time, he feels the surge of his θυμός, an intensification of his own energies. At such moments, he is like the warrior into whom the god breathes μένος at the height of battle. Homer uses the same term, ἐνέπνευσε, "breathed into," for both.[36] Both the bard's performance and the warrior's entrance into battle are what we would call peak experiences; they contain a level of intensity accessible to these gifted figures in demanding circumstances, and so they require an influx of energy from a source beyond their control, or, in Homeric terms, a god. At such times of full concentration, the bard, like the warrior, has access to all the strength and power of which he is capable. Conversely, the Muses, like the gods of the *Iliad*, can deprive their favorite of his special strength. Thus they deprive Thamyris of his bardic memory, that most necessary of all the singer's capacities (*Il.* 2.600: ἐκλέλαθον κιθαριστύν).

The Homeric bard is a singer rather than a maker (ἀοιδός rather than ποιητής) because he is the voice and the vehicle of an ancient wisdom. But if the poet's powers are divine, they are not irrational. There is no trace here of the ideas of the divine madness or Dionysiac frenzy that Plato connects with poetry, or certain kinds of poetry, in the *Ion* or *Phaedrus*. Though the poet's art bears the sign of its divine origin, it is none the less still a social art: He sings for mortals as well as for gods: θεοῖσι καὶ ἀνθρώποισιν ἀείδω (*Od.* 22.346).

Phemius and Demodocus may regard their songs as the result of what a later age will call divine inspiration, but the lyre remains solidly rooted in its physical world of sound, sight, and touch, and the poet remains a vulnerable human being who needs food and drink and has to watch out not to get himself stabbed. Hesiod takes a momentous step away from this attitude in the famous proem to his *Theogony*. As a visible objectification of his music power, the scepter that he receives on Mount Helicon parallels the physical "breath" of inspiration that his Muses have "breathed into" him:

καί μοι σκῆπτρον ἔδον δάφνης ἐριθηλέος ὄζον
δρέψασαι, θηητόν· ἐνέπνευσαν δέ μ᾽ ἀοιδὴν
θέσπιν, ἵνα κλείοιμι τά τ᾽ ἐσσόμενα πρό τ᾽ ἐόντα,

---

[36] For such analogies between bard and warrior, see W. Pötscher, "Die Selbstverständnis des Dichters," 21f.

27

καί μ' ἐκέλονθ' ὑμνεῖν μακάρων γένος αἰὲν ἐόντων
σφᾶς δ' αὐτὰς πρῶτόν τε καὶ ὕστατον αἰὲν ἀείδειν.

They (the Muses) plucked the staff and gave it to me, wondrous branch of blooming laurel, and they breathed into me a voice divine, so that I might sing of the things to come and the things that are, and they bade me hymn the grace of the blessed gods who are always, and to sing of them themselves always, first and last (*Theogony* 30–34).

This scepter, to be sure, is still a concrete object in the physical world, stripped from its tree and presented to the poet at a specific moment in his life. It is not yet Pindar's symbolical Golden Lyre on Olympus, microcosm of divine and aesthetic order (see above). But it does point in that direction. Unlike the lyre of Phemius in *Odyssey* 22, it is bestowed on the poet in a supernatural encounter that he describes in the first person.

Hesiod's Muses do not give the lyre itself. Their gift has no *necessary* connection with poetry or song. It is, rather, a symbol of power in a more general sense, not identical with song, obviously, but signifying the poet's privileged contact with the divine realm of song to which the Muses belong. Hesiod thus detaches the empowering sign of poetic craft from the act of singing and from the immediate performative context. In this respect he is operating in a zone of greater speculative freedom about his art than did Homer. Scepter instead of lyre also alludes to the social function of his poetry, for the kings in the Homeric assemblies hold the scepter to command speech (e.g. *Il.* 1.234ff.). Thus he can make a direct address to the greedy princes in the *Works and Days* (βασιλῆες δωροφάγοι, 248, 264; cf. 38f.). Whereas Hesiod confronts the greedy kings in his own voice, Homer can only set up a fictional attack in a remote period (Achilles confronting Agamemnon in *Iliad* 1, Odysseus confronting Thersites in *Iliad* 2).

The Homeric bard presents himself as more attuned to his audience than to the situation of composition or creation. His chief concern, one could say, is pragmatics, not poetics (which is not to say that he lacks a poetics). His Muses are the repositories of social memory rather than principles of creativity per se. He identifies with his audience rather than claiming (as Pindar, for example, will do) that he is different from or superior to his audience and thus has a right to speak with a special moral authority on his own account. Homer and even Hesiod, though inspired by Muses, do not call themselves their prophet or spokesman, as Pindar does. Nor do they call attention to their own moralizing revisions of the tales that they tell, as Pindar does with the story of the gods' cannibalistic feasting on Pelops in *Olympian* 1 (48ff.). Neither Homer nor Hesiod ever sets himself apart from a large segment of his audience in the way that Pindar does when he labels "the crowd of men, in the largest part," as "blind in heart" and "unable to see the truth" (*Nemean* 7.23f.).

The Homeric bard certainly does convey moral judgments and ethical insights (one need only think of the proem of the *Odyssey*, 1.32–43); but he does not define himself in terms of such tasks. This more critical spirit develops only with the more individualizing, independent, and self-assertive poetics of late archaic lyric (especially Simonides and Pindar); and of course it culminates in the dialogic presentation of myth and the conflictual situations dramatized in tragedy. However much tragedy owes to epic and lyric song, it also represents a radical break with the archaic view of the poet.

The Homeric bard remains, above all, a "singer of tales" (to use Albert Lord's phrase), a purveyor of pleasure (τέρψις), and a preserver of traditions. But in that role he is indispensable to his memory-hungry and pleasure-loving audience, and he is valued and honored accordingly. The Phaeacians, idealized for many of their political and technological skills, are also idealized for their skills as an audience. They are the most eager for song and story, both about the gods and about men; take the most pleasure in hearing the bard; and accord him more honor than we see anywhere else in the poem. Telling his story in this privileged setting (whatever the risks and dangers in the background), even the habitually lying Odysseus exercises the magical spell of an inspired singer (11.333f.); and for all we know he may even be telling them the truth.

CHAPTER TWO

Aristotle's Reading of Homer and Its Background

N. J. RICHARDSON

As CHARLES SEGAL has shown in the first paper in this collection, the Homeric poems themselves can tell us a good deal about the audiences of epic song and their reactions and expectations, thereby raising issues that will become important in the later criticism of Homer. The emotional effects of song; the questions of originality, of poetic technique and inspiration, of credibility, truth, and fiction; the didactic, ethical, and commemorative roles of singers; and whether they themselves should be held responsible for the moral complexities of their narratives are all themes that can already be detected in what is said about singers and audiences in Homer, foreshadowing what is to come.

In the archaic period, what strikes one first is a growing awareness of the problem of epic song as fictional narrative. This is reflected in the famous address of the Muses to Hesiod in his *Theogony* (26–28). If the Muses can sing both truth and also fiction resembling the truth, how and where does one draw the line between the two? Solon's dismissive observation that "poets lie a great deal" (πολλὰ ψεύδονται ἀοιδοί, fr. 29 West) anticipates the more detailed criticisms of the sixth century B.C. philosophers Xenophanes, Heraclitus, and (probably also) Pythagoras, and Stesichorus's explicit rejection of the Homeric and Hesiodic accounts of Helen and the Trojan War. Xenophanes is concerned to combat the epic portrayal of the gods as anthropomorphic and fallible, and the popular acceptance of Homer as a religious teacher (frs. B10–12, 14–16 D-K). Heraclitus attacks the philosophical authority of both Homer and Hesiod (frs. A22, B40, 42, 56, 57, 106 D-K). Hesiod's breadth of learning (πολυμαθίη) should not be mistaken for wisdom (fr. B40), and Homer, although wiser than all other Greeks, was unable to solve a children's riddle, the riddle of the lice (fr. B56). Homer and Archilochus deserved to be expelled from poetic contests and flogged, presumably on moral grounds and for misleading people (fr. B42). According to later legend, Pythagoras was said to have seen Homer and Hesiod being punished in the Underworld, because of their lies about the gods (Hieronymus of Rhodes, fr. 42 Wehrli). Meanwhile Stesichorus produced his own version of the story of Helen, in which she never went to Troy but stayed in Egypt throughout the war whilst a phantom of her appeared at Troy (frs. 192–93 Page [PMG]). The phantom Helen was destined later to have philosophical repercussions as a symbol of human illusion for Euripides, Plato, and the Neoplatonists.

At the same time, such attacks did not prevent people from appealing to Homer as a historical source, for political reasons, as Athens is said to have done early in the sixth century in her dispute with Megara over Salamis (Aristotle *Rhetoric* 1375b30). The Athenians' claim to Sigeum in the Troad was based at least partly on their participation in the Trojan War, as portrayed in the *Iliad* (Herodotus 5.94.2). We hear more of such appeals later, during the Persian Wars (Hdt. 7.161.3, 169, 171, 9.27.4). The authority of Homer in sixth-century Athens is shown most clearly by the regulation that the Homeric poems alone should be recited at the Panathenaia.[1] Although we are never explicitly told that "Homer" means exclusively the *Iliad* and *Odyssey*, that is probably what is meant by the fourth-century B.C. authors who first mention this rule, and it seems quite possible that these two poems were already being distinguished from the other early epics loosely associated by tradition with Homer's name.

Finally, towards the end of the sixth century, we begin to hear of an attempt to meet the attacks of the philosophers on their own ground through allegory, in the work of Theagenes of Rhegium, who is said to have been the first to use this method. The context in which this is mentioned is that of allegorical interpretations of the Theomachy in *Iliad* 20 and 21, in terms of the conflict both of physical elements and also of moral or psychological forces (Theagenes fr. A2 D-K). This episode would make a natural starting point for such interpretations, although the exact nature of Theagenes' own theory is unclear. However, it looks as if he discussed the Homeric text in some detail, because a variant reading is ascribed to him in the scholia (fr. A3), and he is said to have been the first person to write on Homer's poetry, life, and date, as well as on the Greek language in general (frs. A1, 1a). It is interesting to find linguistic study closely linked to allegorical interpretation at this early stage.

The various approaches that we have just reviewed continue through the literature of the fifth century. Pindar, for example, is clearly sensitive to philosophical criticism of the kind expressed by Xenophanes, and he is also more broadly concerned with the problems of truth, credibility, and

---

[1] Lycurgus *In Leocratem* 102, Isocrates *Panegyricus* 159, Plato *Hipparchus* 228b.

the fictional character of poetry. The classic case is his rationalisation of the myth of Pelops in *Olympian* 1 (25ff.), where he comments on the deceptive charm of poetic tales (μῦθοι), their power of lulling us into accepting the marvellous and fabulous as credible. More specifically, in *Nemean* 7 (20ff.) he speaks of Homer's exaggeration of the truth about Odysseus, and the way in which he persuades us to suspend our disbelief: "I think that the story of Odysseus was exaggerated beyond what he experienced, because of the sweet words of Homer: For there is an impressive dignity about his fictions and winged craft, and poetic skill deceives, leading astray with fables: The generality of men has a blind heart." At the same time, however, the shame of the suicide of Ajax was counterbalanced by the honour paid to him by Homer, "who set all his valour upright again, telling of it in accordance with his wand of wondrous verses, as a theme for later singers to play on" (*Isthmian* 4.41ff.). And just before his criticism of Homer in *Nemean* 7, he had referred to the idea of commemorative poetry as a "mirror for noble deeds" (14–16). Here already we see the tension between the ideas of epic song as commemoration, reflecting a true image, and poetic fiction as a distorting medium.

Like Pindar, the historians Herodotus and Thucydides attempt a rationalising approach. Herodotus, for example, argues that Homer's story of Helen at Troy cannot be true (for if she had been there the Trojans would have surely given her back), and he accepts the alternative version that left her in Egypt. Homer, he says, knew the truth, but rejected it as less appropriate (εὐπρεπής) for his poetry (2.112–20). He also observes here that the epic *Cypria* cannot be Homer's work, because it disagrees with the *Iliad* over Paris's journey to Troy (2.117). Elsewhere (4.32) Herodotus doubts whether the *Epigonoi* is Homeric. Thucydides draws detailed deductions about the historical nature of the Trojan War and early Greek society from Homer and other epic poetry, whilst stressing the tendency of poets to exaggeration (1.1–22). Thucydides' respect for Homer as a source is striking, although there is a strong note of disparagement in Pericles' funeral speech, where he says that Athens does not need a Homer to sing her praises, nor any poet whose verses will give a momentary pleasure, only to be contradicted by the truth of history (2.41.4).

So far, we have been dealing largely with attitudes to epic as a whole, rather than with more detailed discussion of Homer or anything approaching literary criticism in a modern sense. Close reading and discussion of problems there must always have been, but it is with the Sophists that they begin to emerge into the foreground.[2] This was encouraged by the Sophists' special interest in language and also in the use of poetic texts to underpin their own theories. Echoes of such discussion can be detected in chapter 25 of the *Poetics* and in the surviving fragments of Aristotle's *Homeric Problems*. Debate about the detailed interpretation of a text (such as Simonides' poem on virtue in Plato's *Protagoras*) led naturally to the search for the *underlying* sense, the ὑπόνοια. For men like Protagoras, the early poets were really Sophists in disguise, clothing their philosophical wisdom in a popular dress.[3] From this could develop more elaborate and extraordinary allegorical constructions, such as that of Metrodorus of Lampsacus, interpreting the whole of the *Iliad* in terms of Anaxagoras's cosmology (Metrodorus frs. A3–4 D-K).[4] Such extreme examples might well have given the whole practice of allegory a bad name!

Anaxagoras himself seems to have been far more cautious: He is said to have been "the first to show that Homer's poetry concerned valour and justice" (fr. A1 D-K). This sounds not so very different from the popular view reflected in Aristophanes' *Frogs*, that Homer teaches "marshalling of armies, forms of valour, arming of men for war" (1034ff.). This kind of moralising approach is echoed by Niceratus in Xenophon's *Symposium* (3.5), when he says that his father Nicias made him learn the whole of Homer's poetry by heart, as part of the education of a gentleman. Later on he claims him as a source of information on all kinds of ethical and practical subjects (4.6–7), as does the rhapsode Ion in Plato's dialogue (*Ion* 537a ff.). It is, incidentally, in these contexts that we hear the names of the various supposedly leading interpreters of the Homeric poems. Apart from Metrodorus, these include Stesimbrotus of Thasos, Anaximander, and Glaucon. It is surely significant that we know so little about most of them: Their views and theories about the poems were overtaken by those of later critics. But Stesimbrotus was the teacher of the first person definitely known to have "edited" the text of Homer, the epic poet Antimachus of Colophon.[5] Here we seem to glimpse the beginnings of scholarship in its later Hellenistic and modern sense.

Many of the major sophists, on the other hand, are known to have used Homeric themes and characters as vehicles for the expression of their own ethical or rhetorical ideas. We see this clearly in the debate between Socrates and Hippias over the relative merits of Achilles' and Odysseus's

---

[2] Cf. N. J. Richardson, "Homeric Professors in the Age of the Sophists."

[3] Plato *Protagoras* 316d–e; *Theaetetus* 180c–e.

[4] For details, see N. J. Richardson, "Homeric Professors," 68–70.

[5] Cf. Rudolf Pfeiffer, *History of Classical Scholarship From the Beginnings*, 35–36.

characters (Plato *Hippias Minor*), in Gorgias's *Helen* and *Palamedes*, or in the *Ajax* and *Odysseus* of Antisthenes. The long list of essays on Homeric subjects ascribed to Antisthenes includes many that probably set out to draw moral lessons from the poems.[6] Socrates himself seems to have been fond of using Homer to illustrate a point, if we can judge from Xenophon and Plato, and sometimes this takes the form of moral allegory: The Sirens' charms strike at those ambitious for fame, and it was gluttony that turned Odysseus's men into swine, and self-restraint that saved Odysseus himself![7]

This early moralising view of Homer perhaps finds its culmination (as far as the classical period is concerned) in the *Mouseion* of Alcidamas, who seems to have collected traditional stories about the early poets, including the old tales of the contest of Homer and Hesiod and their respective deaths, in order to illustrate the moral value of their works: This may well be one of the works that Plato has in mind when he attacks such an approach in book 10 of the *Republic* and questions whether Homer ever was of any practical or civic use to anyone.[8] Alcidamas seems to have admired Homer's poems especially for their ethical realism: He called the *Odyssey* a "fine mirror of human life" (Aristotle *Rhetoric* 1406b12). He also spoke of the honours paid to Homer and other poets, a theme that Plato again treats with sarcastic scepticism.

By contrast with this type of viewpoint, Protagoras himself gives us what is perhaps the first example of interpretative criticism of a more "structural" type, embedded by chance in a papyrus commentary on *Iliad* 21 (fr. A30 D-K). He apparently observed that the battle of Achilles with the river god Scamander was designed to form a transition from Achilles' previous exploits to the battle of the gods ("and perhaps also to increase Achilles' importance," adds the scholiast). Thus, in addition to showing a linguistic interest in Homer (exemplified by his criticism of the poet for addressing the Muse in the imperative: fr. A29 D-K), Protagoras may have taken a broader view of the poet's compositional techniques. But such instances are still rare and hard to detect at this period.

We have reached the threshold of the fourth century and must now consider Plato, whose general views about poetry are both well-known and at the same time very complex and hard to sum up. His attitude to Homer is clearly deeply divided: on the one hand an abiding love of the

[6] See N. J. Richardson, "Homeric Professors," 77–81.
[7] Xenophon *Memorabilia* 2.6.10–12, 1.3.7.
[8] Cf. N. J. Richardson, "The Contest of Homer and Hesiod and Alkidamas' *Mouseion*."

poet, whose influence on him (as 'Longinus' observed: 13.3–4) can be detected at every turn (he quotes him some 150 times);[9] on the other, equally strong misgivings about the role of poetry in the philosophical life. His own work may well be viewed as a philosophical alternative to traditional literary forms, especially epic and drama, and his own myths as designed to replace those of Homer and Hesiod. At the end of the *Republic*, the story of Er is said to be "not a tale told to Alcinous, but rather that of a courageous man" (οὐ . . . Ἀλκίνου γε ἀπόλογον. . . . ἀλλ' ἀλκίμου μὲν ἀνδρός *Rep.* 614b2–3). Thus Homeric fiction gives way to a tale that conveys philosophical truth, even if in mythical form.

For Plato, although he toys with the idea from time to time, allegory is no answer to the problem of poetry. There is no way of discovering whether or not a particular interpretation of the text is correct. You cannot prove this philosophically, and even if you could ask the poet, he could not tell you. Poets are mouthpieces of divine inspiration, hence essentially irrational, unable to give an account (λόγος) of what they mean. Poetry is of no use as a direct source of knowledge.[10]

On the other hand, the emotional power of epic and dramatic poetry is immeasurable. The intense sensations of pity and fear, already noted by Gorgias in his *Defence of Helen* (fr. B11.9 D-K), are also experienced by Ion the rhapsode and his audiences at the high points of his recitation of Homer (*Ion* 535b–c). In the *Republic* the potentially damaging effect of such emotional scenes in Homer and tragedy on our own characters is one of the main themes in Plato's attack on poetry, combined with the more direct onslaught on the falsehood of poetic portrayals of gods and heroes. The stories, untrue and immoral as they are, influence our own behaviour in turn, and the insidious pleasure that they arouse must be resisted. Finally, in book 10, we have the deeper attack on artistic μίμησις as a whole, as an illusory portrayal of what is itself only a world of appearances. Here the old idea of narrative or dramatic poetry as a mirror of life, and hence as morally valuable, is explicitly rejected.

Despite the attack on Homer as the "first of the tragedians" in the *Republic*, Plato clearly has a deeper admiration for him than for the tragedians themselves: In the *Laws*, for example, he dismisses tragedy as suitable for women, teenagers, and the general crowd, whereas epic is for older and wiser men (658d–e). The end of the *Republic* sets the scene for Aris-

---

[9] Cf. G. E. Howes, "Homeric Quotations in Plato and Aristotle"; and Jules Labarbe, *L'Homère de Platon*.

[10] For Plato's views on allegory, cf. J. Tate, "Plato and Allegorical Interpretation," and S. Weinstock, "Die Platonische Homerkritik und seine Nachwirkung."

totle's defence of both Homer and tragedy, when Socrates invites poetry to produce a defence of her value, "as we are conscious of the fascination which she holds for us," especially when she is approached through the medium of Homer (607b–608b).

Plato's philosophical views hardly really constitute a "reading" of Homer in the modern sense. Aristotle, on the other hand, is said to have "discussed Homer in detail in many dialogues, admiring and praising him" (Dio Chrysostom *Or.* 53.1). There was a strong ancient tradition that Aristotle gave his pupil Alexander the Great a special text of the *Iliad*. Alexander's own passion for Homer must derive in part from Aristotle's influence, and the work *On Kingship* that he wrote for Alexander can hardly have failed to make use of Homer for this purpose.[11] In his surviving works Aristotle quotes Homer some 114 times, with a strong bias towards the *Iliad* (as in the case of Plato), and these quotations show his fondness for the poet, whom he often uses to illustrate a point.[12] For example, in the *Nicomachean Ethics* the observation that people do not like to be reminded of benefits conferred on them is backed up by a reference to the scene of Thetis's supplication of Zeus in *Iliad* 1, where she tactfully omits to mention the service she had done for him in the past in rescuing him from an Olympian conspiracy, although Achilles had reminded her of it (1124b12–17). This surely shows a close and sensitive psychological reading of the text, whether or not the observation is originally due to Aristotle himself.

The Aristotelian work entitled *Homeric Problems* (frs. 142–79, Rose) must reflect the whole tradition of detailed discussion of the text down to Aristotle's time as well as his own observations, and chapter 25 of the *Poetics* is a summary of the same subject, with an attempt for the first time to systematise the methods that can be used to solve difficulties.[13] Here he states the fundamental principle, so often ignored by both earlier and later critics, that poetry is not subject to the same criteria as are other arts and sciences (1460b13–15). If a scene achieves the kind of effects that are described in the *Poetics* as desirable, then minor faults of accuracy, coher-

[11] Cf. R. Pfeiffer, *History of Classical Scholarship From the Beginnings*, 71–72; Aristotle *Fragments*, ed. Rose, 408–09.

[12] Cf. Adolph Römer, "Die Homercitate und die Homerischen Fragen des Aristoteles," and G. E. Howes, "Homeric Quotations."

[13] Cf. R. Pfeiffer, *History of Classical Scholarship From the Beginnings*, 69ff., and also A. Römer, "Die Homercitate"; R. Wachsmuth, *De Aristotelis studiis Homericis capita selecta*; M. Carroll, *Aristotle's Poetics ch. xxv in the Light of the Homeric Scholia*; A. Gudeman, "Λύσεις"; H. Hintenlang, *Untersuchungen zu den Homer-Aporien des Aristoteles.*

ence, and so on are irrelevant. With this simple observation most of the trivial objections of earlier pedants such as Zoilus are swept away. Thus, the pursuit of Hector by Achilles is impossible in practice, but the dramatic effect is overwhelming (1460b23–26). Moral criticisms (such as those raised by Plato and others) can be answered by appealing to historical context or the conventions of the poet's day: For instance, in the *Problems* Aristotle compares Achilles' brutal treatment of Hector's body with a later Thessalian practice, to show that it was not unique to this scene in Homer (fr. 166). Religious beliefs may simply reflect those of Greek society at that stage of development, and so to attack them from a modern viewpoint is misguided. Careful examination of the poetic context is also important in dealing with moral issues. For instance, Agamemnon lets Echepolus off military service in return for a horse, and this sounds like bribery (*Il.* 23.295ff.); but he was right, said Aristotle in the *Problems*, to prefer a good horse to a useless man (fr. 165)! Alternatively, if something is untrue or historically impossible, it may be justified as idealisation. Finally, many minor problems of interpretation and consistency can be solved by adopting a more flexible approach to the text and considering alternative ways of taking it, instead of assuming that the first or most obvious interpretation must be correct. To us these principles may seem largely obvious, but it is surprising how easily they can be forgotten by modern as well as ancient critics.[14]

The *Homeric Problems* constituted a preliminary ground-clearing exercise of a practical kind in preparation for the more theoretical approach of the *Poetics* as a whole. In the main body of this work, Aristotle is primarily interested in tragedy and sees Homer very much in dramatic terms. But, despite his eventual conclusion (in chapter 26) that tragedy is superior to epic because of its greater dramatic immediacy and concentration (reversing Plato's preference for epic), his intense admiration for Homer shines through again and again. Here for the first time the fundamental differences between the *Iliad* and *Odyssey* and other epic poems are clearly stated. Homer is outstanding for his dramatic qualities and his portrayal of character through speeches (1448b34–36, 60a5–11). His plots, even if by necessity less strictly unified than those of tragedy, are far more so than those of other epic poets, whose works are essentially episodic and often centred on a single character or concerned with a sequence of unrelated actions, rather than aiming at unity of action (51a16–30, 59a30–b7, 62b3–11). He was the first to use all the forms and parts of

---

[14] Cf. W. B. Stanford's lively book *Enemies of Poetry* for a demonstration of this fact!

epic (as defined in Aristotle's chapters on tragedy) and to do so success-
fully, and he surpasses all others in style and thought (59b12–16). Moreover, he has taught other poets the art of making fictions plausible (60a18
ff.). In view of the generally evolutionary approach of Aristotle, it is
really very remarkable that he should see the Homeric poems as so highly
developed artistically, although they stand relatively early in his conspec-
tus of literary development.

Aristotle provides the answers to Plato's main attacks on epic and tragedy in his discussion of the nature of poetic imitation and in his account
of the "catharsis" ($\kappa \acute{\alpha} \theta \alpha \rho \sigma \iota \varsigma$) achieved by tragedy. The first reinstates poetry in general as a philosophically serious pursuit, and the second gives
to tragedy a special value on the emotional plane. Aristotle never explicitly ascribes to epic a similar cathartic function, but the close analogies he
draws between epic and tragedy do surely imply that epic can act in a
similar way. More specifically, the fact that epic in his view should have
reversals, recognitions, and "sufferings" ($\pi \alpha \theta \acute{\eta} \mu \alpha \tau \alpha$) and should produce
similarly powerful effects of $\breve{\epsilon} \kappa \pi \lambda \eta \xi \iota \varsigma$ must (I think) point this way. The
implication of Aristotle's final comparison of epic and tragedy is most
probably that the kind of pleasure that both should arouse is similar and
should be associated with an emotional $\kappa \acute{\alpha} \theta \alpha \rho \sigma \iota \varsigma$, but that tragedy does
this more powerfully and effectively than epic does. At the same time,
the *Iliad* is evidently much closer to tragedy than the *Odyssey* is, for it is
concerned above all with suffering and emotion ($\pi \acute{\alpha} \theta o \varsigma$), whereas the *Odyssey* is primarily concerned with character ($\mathring{\eta} \theta o \varsigma$, 59b14–15), and its
happy ending is more like that of a comedy (53a30–39). Where the *Od-
yssey* seems to come closest to tragedy (in Aristotle's view) is in its recur-
rent use of the device of *recognition* (59b15). This is a theme to which
Aristotle devotes considerable attention, and it surely deserves more attention than it has received in recent criticism of both Homer and the
Poetics.[15]

Aristotle's admiration for Homer is focused especially on the extraordinary skill with which he creates a single, unified story out of a vast and
highly diversified body of material, incorporating many subsidiary episodes without allowing us to lose sight of the main theme. When he
comes to discuss the differences between epic and tragedy (in chapter 24),
he shows that epic has certain advantages because of its much greater

[15] Terence Cave's book *Recognitions*, however, redresses the balance; cf. also Sheila Murnaghan's *Disguise and Recognition in the Odyssey*, and N. J. Richardson, "Recognition Scenes
in the *Odyssey* and Ancient Literary Criticism."

scale, which gives it grandeur (and the heroic metre adds to this by its more stately character) and also allows for more variety, which is linked to its more "episodic" nature. The chief technique for creating this variety is the description of different sequences of events that are happening at the same time, i.e., the epic poet's ability to freeze one sequence and shift the scene, returning later to the point where he left off. This advantage in epic is linked to its narrative mode, because events do not have to be enacted visually, and also gives greater scope to "the marvellous" (τὸ θαυμαστόν), as in the pursuit of Hector (which would be impossible on the stage). Here Aristotle picks up the criticisms by earlier readers (Pindar, Thucydides, etc.) of the tendency of epic poetry to exaggeration but makes a special poetic virtue out of this. He links it with Homer's exceptional skill in creating plausible fictions, which is based on the accumulation of enough realistic circumstantial detail to make his fantasies credible, again (presumably) a particular feature of the more leisurely descriptive and narrative mode of epic as opposed to tragedy.

Although much of what Aristotle says here apparently applies to epic in general, it is clear that he really has Homer in the forefront of his mind throughout. This of course does not mean that he would have recommended taking Homer's work as the model for a new epic poem, which he explicitly says should be much shorter, roughly in fact the length of Apollonius's *Argonautica* (1459b17–22). There is an underlying conflict here between his intense admiration for the Homeric poems, which prevents him from criticising them as too long and complex or too "episodic," and his preference for a more compressed and more clearly unified structure. But he did not set out to write a treatise on epic in the *Poetics*, and so we must not press him too hard for consistency on this subject. Doubtless he could have replied that in works on the scale of the Homeric poems one must take a broad view of the overall effect and not subject them to the kind of detailed scrutiny that might be appropriate to more compressed and briefer works.

Where, then, does this necessarily rather rapid survey of approaches to Homer down to and including Aristotle leave us, and how does Aristotle's own "reading" relate to what has gone before? Clearly his whole approach to poetry is conditioned by his status as Plato's successor, and this affects his view of Homer too. He shares Plato's intense love and admiration for the poet and wishes to rescue him from the attacks of Plato and earlier philosophers and critics. To do so, however, he shifts the focus right away from the preoccupation with the gap between Homer's portrayal of divine or heroic ethics and later moral beliefs, and also between the aesthetics suitable for an eighth-century epic poem and those governing the literature of the classical period. The criterion is no longer that of literal truth, but of dramatic effectiveness and credibility, and in aesthetic terms Aristotle's approach, although highly technical, is also extremely flexible. As the ancestor of tragedy, Homeric epic anticipated in many respects the most powerful form of poetry ever conceived, and at the same time the use of the epic narrative mode gave Homer a wider scope, which enabled him to become the supreme "master of fiction" at a remarkably early stage in its development.

CHAPTER THREE

Stoic Readings of Homer*

A. A. LONG

I

How did the Stoics read Homer? Common sense suggests that the question must be complex. The evidence confirms this. Are we asking about Zeno or Posidonius? Should we mention Aristo's brilliant parody of Homer's line about the Chimaera (*Il.* 6.181) to mock the Academic philosopher Arcesilaus (Diogenes Laertius 4.33)? Or Strabo's ingenious efforts to demonstrate Homer's geographical expertise? Or Epictetus's remark that the *Iliad* is nothing but an idea (φαντασία), because it would not have occurred if Paris and Menelaus had not made their respective mistakes in regard to Helen (*Discourses* 1.28.10ff.)? Stoic philosophers, like all educated Greeks, knew Homer intimately and could use him as they saw fit. Were they also, however, united in their acceptance of a general theory about the meaning and interpretation of the epics and the philosophical value of these poems from a Stoic viewpoint? The question cannot be settled decisively from the surviving words of the early Stoics, but modern scholars are not deterred from arriving at a virtual consensus about how it should be answered. Their theory, generally asserted as a fact, is that Stoic philosophers, beginning around 300 B.C. with Zeno, the founder of the school, interpreted Homer himself as a crypto-Stoic. In

* In drafting and revising this paper, I have been helped by many people. It would not have become even an embryonic idea but for the invitation from Bob Lamberton to write on this topic. Before the paper was read to the Princeton conference, Tom Rosenmeyer gave me detailed criticisms and encouraged me in my heresies. Like all the conference participants, I benefited from the excellent discussions our work received. Subsequently, Alan Bowen, Denis Feeney, and Jim Porter sent me further comments, all of them trenchant and helpful, which I have tried to absorb and answer, and I learned much from further discussion of the paper by audiences at Leiden and Utrecht Universities. I am also grateful to Glenn Most, who gave me a copy of his fine study "Cornutus and Stoic Allegoresis" before it appeared in *ANRW* 2.36.3 (1989). Finally I thank my colleagues at Leiden University for housing me so graciously during the final work of revision, and the National Endowment for the Humanities, which provided me with a fellowship at this time.

this paper I shall cast doubt on this theory and offer a different interpretation of the Stoics's generic interests in Homer.

According to this received opinion, the Stoics took Homer (and other early Greek poets, especially Hesiod) to have a correct understanding of the world—its physical structure and processes, its god(s), its basic causes and purposes—a correct understanding because it coincided with the Stoics' own philosophy of nature.[1] Thus, so the theory goes, the Stoics interpreted certain episodes in Homer, for instance the story at the beginning of *Iliad* 15 that Zeus punished Hera by hanging her from the sky by a golden chain, as deliberately *disguised* references to astronomy and natural phenomena. Crucial to this theory is the supposition that Homer often *means* something other than he *says*. Homer, the Stoics are supposed to have thought, really understood the world in the Stoics' way; but because he was a poet, he does not express Stoicism directly. He composed, in other words, on two levels: On the surface he offers an epic narrative about the deeds of gods and heroes, but what he is *really* talking about, and understands himself to be talking about, is the physical world in a sense acceptable to Stoic philosophers.

We can sum up this theory by the term "allegory," taking allegory in its standard ancient definition: "saying what is other—i.e., saying or meaning something other than what one seems to say."[2] The Stoics, we are asked to believe, took Homer to be an allegorist; they interpreted the epics "allegorically" because of assumptions that they made concerning the poet's philosophical understanding and methods of composition. That is the theory I propose to contest, but its proponents have never, to the best of my knowledge, made its implications fully explicit. Part of the difficulty of understanding what the Stoics were doing arises from the vagueness of the modern claim that they allegorized Homer.

[1] Because the theory, as I call it, has been taken to be a fact, no publication that I know of seeks to prove it, and I have to confess to endorsing it myself in "Stoa and Sceptical Academy," 165–66. Characteristic statements of it can conveniently be found in Phillip De Lacy, "Stoic Views of Poetry," esp. 256–63, and in Rudolf Pfeiffer, *History of Classical Scholarship From the Beginnings to the End of the Hellenistic Age*, 237, which I discuss below. Some qualified dissent is offered by Peter Steinmetz, "Allegorische Deutung und allegorische Dichtung in der alten Stoa"; cf. also J. Tate, "Plato and Allegorical Interpretation [2]," 7–10. The other studies that I have found most helpful are Glenn Most's article "Cornutus and Stoic Allegoresis," and Fritz Wehrli, *Zur Geschichte der allegorischen Deutung Homers im Altertum*. For further references see the bibliographical citations given by Steinmetz and Most.

[2] Cf. Heraclitus, *Quaest. Hom.* 5.2, and Anon., Περὶ ποιητικῶν τρόπων under ἀλληγορία in *Rhetores Graeci* 3, 207, 18–23 (Spengel). In the second passage, allegory is exemplified by the "idea of devil" as signified by the word *snake*.

Allegory is a very complex notion. Some preliminary clarification of it can be reached once we recognize that a text might be called allegorical in a strong sense or in a weak sense.[3] A text will be allegorical in a *strong* sense if its author composes with the intention of being interpreted allegorically. Familiar examples of such texts are Dante's *Divine Comedy*, Spenser's *Faerie Queen*, and Bunyan's *Pilgrim's Progress*. Such texts require their reader to take them allegorically; they are composed as allegories. A text will be allegorical in a *weak* sense if, irrespective of what its author intended, it invites interpretation in ways that go beyond its surface or so-called literal meaning. Examples include the stories of Pandora's box in Hesiod and Adam and Eve in Genesis. Such stories, as we today read them, seem to signify something general about the human condition which is quite other than their narrative content; but they are weak allegories because, in these cases, the allegorizing is a contribution by us, the readers, and not something that we know to be present in the text as originally constructed. In some sense, all literary interpretation is weak allegorizing—our attempt to say what a narrative *means*.[4] As we shall see in detail later, Heraclitus, the author of *Homeric Problems*, interpreted Homer as a strong allegorist. Yet even Heraclitus did not take Homer to be the author of an "allegory." As a literary genre, allegory is scarcely attested in antiquity before Prudentius (fourth century A.D). Medieval and later allegories need to be put on one side in considering the scope of allegorizing in classical antiquity.

· · · · ·

According to the theory I propose to reject, the Stoics as a school took Homer to be a strong allegorist in the way just explained. Instead, I shall argue, it is doubtful whether they even took themselves to be allegorizing *Homer's* meaning, i.e., interpreting the epic narratives, in a weak sense. As the paper develops, I will offer a different account of the Stoics' generic interest in Homer, and also, by the way, in Hesiod. Before we come

---

[3] The distinction is my own but influenced by the work of others, especially Maureen Quilligan, *The Language of Allegory*, who (25–26) acutely distinguishes allegorical narrative from allegoresis, "the literary criticism of texts." See also D. Dawson, *Allegorical Readers and Cultural Revision in Ancient Alexandria*. For good remarks on the Greek terminology and recognition of how it may differ from "allegory in the modern sense," cf. N. J. Richardson, "Homeric Professors in the Age of the Sophists."

[4] Cf. Northrop Frye, *Anatomy of Criticism: Four Essays*, 89, and Robert Lamberton, who observes, in *Homer the Theologian*, 20, that allegorical interpretation "can comprehend virtually the whole of what we call 'interpretation' beyond mere parsing."

to grips with the details, something needs to be said about why the question matters: What is at stake in our asking how the Stoics read Homer?

II

Homer was *the* poet for the Greeks. Children learned large parts of the *Iliad* and *Odyssey* by heart as part of their primary education. All Greek literature and art, and just about all Greek philosophy, resonate against the background of Homer. Throughout classical antiquity and well into the Roman Empire, Homer held a position in Mediterranean culture that can only be compared with the position the Bible would later occupy. The comparison is important if we are to understand why, from as early as 500 B.C., the status and meaning of Homer were central questions for philosophers. Like the Bible for the Jews, Homer offered the Greeks the foundation of their cultural identity. Such texts, however, can only remain authoritative over centuries of social and conceptual change if they can be brought up to date, so to speak—I mean they must be capable of being given interpretations that suit the circumstances of different epochs.[5] When read literally, Homer was already out of date—physiologically and ethically unacceptable—for the early Ionian thinkers Xenophanes and Heraclitus. It was probably their criticism that evoked the first so-called allegorical defence of Homer. In the fifth century, Metrodorus of Lampsacus (frs. A3–4 D-K) "interpreted the heroes of the *Iliad* as parts of the universe, and the gods as parts of the human body. Agamemnon represented the $\alpha i \theta \acute{\eta} \rho$, Achilles the sun, Helen the earth, Paris the air, Hector the moon."[6] Crazy though this kind of allegorizing seemed to many in antiquity, Metrodorus was not alone in his style of interpretation. Plato a few decades later (*Theaetetus* 153c) makes Socrates refer ironically to a proposal that the golden chain (with which Zeus challenges the other Olympians to a tug-of-war, *Il.* 8.18–27) is "nothing else but the sun."

Metrodorus and his like seem to have taken Homer to be a strong allegorist—a poet who was really au courant with scientific theories but who chose to disguise them in a misleading narrative. Why would anyone

[5] The point is well stated by Albert Henrichs, "Philosophy, the Handmaiden of Theology," 439.

[6] Cf. N. J. Richardson, "Homeric Professors," 69. Tatian (Metrodorus fr. A3 D-K) describes Metrodorus as "converting everything to allegory" ($\pi \acute{\alpha} \nu \tau \alpha$ $\epsilon i \varsigma$ $\dot{\alpha} \lambda \lambda \eta \gamma o \rho \acute{\iota} \alpha \nu$ $\mu \epsilon$-$\tau \acute{\alpha} \gamma \omega \nu$).

suppose that a poet would do such a thing? Plato (*Protagoras* 316d) makes Protagoras say that Homer, Hesiod, and Simonides were really sophists—possessors and teachers of practical wisdom—who used poetry as a "cover" for their real purposes in order to avoid unpopularity. Plato is probably ironical again here, but the kind of explanation he ascribes to Protagoras is essential to anyone who proposes, against the evidence of historical change, that an ancient author actually *intends* to give a contemporary message or a message that differs from the literal sense of his text. The message must be covert, esoteric, allegorical in the strong sense— and yet, somehow or other, open to the expert interpreter to disclose.

Later antiquity reveals many examples of such allegorical readings. One of the most famous is that of the Neo-Platonists who interpreted the *Odyssey* as a spiritual journey through the Neo-Platonic universe. Another example is the Jew Philo of Alexandria's interpretation of whole episodes in the Pentateuch, for instance Noah's construction of the ark, by means of Stoic and Platonic concepts. The author I want to focus on is the Heraclitus (not the famous Ephesian philosopher) who wrote a work called *Homeric Problems—Homer's Allegories Concerning the Gods*.[7] Nothing is known about this man's life or background or precisely when he wrote. His work probably dates from the first or second century A.D.

. . . . .

Heraclitus announces his purpose very clearly at the beginning of his book. He intends to rescue Homer from the charge that his account of the gods is blasphemous. He states his primary point in his second sentence: "If Homer was no allegorist, he would be completely impious."[8] That is to say, if Homer's apparent meaning is his real meaning, his gods are violent, sexually corrupt, the very reverse of moral exemplars. As Heraclitus knows very well, Plato had banned Homer from his ideal state for just this reason. By interpreting Homer as a strong allegorist, Heraclitus sets out to save Homer from Plato's criticism (and also from Epicurean disparagement). He proceeds systematically through the epics, book by book, to illustrate Homer's "allegorizations concerning the gods." One example will suffice because Heraclitus's methods are monotonously similar. The "theomachy"—the battle between the gods in *Iliad* 21—is not to be taken literally; rather, the warring gods are to be

---

[7] The text has been excellently edited in the Budé series by Félix Buffière, *Héraclite: Allégories d'Homère*.

[8] [Ὅμηρος] πάντα ἠσέβησεν, εἰ μηδὲν ἠλληγόρησεν.

interpreted as natural elements and heavenly bodies: Apollo is the sun, Poseidon is water, Hera is air, etc. What Homer is really talking about in this passage is cosmology.

For Heraclitus, allegory is not an importation by the interpreter; it is not the interpreter's reading of a text but central to the text's, or rather, to the author's intent. He characterises allegory as "a trope that consists in saying one thing but meaning something different from what one says" (5.2), or a disjunction between "what is said" (λεγόμενον) and "what is thought" (νοούμενον, 5.16). As justification for applying it to Homer, he gives examples from other poets—Archilochus's use of a storm at sea to signify the perils of war and Anacreon's image of a frisking horse as a way of insulting a girl-friend (5.3–11). These examples, from our point of view, are cheating. They are metaphors, not allegories; or, if you want to say that all metaphors are allegories, then Homer is an allegorist (because he uses metaphors) but not the kind of allegorist Heraclitus needs to prove. However, Heraclitus is not interested in Homer's metaphors, but in his supposedly deliberate treatment of the gods as veiled references to natural phenomena. This is evident, for instance, in the following quotations: "Homer conceals his philosophical mind," "the hidden truth in [Homer's] words," and "[Homer] has signified to us the primary elements of nature."[9] Heraclitus knows there are obvious objections to reading Homer in this way. He defends his position by alleging that philosophers such as Heraclitus, his Ephesian namesake, and Empedocles use allegory, and so there should be nothing surprising if the poet Homer does so too (24.8).

Heraclitus's allegorical reading of Homer can rest there for the present. We now come to the Stoics. Scholars have generally supposed that Heraclitus was a Stoic or that he at least followed Stoic precedent in his allegorization of Homer.[10] If that were so, and if (as was also supposed), Heraclitus was transmitting a Stoic reading of Homer that had been orthodox for centuries, there would be nothing to argue about: The Stoics will have interpreted Homer as a strong allegorist. Why does correctness on this point matter? If the standard theory is correct, the Stoics will have been primarily responsible for authorizing the allegorical interpretations of literature that we find in Philo, the Neoplatonists, and others because the Stoics were far and away the most influential philosophers during the

<hr/>

[9] ὑποκρύπτεταί τις Ὁμήρῳ φιλόσοφος νοῦς (26.3); τὴν ὑπολελησμένην ἐν τοῖς ἔπεσιν ἀλήθειαν (6.5); ὑπεσήμηνεν ἡμῖν τὰ πρωτοπαγῆ στοιχεῖα τῆς φύσεως (23.14).

[10] This is particularly evident in P. De Lacy's influential study, "Stoic Views of Poetry."

Hellenistic and early Roman period. In that case, we learn something very important concerning both Stoicism and the interpretation of Homer. However, to anyone who respects the Stoics as serious philosophers this finding should be unwelcome. The Stoics were rationalists and they were also empiricists. They don't talk nonsense, and it is frankly nonsensical to suppose that Homer was a crypto-Stoic. In addition, what motivation could the Stoics have for such an enterprise as Heraclitus is engaged in? Why should it matter to them to save Homer's theological credit at the cost of claiming, against all reason, that he is a strong allegorist?[11]

However, if Heraclitus were an orthodox Stoic, that would seem to settle the question. In fact, as Félix Buffière, the latest editor of Heraclitus, has carefully argued, there are no good grounds for thinking that Heraclitus was a Stoic.[12] Although he often draws on Stoic physics for the cosmology that his allegories ascribe to Homer, that alone does not make him a Stoic; by this date Stoicism has become a lingua franca for technical writers who are not themselves Stoics. In addition, Heraclitus includes doctrines that are non-Stoic and inconsistent with orthodox Stoicism.[13] Buffière concludes that Heraclitus was not affiliated with any specific philosophical school, and his arguments seem to me utterly convincing.[14]

[11] No satisfactory answer to this question has been proposed, as G. Most recognizes in a careful discussion of the "motivations" of Stoic "allegoresis," "Cornutus and Stoic Allegoresis," 2018–23. The favorite answer is that the Stoics wanted Homer's support for their own philosophy. If, however, they had to allegorize Homer in order to make him appropriately Stoic, their procedure was egregiously circular, as Most points out. There is no evidence that the Stoics took Homer to be a philosopher or a Stoic sage. Indeed, Seneca, *Epistle* 88.5, pokes fun at the whole idea of Homer's being a philosopher of any persuasion, including a Stoic. The joke would be in bad taste if the school of his allegiance had allegorized the poet in the way commonly proposed, though Seneca's position is compatible with the Stoic interpretation of Homer's poetry as a φιλοσόφημα, which Strabo (1.2.7) takes to be universally accepted.

[12] F. Buffière in *Héraclite: Allégories d'Homère*, xxxi–xxxix. Buffière's detachment of Heraclitus from Stoicism is unknown to or ignored by Michael Hilgruber, "Dion Chrysostomos 36 (53), 4–5 und die Homerauslegung Zenons." Hilgruber, 22, invokes Heraclitus in order to support his claim that Dio Chrysostom's account of Zeno ad loc. refers to Zeno's allegorization of Homer.

[13] E.g., he invokes Plato's tripartite psychology (17.4–18.8) in order to explain various lines in the *Odyssey* and, unlike the Stoics, locates rationality in the head (19.1–19). The Stoic doctrines that he uses he takes over without acknowledgement or attributes to "the greatest philosophers" (22.13; cf. 25.2), citing Stoics only once by name (33.1) for their interpretation of Heracles.

[14] He notes that many of Heraclitus's allegories recall interpretations current before the

There is a further crucial point that he does not make. If Heraclitus were simply drawing upon Stoic orthodoxy, his whole essay would be redundant and disingenuous. Because he does not support his approach to Homer by any appeal to the Stoics or, for that matter, to other authorities, the obvious implication is that he takes himself to be doing something not readily accessible in the way the standard theory would have us suppose. We are in no position, then, to infer from the work of Heraclitus that official Stoics interpreted Homer in his manner. He offers no confirmation for the theory that the Stoics took Homer to be a strong allegorist.

Unquestionably, Homer was important to the Stoics. The founding fathers of Stoicism—Zeno, Cleanthes, Chrysippus, none of whom were from mainland Greece—developed a philosophy that would appropriate, as far as possible, traditional Greek culture. Contrast the Athenian Epicurus, who rejected Homer as part of his radical program to abandon all παιδεία (*Epicurea* 228–29 Usener). The Cypriot arriviste Zeno could not have been more different. He wrote five books of *Homeric Problems* (Diogenes Laertius 7.4), perhaps his most extended work on any subject.

Zeno's work on Homer is totally lost. The one thing we can say about it for certain is that he discussed standard philological cruxes, which reminds us that Homeric philology had just become extremely fashionable through the work of scholars in Alexandria.[15] In the case of Chrysippus, some few generations after Zeno, there survive eight examples of his work on Homer (cf. n. 15). They are all emendations to the text or grammatical explanations. In none of them does he draw upon doctrinaire Stoicism. He contributes intelligent philology, and the Homeric scholia record this, mentioning his name alongside the famous grammarian Aristarchus. Like all educated Greeks, of course, the Stoics had lines of Homer and other poets in their heads which they could use to make an ethical point and to show that their philosophy accorded with "the com-

---

Stoics—"Les stoïciens ne sont donc qu'un des derniers chaînons de la grande chaîne" (xxxvii)—and sums up Heraclitus's relation to Stoicism by saying (xxxix), "La teinte de stoïcisme qu'il offre par endroits, n'est rien de plus, chez lui, qu'un vernis récent sur un meuble ancien." Because Buffière accepts the traditional doctrine on Stoic allegoresis, he has no vested interest in detaching Stoicism from Heraclitus.

[15] For the evidence, cf. SVF 1.275 (Zeno's proposal to emend καὶ Ἐρεμβούς to Ἀραβάς τε, *Od.* 4.84), and SVF 3.769–77 (von Arnim's collection of passages documenting Chrysippus's interpretations of Homer). For discussion, cf. P. Steinmetz, "Allegorische Deutung," 19–21, 26–27. A recently published papyrus of a commentary dealing with passages from *Odyssey* 11 probably includes Chrysippus's name; cf. CPF 1, 421 (Chrysippus 5T).

mon conceptions" of people. Although the voluminous writings of Chrysippus have not survived, we possess fragments of them in which some seventy lines of Homer are quoted. In all of these, Chrysippus cites Homer in order to support a Stoic doctrine—for instance the mind's location in the heart—and in all cases he takes Homer literally, not allegorically.[16]

. . . . .

For what reason, then (apart from the misconception concerning Heraclitus), have scholars propagated the belief that the Stoics took Homer to be a strong allegorist? The principal reason is a misleading focus upon just one text, to the neglect of all evidence that tells a rather different story. I will illustrate the point by reference to Rudolf Pfeiffer in his highly influential *History of Classical Scholarship From the Beginnings to the End of the Hellenistic Age*.

Pfeiffer (237) writes, "Orthodox Stoics were necessarily allegorists in their interpretation of poetry." He does not explain what he means by allegorist, though without elucidating the terms he writes of "genuine allegory" and "true allegorist." Pfeiffer justifies his claim about the Stoics with a selective quotation in Latin from Cicero's *De natura deorum* 1.41: [Chrysippus] "volt Orphei Musaei Hesiodi Homerique fabellas accommodare ad ea quae ipse . . . de deis immortalibus dixerat, ut etiam veterrimi poetae . . . Stoici fuisse videantur." As translated, this says, "Chrysippus . . . wanted to fit the stories of Orpheus, Musaeus, Hesiod, and Homer to his own statements about the immortal gods [namely in his first book *On the Nature of the Gods*] in order that even the most ancient poets . . . might seem to have been Stoics." Pfeiffer leads his readers to suppose that this is a totally objective remark about the Stoics. But it is not. Actually, it is a piece of anti-Stoic polemic by the Epicurean spokesman in this Ciceronian book, and we know Cicero's source for it. Cicero got the remark from the Epicurean philosopher Philodemus, but Cicero himself has subtly altered the original. What Philodemus said is this: "Chrysippus just like Cleanthes tries to harmonise the things attributed to Orpheus and Musaeus, and *things* in Homer, Hesiod, Euripides and other poets" with Stoic doctrine.[17] The "things" in question, as Philode-

---

[16] The point is made by P. Steinmetz, "Allegorische Deutung," 27: "Alle diese Verse werden nicht anders als die Zitate aus den Lyrikern und aus den Tragikern im Wortsinn verstanden. Kein einziger Vers wird in einer irgendwie gearteten Allegorese ausgelegt."

[17] Philodemus, *De pietate* col. vi (ed. in Albert Henrichs, "Die Kritik der stoischen Theologie im PHerc. 1428," 17): ἐν δὲ τῶ[ι] δευτέρ[ωι] τὰ εἰς Ὀρφέα [καὶ] Μουσαῖον

mus indicates, were divine names and myths *transmitted by the poets*. Philodemus, hostile to Stoicism though he is, does not imply that Chrysippus took Homer and the other poets to be crypto-Stoics or strong allegorists. This is an addition by Cicero on behalf of his Epicurean critic.

Cicero, or his source, also adds to Philodemus a very damning clause that Pfeiffer omits; the full Latin text reads, "in order that even the most ancient poets, *who did not even suspect this [qui haec ne suspicati quidem sunt]* might seem to have been Stoics."[18] There, in a nutshell, we have the principal basis for the modern theory about the Stoics' allegorical interpretation of Homer—a text that, in reality, is a Ciceronian distortion of Epicurean polemic.[19]

Still, one may retort, there must be some foundation to the Epicurean criticism. There is, as we shall see, but ancient philosophical polemic did not operate with any rules of fair play. Before taking the Epicurean critique of the Stoics at face value, we should let the Stoics speak for themselves. Cicero himself provides us with one means of doing so in a passage he writes for the Stoic Balbus in book 2 of his *De natura deorum*. As we shall see, this passage does not sit well with the traditional account of Stoic allegoresis, and it is generally ignored in discussions of the subject. Before setting it alongside the Epicurean critique just examined, we need to consider what is unambiguously attested concerning the Stoics' attitude to early Greek poetry.

III

So far as Homer is concerned, the Stoics' interest in his poems was plainly complex. As I have mentioned, Zeno and Chrysippus contributed to Homeric philology; and we also know that Zeno had views about the whole

---

ἀναφερ[όμ]ενα καὶ τὰ παρ᾽ ['Ο]μήρωι καὶ Ἡσιόδω[ι] καὶ Εὐριπίδη καὶ ποιητα[ῖ]ς ἄλλοις [ὧ]ς καὶ Κλεάνθης [πει]ρᾶται σ[υ]νοικειοῦ[ν] ταῖς δόξ[αι]ς αὐτῶ[ν]. This passage is often overlooked when the Cicero text is cited, and Cicero's divergence from it has never, to the best of my knowledge, been noted.

[18] I read *sunt* rather than *sint*, which would most naturally make the relative clause a comment by Chrysippus. *Sunt* is reported as a reading of some mss. by the Loeb editor of Cicero's *De natura deorum*, though it is not recorded in the Teubner edition or that of A.S. Pease ad loc.

[19] For other examples of unqualified reliance on Cicero's comment here, cf. J. Tate, "Cornutus and the Poets," 42; S. Weinstock, "Die platonische Homerkritik," 137; P. Steinmetz, "Allegorische Deutung," 27; M. Hilgruber, "Dion Chrysostomos," 19, n. 33; P. De Lacy, "Stoic Views of Poetry," 263, actually referring to Cicero, *De nat. deor.* 1.36.

corpus of Homeric poetry because he judged the *Margites* to be a youthful work by the poet (SVF 1.274). But our central question is the Stoics' approach to early Greek poetry generically. For if they interpreted Homer allegorically, they also approached Hesiod in the same way. The question of how, in general, the Stoics interpreted passages in Homer is a question about what they thought early Greek poetry could contribute to the history of ideas.

Contexts in which we learn about this are not philological or literary, but theological and cosmological.[20] Like the Epicureans, the Stoics were much concerned with the anthropology and aetiology of religion. Both schools found elements of truth in traditional Greek religion but saw them as overlaid by superstition and myth. The Epicureans thought people were right to picture the gods in human form but wrong to involve them in the world. Stoics took the opposite view. They rejected anthropomorphic gods but retained a divine presence throughout nature. As theologians and cosmologists, they took on the task of studying Greek mythology for traces of their own views. This prompted them to investigate the factors that led people to conceive of gods in the first place. A doxographical summary shows the role they assigned to poetry in this study.[21]

The author attributes to the Stoics three "forms" that have mediated reverence for the gods:

> The physical is taught by philosophers, the mythical by poets, and the legislative is constitued by each city.[22] The entire discipline has seven divisions. The first one deals with phenomena and the heavens. People got a conception of god from the sight of the stars; they observed that these are responsible for great harmony, and they noticed the regularity of day and night, winter and summer, risings and settings, and the earth's production of animals and plants. Therefore they took the sky to be a father and the earth a mother . . . father because the outflow of waters is the same type of thing as sperms, and mother because of her receiving the waters and giving birth. . . .
> To the second and third topic they [the Stoics] distributed gods as

[20] This point is well taken by G. Most, "Cornutus and Stoic Allegoresis," 2025–26.

[21] Ps.-Plutarch, *De placitis philosophorum* 879c–880d = Aetius, *De placitis* 1.6 = SVF 2.1009. The importance of this neglected testimony was brought to my attention by F. Wehrli, *Zur Geschichte der allegorischen Deutung*, 52–53.

[22] Dio Chrysostom 12.44 adopts a version of this tripartite division, substituting ἔμφυτον for φυσικόν and then adding a fourth category in order to accommodate the plastic arts.

benefactors and agents of harm—as benefactors Zeus, Hera, Hermes, Demeter, and as agents of harm Poinai, Erinyes, Ares. . . . .The fourth and fifth topics they assigned to things and to passions, as passions Eros, Aphrodite, Pothos and as things Hope, Justice, Eunomia. As the sixth topic they included the poets' inventions (τὸ ὑπὸ τῶν ποιητῶν πεπλασμένον). For Hesiod, because he wanted to construct fathers for the generated gods, introduced such progenitors for them as "Koios and Krios and Hyperion and Iapetos" (*Theogony* 134);[23] hence this topic is also called myth. The seventh topic is . . . [here I summarise] apotheosized men who were great benefactors, such as Herakles.

In this sophisticated and perceptive passage, myth and poetry are mentioned as just one of many sources of theological notions. The text does not say that Hesiod—the one poet named—really understood the gods to be different from what he said they were. It simply registers the fabricated character of his account, and his wish to construct divine genealogies.

A much fuller statement of the same topics is to be found in Cicero, *De natura deorum* 2.63–72. After dealing with the apotheosized humans, Cicero's Stoic spokesman Balbus turns to myth and poetry, and he adds a central point omitted by the doxographical text. Stories such as Hesiod tells, for instance the castration of Ouranos by Kronos and the fettering of Kronos by Zeus, are utterly erroneous and stupid. However, that story is actually a fictional and superstitious perversion of an intelligent and correct understanding of certain natural phenomena ("physica ratio non inelegans inclusa est in impias fabulas"): that the highest entity, the aether, does not need genitals in order to procreate, and that Kronos, i.e., χρόνος ("time"), is "regulated and limited."[24]

Cicero's Stoic spokesman is not interested in saving the veracity of poets including Homer. He dismisses anthropomorphic gods—and their involvement in the Trojan war—as absurd (*De nat. deor.* 2.70). What he

---

[23] I translate the received text, Ἡσίοδος γὰρ βουλόμενος τοῖς γενητοῖς θεοῖς πατέρας συστῆσαι εἰσήγαγε τοιούτους αὐτοῖς γεννήτορας, "Κοῖον κτλ." Von Arnim in SVF 2.1009 prints θεούς, an emendation of the transmitted text by Hermann Diels (*Doxographi Graeci*, 296) and also accepted by J. Mau in the Teubner edition of Plutarch, *Moralia* V, fasc. 2 Pars 1 (Leipzig, 1971), but sense and flow of the Greek are against this. The Titans named are from the first generation of gods and are sires of gods themselves; cf. Hesiod, *Theogony* 404.

[24] Cicero twice uses *voluerunt* in *De nat. deor.* 2.64 to refer to the meaning intended by those who developed the "physica ratio non inelegans." He does not imply that this meaning was understood by those who told the "impias fabulas."

commits himself to is a theory of cultural transmission, degeneration, and modification. At some time in the remote past, on this view, certain people intuited basic truths about nature. They expressed these, however, in a symbolical mode that was easy to misinterpret as independently valid.[25] Hence the emergence of misleading myths. The task of the Stoic interpreter of religious history is to identify and articulate the correct beliefs that directly gave rise to such myths but are not evident in their superficial narrative content. Far from suggesting that Homer and Hesiod were proto-Stoic cosmologists, this passage implies that the poets propagated misleading myths as if they were truths.

Cicero's Balbus, giving the official Stoic view, does not match well with the Epicurean account in *De natura deorum* 1.41, the passage on which Pfeiffer and others chiefly rely for their theory about the Stoics' allegorization of Homer. Here, in the Stoics' own account, nothing is said about what *Homer or Hesiod themselves meant*. The Stoics are interested in their poems as *sources* of pre-existing, pre-philosophical views of the world—what we may call "true myths," which in the later poems take on a narrative life of their own and are thus misunderstood.[26]

The two pieces of evidence I have just analyzed give a clear and coherent account of the Stoics' generic interests in early Greek poetry. However, they can be supplemented by something else, which, until recently, had been curiously neglected in the discussion of this whole topic.[27] From the first century A.D. there survives an entire book by the Stoic philosopher Cornutus, entitled *Compendium [Ἐπιδρομή] of the Tradition of Greek Theology*. Cornutus wrote this work, as he remarks, for young students. His topic is the transmitted names, epithets, cults, and myths pertaining to particular divinities. He draws on poetry, especially Hesiod's, simply because poetry is a primary vehicle for the transmission of theology.

Cornutus has a methodology for analyzing his data. It is not allegory

---

[25] "Videtisne igitur ut a physicis rebus bene atque utiliter inventis tracta ratio sit ad commenticios et fictos deos? Quae res genuit falsas opiniones. . . ."

[26] When referring back to these Stoic activities, the Academic critic of the Stoics (*De nat. deor.* 3.63) does not refer to their "allegorization" of the *poets* but to their pointless efforts "to rationalize the mendacious stories and explain the reasons for the names by which each thing is so called" ("commenticiarum fabularum reddere rationem, vocabulorum cur quidque ita appellatum sit causas explicare").

[27] G. Most's study, "Cornutus and Stoic Allegoresis," has ensured that Cornutus will not be neglected in the future. Although Most endorses the notion of Stoic "allegoresis," what he understands by this seems to be largely compatible with the thesis of my paper.

(to which he never refers) but etymology. He assumes (as the earliest Stoics had also assumed) that the Greek gods have the names and epithets that they do—"earthshaking Poseidon," etc.—because in their original usage these names represented the way people understood the world. Etymology, that is, analysis of the original meaning of names, enables the Stoic philosopher to recover the beliefs about the world held by those who first gave the gods their present names. From our modern perspective, Stoic etymologies often seem fantastic. From the same perspective, we have to say that the Stoics were far too bold in relying on etymology as they did and in presuming a coincidence between the original meaning of divine names and aspects of their own philosophy of nature. More on this point later. What I want to emphasize now is that etymology is not the same as allegory, although allegories may make use of etymology. Etymology offers explanations of single names and phrases—atomic units of language, as it were. But to have allegory, it seems, we need a whole story, a narrative—Pandora's box, the Garden of Eden, etc. Only rarely does Cornutus offer an interpretation of any extended episodes in early Greek poetry.[28] He is an etymologist, not an allegorist.[29]

Cornutus's etymologies are based upon the same cultural assumption that we found just now in Cicero. Greek poetry is not the bottom line for recovering primitive beliefs about the gods and cosmology. Behind the earliest Greek poetry, and distortedly present in it, are ways of understanding the world whose basic correctness the Stoic interpreter, through etymology, can reveal. Cornutus's principal source is Hesiod, and he also refers to Homer a number of times. Fortunately for our purposes, he is explicit about his approach to poetic texts and about his methodology. In section 17 (Lang), Cornutus begins by noting the number and variety of myths generated among the ancient Greeks and other peoples. As an example he takes two stories from Homer: Zeus's suspending Hera by the golden chain (Il. 15.18–24) and Thetis's support of Zeus against the rebellion of the other Olympians (Il. 1.396–406). Of the first of these he writes, "The poet seems to cite (or, possibly, pervert, παραφέρειν) this fragment of an ancient myth, according to which Zeus was fabled to have

---

[28] The points I have just made are well developed in the forthcoming book by D. Dawson, *Allegorical Readers and Cultural Revision.*

[29] Contrasting Cornutus's methodology with that of Heraclitus, F. Buffière notes, "Cornutus ne s'attarde guère aux allégories proprement dites et ne se limite point aux données d'Homère, pour les dieux qu' il étudie," *Héraclite,* xxxi. An interesting feature of Cornutus's etymological analysis, as G. Most points out, 2027–28, is his frequent mention of and refusal to choose betwen alternative etymologies.

suspended Hera from the sky with golden chains, since the stars have a golden appearance, and to have attached two anvils to her feet, i.e., evidently earth and sea, by means of which the air is stretched down and cannot be removed from either of them." Cornutus bases his interpretation on the traditional etymology of ἀήρ, "air," as Hera.[30]

Cornutus then adduces the second myth, that of Thetis, and says: "Clearly each of these gods was privately plotting against Zeus continuously, intending to prevent the world's origin. And that would have happened if the moist had prevailed and everything had become wet, or if fire had prevailed and everything had become fiery, or if air had prevailed. But Thetis, who disposes everything properly, positioned the hundred-handed Briareus against the gods mentioned—Briareus, who perhaps controls all exhalations from the earth." For this interpretation Cornutus relies on etymologies of the names Thetis (τίθημι) and Briareus (βορά and αἴρειν). Thus he finds germs of Stoic cosmogony in Homer's story, but he does not suggest that Homer himself did so.[31]

Immediately following this passage, Cornutus gives the following instruction: "One should not conflate myths, nor should one transfer names from one to another; and even if something has been added to the transmitted genealogies by people who do not understand what the myths hint at (αἰνίττονται) but who handle them as they handle narrative fictions, one should not regard them as irrational."[32] Cornutus is addressing would-be students of the history of religion. Not unlike a modern ethnographer or cultural anthropologist, he warns against tampering with the recorded data. He recognizes that the data, as transmitted, may distort the original beliefs that he takes to underlie existing

---

[30] Cosmological readings of this passage are ancient. F. Buffière thinks they may go back to the time of Anaximenes, *Les Mythes d'Homère*, 115–17. Socrates cites a version in Plato, *Theaetetus* 153c, and the etymology of Hera as ἀήρ is found in *Cratylus* 404c. Heraclitus (40) elaborates the interpretation along the same lines as Cornutus but conjoins it (41.1) with an allegorization of Hera's oath (*Il.* 15.36–37), where he also locates the four elements, thus he thinks himself entitled to say that: "Homer continuously allegorizes them" (41.12).

[31] Heraclitus (25) explains this story as an allusion to the eventual destruction of the world by deluge or conflagration, which are, of course, Stoic ideas.

[32] Cornutus 27, 19 Lang: δεῖ δὲ μὴ συγχεῖν τοὺς μύθους μηδ᾽ ἐξ ἑτέρου τὰ ὀνόματα ἐφ᾽ ἕτερον μεταφέρειν μηδ᾽ εἴ τι προσεπλάσθη ταῖς παραδεδομέναις κατ᾽αὐτοὺς γενεαλογίαις ὑπὸ τῶν μὴ συνιέντων ἃ αἰνίττονται, κεχρημένων δ᾽αὐτοῖς ὡς καὶ τοῖς πλάσμασιν, †ἀλόγως† τίθεσθαι. Tom Rosenmeyer has convinced me that the sense requires ἀλόγους (referring to μύθους) and I translate the text accordingly. Cornutus, as Rosenmeyer notes in written comments he gave me, is "talking about methods of looking at myth, not about the mentality of the one who looks at the myth."

myths, but the problems of transmission are not sufficient to rule out recovery of the myths' original rationale. In the next part of this section, he turns to Hesiod's "mythical" cosmogony and interprets its details in terms of Stoic physics. He concludes with these remarks: "I could give you a more complete interpretation of Hesiod's [genealogy]. He got some parts of it, I think, from his predecessors and added other parts in a more mythical manner, which is the way most of the ancient theology was corrupted."[33] Reading this passage in the light of Cornutus's previous instructions, we can see that Hesiod is one of the people who made inappropriate additions through his failure to see the theological physics implicit in his inherited material. For Cornutus neither Homer nor Hesiod is a crypto-Stoic. Both are the transmitters of myths.

In his interpretation of those myths, Cornutus intends to elucidate neither the scientific acumen of Homer and Hesiod nor their poetic intentions. He is interested in what we might call proto-myth, myth detached from narrative context in a poem, myth as interpretable evidence of pristine cosmological beliefs. At the end of his book, he tells its young addressee to realize that "the ancients were not nobodies but competent students of the world, and well equipped to philosophize about it via symbols and riddles" (Cornutus 76, 2–5 Lang).[34] Does Cornutus take the wise ancients to have been deliberate allegorists—practitioners of indirection—and to be identical with the early Greek poets? Surely not. He is saying that proto-myth, in the sense just explained, is the form in which the ancients expressed their serious thoughts about the world. The Stoic exegete seeks to recover these by removing the veneers created by poetic fictions and superstitions.

The evidence of Cornutus, an official Stoic, tells decisively against the

---

[33] I give the Greek of the concluding parts of this translation, Cornutus 31, 14–17 Lang: τὰ μέν τινα, ὡς οἶμαι, παρὰ τῶν ἀρχαιοτέρων αὐτοῦ παρειληφότος, τὰ δὲ μυθικώτερον ἀφ᾽ αὐτοῦ προσθέντος, ᾧ τρόπῳ καὶ πλεῖστα τῆς παλαιᾶς θεολογίας διεφθάρη.

[34] Cornutus 76, 2–5 Lang: οὐχ οἱ τυχόντες ἐγένοντο οἱ παλαιοί, ἀλλὰ καὶ συνιέναι τὴν τοῦ κόσμου φύσιν ἱκανοὶ καὶ πρὸς τὸ διὰ συμβόλων καὶ αἰνιγμάτων φιλοσοφῆσαι περὶ αὐτῆς εὐεπίφοροι. It is not necessary to take Cornutus's words to endorse Posidonius's controversial position on the existence of full-fledged philosophers in the Golden Age (Seneca, Epistle 90.4 ff.). For discussion of Stoic views on cultural history, cf. G. Most, "Cornutus and Stoic Allegoresis," 2020–23, and Michael Frede, "Chaeremon der Stoiker," 2088. Strabo (10.3.23) makes a similar point to Cornutus, but he also emphasizes the difficulty of extracting primary theological truths from mythical material that is not internally consistent. The passage is mentioned by R. Lamberton, Homer the Theologian, 26 (and above, "Introduction," p. xix).

evidence of Heraclitus, a contemporary perhaps but a dubious Stoic at best. Thus far we have found no shred of evidence from unimpeachable Stoic sources to suggest that Stoics in general interpreted Homer allegorically or took Homer himself to be an allegorist. They had many interests in Homer; insofar as they asked themselves what cosmological truths he expressed, they took themselves to be interpreting pre-Homeric myths within the poem, not the poem's narrative content or Homer's own knowledge or purposes.[35]

At this point, however, an obvious question arises. It may seem that my account of the Stoics' interpretative interests in Homer and Hesiod has merely pushed matters one stage further back. The new theory saves the Stoics from taking Homer to be a crypto-Stoic, but it does so at the cost of positing crypto-Stoics prior to Homer—the original enlightened ancients whose names for the gods display their correct understanding of nature. That challenge demands an answer and I will give it at the end of the paper. For the present, I want to leave it in abeyance because some further evidence requires consideration.

IV

So far, my case against the standard theory of the Stoics as allegorists of poetic meaning has largely rested on the following points: rejection of Heraclitus as an official Stoic, rejection of the polemical evidence of the Epicurean in Cicero, and reliance on the three witnesses who explain the Stoics' interest in the myths expressed in poetry. This material is all relatively late within the history of Stoicism. What reason do we have for thinking that it correctly represents the views of the earliest Stoics, the founders of the school? Is it not possible that they, or some of them, were

---

[35] The thesis I am advancing has affinities with the positions of both P. Steinmetz, "Allegorische Deutung," and G. Most, "Cornutus and Stoic Allegoresis," though I differ from both of them in my view of the Stoics's attention to myth rather than poetry. Most (2023–36) criticizes Steinmetz for attacking a straw man, "allegorical interpretation of poetry as poetry"; but Steinmetz has good reason to do this within the context of the traditional theory, because it enables him to shift the focus of the Stoics' interests to the myths incorporated by the poets. However, Steinmetz continues to think (23), incorrectly I believe, that the Stoics took themselves to be uncovering via etymology the poet's meaning. Most, though he writes of the Stoics' allegoresis of poetry, comes close to my position when he notes (2026, n. 80), "The figures of mythology ultimately have an explanation in terms of physical allegoresis which is their ἀλήθεια; but in many details this has been misunderstood, presumably already by the poets themselves, and the result is the δόξα of superstition."

allegorists as the standard doctrine proposes, and that it is Cicero's Stoic spokesman and Cornutus who are aberrant?[36] I cannot decisively disprove this suggestion because what we know of Zeno, Cleanthes, and Chrysippus on this matter is so fragmentary, but the evidence we have seems to offer nothing unambiguously in its favour.

. . . . .

First Chrysippus. It was he, above all, who represented orthodoxy for later Stoicism. As I have already said, his eight recorded contributions to Homeric exegesis are all philological. I also pointed out that in all cases where he cites Homer in support of a doctrine he takes Homer's text at its surface or literal meaning. The only cosmological allegory he is known to have advanced concerns not a text but a painting. There was a famous and obscene painting at Argos that showed Hera fellating Zeus (SVF 2.1071–74). Chrysippus explained this (Do we know he was utterly serious in doing so?) as an interaction between the two Stoic principles, Zeus/god and Hera/matter. Interestingly enough, this interpretation does not invoke the standard Stoic etymology, Hera/$\dot{\alpha}\dot{\eta}\rho$.

When it was a question of choosing between interpretations of a myth, Chrysippus was skillful at exploiting the literal sense of a passage. He wanted to show that Hesiod's account of Athena's birth from the head of Zeus does not contradict the Stoic doctrine of the heart as the mind's center.[37] "Some people," he says, "take this story to be a symbol of the mind's location in the head." But they fail to attend properly to Hesiod's text. Chrysippus notes that Hesiod gives two versions of Athena's birth and that a common feature of both is Zeus's swallowing of Metis.[38] So Athena is generated from Metis, present in the belly of Zeus, and not *simpliciter* from the head of Zeus. Therefore, the myth in Hesiod confirms Chrysippus's view on the central location of the mind. This piece of ex-

[36] This is the view of J. Tate, "Cornutus and the Poets," but only so far as Cornutus is concerned, because Tate overlooks Cicero, *De nat. deor.* 2.63–72. Tate claims that earlier Stoics believed "Homer and Hesiod to have been original thinkers, who expressed sound doctrine in the mythical style proper to the primitive times in which they lived." The evidence he cites to support this is our old favourite, Cicero *De nat. deor.* 1.41, and other indirect testimonies—Strabo 1.1.10 and 1.2.9, Dio Chrysostom 55.9 ff., and Heraclitus. Yet Cornutus himself, apart from his coherence with the other Stoic evidence discussed above, says that his book is only a summary of works by earlier philosophers (Cornutus 76, 6–8 Lang).

[37] Galen, *De plac. Hipp. et Plat.* 3.8.1–28 = SVF 2.908–09.

[38] Chrysippus's text of the *Theogony* included lines that modern scholars excise; cf. fr. 343 Merkelbach-West.

egesis may be overingenious, but it approaches the text in ways that are scrupulous, closely argued and even, perhaps, ironical.

Galen characterises Chrysippus's practice here in language that modern scholars conventionally call allegorizing.[39] But Galen has correctly seen that what interests Chrysippus is the interpretation of a myth, and *interpretation* is a much better term than *allegorization* for what Chrysippus is doing. Chrysippus does not take himself to be identifying a gap between surface meaning and hidden meaning. His interpretation demythologizes Hesiod but it does so in ways that retain the obvious link in the text between Metis as goddess and μῆτις as a word signifying intelligence.

. . . . .

Next Zeno. In his fifty-third oration, "On Homer," Dio Chrysostom speaks briefly about Zeno's judgment of the poet. Dio's context is this: Most philosophers and grammarians are unequivocal in their admiration of Homer. Plato, however, although sensitive to Homer's charm, criticizes the poet severely for his myths and statements about the gods. This is not an easy matter to assess. Did Homer err, or did he merely "transmit certain physical doctrines present in the myths according to the custom of his time"?[40] Dio seems to allude to the Stoic theory of cultural transmission and not to Heraclitus's treatment of Homer as an allegorist. He then observes that Zeno wrote on both Homeric poems and found nothing to criticize in them. Zeno's object, according to Dio, was to save Homer from the charge of self-contradiction. He did this by showing in detail that Homer wrote "some things in accordance with opinion (δόξα) and other things in accordance with truth (ἀλήθεια)."[41] Dio then notes that Antisthenes anticipated Zeno in this approach to Homer. It was Zeno, however, and others including Zeno's follower Persaeus, who expounded Homer in this way, point by point. Unfortunately, Dio gives no example of Zeno's procedure. We are left to infer what apparent inconsistencies he sought to remove and how he did so.

[39] Cf. *De plac. Hipp. et Plat.* 3.8.34 on Chrysippus's concern to explain the ὑπόνοιαι of myths. Cf. above ("Introduction"), p. xvii, n. 34.

[40] Dio Chrysostom 53.3: πότερον Ὅμηρος ἥμαρτε περὶ ταῦτα ἢ φυσικούς τινας ἐνόντας ἐν τοῖς μύθοις λόγους κατὰ τὴν τότε συνήθειαν παρεδίδου τοῖς ἀνθρώποις. Cf. Cicero *De nat. deor.* 2.64, "physica ratio non inelegans inclusa est in impias fabulas."

[41] Dio Chrysostom 53.4 (SVF 1.274): ὁ δὲ Ζήνων οὐδὲν τῶν Ὁμήρου ψέγει, ἅμα διηγούμενος καὶ διδάσκων ὅτι τὰ μὲν κατὰ δόξαν, τὰ δὲ κατὰ ἀλήθειαν γέγραφεν, ὅπως μὴ φαίνηται αὐτὸς αὑτῷ μαχόμενος ἔν τισι δοκοῦσιν ἐναντίως εἰρῆσθαι.

Given Dio's context, the inconsistencies should above all include apparently incongruent statements in Homer about the gods. If Zeno harmonised these by distinguishing "opinions" from "truths," he presumably wanted to show that Homer's treatment of the gods is epistemologically complex, containing both identifiable truths and identifiable fables or falsehoods. Coherence would be established by distinguishing these two modes of discourse and by appropriately assigning passages to (false) opinion or to truth. There is good reason to attribute this procedure to Antisthenes. He distinguished, as the Stoics later did, between the many gods of popular religion and a single divinity in nature (Cicero, *De nat. deor.* 1.32). Ethically impeccable passages in Homer about the gods collectively or about Zeus in particular could seem to justify the application of this distinction to the poet.

There is no good evidence that Antisthenes offered physicalist allegories of the Homeric gods in the manner of Metrodorus of Lampsacus.[42] His well-known interest in the figures of Odysseus, Ajax, and Herakles was ethical. Is allegory implied by or consonant with Zeno's use of the distinction between truth and opinion? Many have thought so,[43] but there are strong reasons for doubt. Fritz Wehrli states the obvious objection: "It is false to take this as evidence for allegory since allegory creates truth out of everything mythical."[44] His point is that Antisthenes and Zeno would not have distinguished between Homer's true and opining statements if they had taken the opining ones to express covert truths.

Peter Steinmetz goes a step further than Wehrli: "It is unclear how physico-cosmological allegory or psychological-ethical allegory could help in resolving inconsistencies between two Homeric passages."[45] Steinmetz interprets Zeno's concern as philological. On this view, Zeno was primarily interested in close textual analysis of Homer—in resolving apparent inconsistencies such as the description of Ithaca as "low" and "very high" in adjacent words (*Od.* 9.25).

It is highly likely that Zeno's five books of *Homeric Problems* did address such points. We have no evidence that this work included allegorization, and Steinmetz could have helped himself to an additional point. Cicero

---

[42] Cf. F. Wehrli, *Zur Geschichte der allegorischen Deutung*, 65 ff.; N. Richardson, "Homeric Professors," 77–81; M. Hilgruber, "Dion Chrysostomos," 15–18.

[43] Cf. M. Hilgruber, "Dion Chrysostomos," who is the latest to take Dio's text to refer to Zeno's allegorizing, but in my opinion he fails to overturn the arguments of Tate (cf. n. 46 below). He adduces no new evidence for the thesis and saddles himself with a view of the passage that makes Zeno, but not Antisthenes, an allegorist of Homer.

[44] F. Wehrli, *Zur Geschichte der allegorischen Deutung*, 65.

[45] P. Steinmetz, "Allegorische Deutung," 20.

tells us, on Stoic authority, that the separation of proto-science from legend and superstition was treated more fully by Cleanthes and Chrysippus
than by Zeno (*De nat. deor.* 2.63). It can hardly, then, have formed a major
part of his five-book work *Homeric Problems*. However, Steinmetz's
strictly philological reading of Dio's testimony will not do. That interpretation does not fit Zeno's distinction between "truth" and "opinion,"
nor does it chime with Dio's theological context.

The most obvious point was made by J. Tate in an article written sixty
years ago: The distinction between "truth" and "opinion" or fiction was
a commonplace in the interpretation of Homer.[46] Strabo uses it (1.2, etc.)
to save Homer's credit as a geographer against Eratosthenes' opinion
that the poet is entirely concerned with fiction. According to Strabo,
Homer regularly combines truth and falsehood (1.2.7–9, 1.2.19, etc.). In
addition, the poet sometimes overlays truths with a mythical covering to
flavour his style and enchant his audience. Strabo is confident, too confident, that he can remove Homer's mythical accretions and exhibit the
kernel of his factual knowledge. He treats Homer as fully in control of
his (Strabo's) distinction between truth and falsehood; perhaps Zeno did
so too. However, Strabo does not maintain, as Heraclitus does, that
Homer's myths are regularly reducible to covert truths.[47]

Another author who can illuminate Zeno's approach to Homer is Plutarch. In his essay *On How to Study Poetry*, Plutarch rejects astrological
and cosmological allegory as the way to clear Homer from the charge of
representing the gods immorally (19e–20a). In this context he is clearly
talking about the likes of Heraclitus, but he does not name the Stoics. For
Plutarch one correct response to this charge is to recognize that Homer
includes "healthy and true theological doctrines" and others "that have
been fabricated to excite people" (20f). Setting the former against the
latter enables the poet's own voice to be distinguished. This comes as
close as possible to the simplest interpretation of Zeno's distinction between "truth" and "opinion."

A second recommendation of Plutarch is also relevant to the Stoics'

---

[46] "Plato and Allegorical Interpretation [2]" 7–10. Tate's view is summed up in these remarks of his ad loc.: "As spokesman for the multitude [Homer] may contradict the truths
he knew and expressed elsewhere. But this contradiction is only apparent, for in this case it
is not Homer who is wrong but the multitude whose views he is expressing." Diogenianus
criticizes Chrysippus for his selective quotations from Homer, which obscure the fact that
Homer does not consistently support Chrysippus's doctrine that everything is fated; cf.
Eusebius, *Praeparatio evangelica* 6.8.1–7, and above ("Introduction"), xvii, n. 34.

[47] For a well-balanced account of Strabo's treatment of Homer, cf. D. M. Schenkeveld,
"Strabo on Homer."

procedures. He emphasizes the importance of recognizing how poets use the names of the gods (23a). Sometimes a divine name is to be taken as a direct reference to the god himself. Frequently, however, poets use the names of gods, by metonymy, to refer to impersonal states of affairs— for instance, Zeus to denote fate or fortune, Ares to signify war, Hephaestus to signify fire. Plutarch does not call this allegory and nor would I. The second kind of usage does not invoke a hidden meaning. It is a transparent application of names, and one that belongs to the Greek language from its recorded beginnings. Plutarch offers it as a way of "correcting" most of the seemingly out-of-place statements made in Homer about Zeus (24a).

Plutarch may have drawn heavily on Stoicism in his writing of this essay. However that may be, Zeno could certainly have availed himself of Plutarch's two procedures in his process of removing apparent inconsistencies from Homer. Unlike allegory, these procedures clearly fit his distinction between truth and opinion, and both are set by Plutarch within a theological context, as Dio's citation of Zeno requires.

Before we leave Plutarch, a further word on his approach to Homer is in order. He has no time for allegorical euhemerism, as we have seen. Yet, as far as I know, Plutarch never launches any attack on allegorical interpretation of poetry by the Stoics.[48] Because his knowledge of Stoicism was second to none, and because he uses every opportunity to make fun of Stoic extravagances, his silence on this point should embarrass proponents of the standard theory about the Stoics, represented by R. Pfeiffer, as "necessarily allegorists in their interpretation of poetry."

V

However Zeno read Homer, he certainly sought to demythologise Hesiod by means of etymology.[49] What survives of Zeno's work on the *Theogony* has close affinities with Cornutus. Zeno interpreted Hesiod's χάος as primal water, deriving the word from χύσις or χέεσθαι (SVF 1.103–04), meaning "pouring." He identified four of Hesiod's Titans (children of Earth and Heaven) with cosmic powers, justifying this by etymology,

---

[48] Plutarch does complain (*De aud. po.* 31e) about the "childishness" or "irony" Cleanthes exhibits in his physicalist etymology of ἄνα Δωδωναῖε [see main text below]. Immediately later he criticizes Chrysippus for an implausible, but not physicalist, etymology of Κρονίδης.

[49] Cf. P. Steinmetz, "Allegorische Deutung," 21–23.

and treated the names of the Cyclopes similarly (SVF 1.100, 118). Above all, he set a pattern for later Stoics in explaining the names of the Olympians as primary allusions to the physical elements—Hera/air, Zeus/aither, Hephaestus/fire, etc. Like Cornutus, Zeno seems to have focused on divine names and epithets rather than the extended episodes of the poem.

It seems quite credible that Zeno applied this approach to Hesiod, as he is said to have done (Cicero, De nat. deor. 1.36), but not to Homer.[50] Unlike Homer, Hesiod has an explicit cosmogony. His divine genealogies include many items that we today would call abstract powers or that have a straightforward reference to physical phenomena. His narratives are much simpler than Homer's. The whole tenor of his work is descriptive rather than dramatic. As modern studies of myth and the beginnings of philosophy have shown, Hesiod lends himself to treatment as a pioneer in speculative thought.

Homer was more hallowed and more complex. He had been interpreted allegorically long before the Stoics, but not with results that any major thinker took seriously. For Cornutus's theology Hesiod is far more significant than Homer. Cornutus does show, however, that Stoicism by his time was accommodating some cosmological interpretations of episodes in the Iliad. Peter Steinmetz is probably right to give Cleanthes the credit or discredit for adumbrating these.[51] In Cleanthes' case, unlike that of Zeno, we have clear evidence of reading isolated words in Homer through Stoic eyes. Cleanthes derived ἄνα Δωδωναῖε, "O lord of Dodona," an invocation of Zeus in the Iliad, from ἀναδίδωμι, and related this to the Stoic doctrine of air vaporising from the earth (SVF 1.535). He wanted to make Atlas's epithet in Odyssey 1.52 ὀλοόφρων, "mindful of everything," instead of "malevolent," ὀλοόφρων, in order to indicate Atlas's providential concern for the world (SVF 1.549). And he interpreted the mysterious plant μῶλυ (Od. 10.305) as signifying "reason," deriving it from the verb μωλύεσθαι, "to relax" (SVF 1.526).[52] Thus he could ex-

---

[50] P. Steinmetz makes this point, loc. cit.

[51] P. Steinmetz, "Allegorische Deutung," 23–25.

[52] According to Apollonius Sophistes, the source of this evidence, "Cleanthes says that reason (λόγος) is signified allegorically (ἀλληγορικῶς)." The absence of any offical Stoic account of "allegory" makes it likely that this is a scholiast's report of Cleanthes rather than his own verbatim statement. In any case, as I have tried to emphasize throughout, the important point is not the ancient terminology applied to Stoic interpretations but whether they should be termed allegorical from our perspective. Sometimes ἀλληγορέω is simply synonymous with ἑρμηνεύω; cf. Metrodorus fr. A6 D-K with Plutarch, De Iside 363d.

plain why μῶλυ protected Odysseus from the passions that Circe exploited in his followers.

This is not allegory, as Heraclitus uses it, but etymology. For Heraclitus it is crucial that Homer means something different from what he says—that he intends his stories to be taken not literally but as *covert* references to natural phenomena. No such assumption is required by Zeno or Cleanthes. Their explanations of divine names are based upon etymologies whose validity is quite independent of anything Homer or Hesiod may have thought. For all we know, Cleanthes may have supposed that Homer wrote ὀλοόφρονος. His emendation could have aimed at restoring a truth not evident to Homer but familiar to Homer's wiser predecessors.

VI

The lines between poetry and myth and between poetic meaning and mythological interpretation are fine ones to draw. It would be a mistake to presume that the Stoics never overstepped them or that they always tried to keep them apart. Nonetheless it does appear that we have failed to distinguish between the Stoics' interest in myth and their understanding of literature. They were well aware that poets combine truth *and* fiction at the surface level of meaning. As students of Hesiod, they will have known *Theogony* 27–28, where the poet himself seems to alert his audience to the fact that he is about to recite just such a combination. What passes under the name of Stoic allegorizing is the Stoic interpretation of myth. The Stoics seem to have recognized that *myths are allegories*, stories told in order to explain problematic features of the physical world. They thought that elucidation of these myths could help to confirm their own understanding of nature. Interpretation of the meaning and composition of Homer or Hesiod per se was not their concern. As even the hostile Philodemus says (*De Pietate* col. vi), "It was *things in* Homer and Hesiod" that Chrysippus tried to harmonise with Stoic doctrines. The things in question were divine names and myths transmitted by the poets, and not the poets' own use of these. By taking the latter to have been the Stoics' concern, we have come to believe that they advertised Homer and other early poets as proto-Stoics.

The evidence I have reviewed—drawn from Stoics and not their detractors—tells decisively against the pertinence of this assessment. Some Stoics, though perhaps not Zeno, used Homer among other poets as a source of myth pertaining to cosmology. They did this as students of natural theology, believing, most reasonably, that divine names and epithets and myths *are* serious evidence of how early people interpreted the world. They assumed, less reasonably, that etymology is the best device for recovering the beliefs of the primary users of names and that etymology could line up those beliefs with some of their own views on nature. They had enough confidence in their own cosmology and human rationality to presume that many of their own findings were not original; this was naive perhaps, but it is an approach that should appeal to cultural historians and anthropologists. In all of this, the Stoics treated early Greek poetry as ethnographical material and not as literature in, say, an Aristotelian sense.

So, to conclude, has my revision of the standard theory merely pushed the problem one stage further back, so that instead of Homer and Hesiod being crypto-Stoics that role is now being played by the anonymous mythmakers who preceded them? I think not. For one thing, on my explanation, the ancient sages are not crypto-Stoics. They are not deliberately concealing truths about nature in misleading myths. Myth, in the theory I am offering, *is* the early people's mode of interpreting the world. Second, up to quite a large point, the Stoics were right about this. Many Greek myths *are* cosmological—ways of ordering the physical world. To have had the insight to see this is greatly to the Stoics' credit, and gives them a theory very different from the standard one that Homer's epic narrative is a Stoic cosmology in disguise. Many anthropologists take allegory to be central to a myth's mode of signification. The Stoics clearly had an inkling of this. They did not make the mistake of supposing that a myth's meaning is identical either to its function in a larger story (the personification of concepts) or to a secret message inscribed by the storyteller.

Allegory, so we are often told today, covers everything written. All texts are codes, no meaning is objective or stable, authorial intentions do not count, what *we* find in a text *is* what the text says. Although this modern fashion might seem to suit the Stoics, they should firmly reject it. Their hermeneutic is fundamentally historicist. That is why it depends on etymology, the search for original meanings. Independently of the Stoics, the idea had developed that Homer was his own allegorist; the task of the exegete then became one of demonstrating Homer's knowledge of philosophical truths.[53] This is the position of Heraclitus, and it is also

---

[53] This practice seems to be well under way by the end of the fifth century, on the evidence of Metrodorus of Lampsacus, and it can also be observed in the Derveni papyrus, whose

evident in that curious work, attributed to Plutarch, *On the Life and Poetry of Homer*.[54] Once Homer was his own allegorist, he could be turned into any philosopher one liked, as he is by pseudo-Plutarch. The scene was set for Neoplatonist allegorical readings.

The contribution of Stoicism to this was partly substantive but also accidental and indirect. It was substantive because the Stoics had shown how to give cosmological readings to certain myths by etymologizing the names of their divine agents. Their philosophy of nature is a strong presence in Heraclitus. But an element of accident is also evident there. Stoicism simply was the most powerful philosophy at his time. If Heraclitus was to use philosophy as the way of exonerating Homer, he had to turn to the Stoics. Mutatis mutandis, the same holds for Philo's allegorical readings of Scripture. These do not make him a Stoic. The Stoic contribution is indirect for the reason I have emphasized throughout this paper—the shift from interpreting the earliest poets' myths as sources for archaic beliefs to interpreting Homer as an allegorist.

---

author takes Orpheus to have had access to truths about the world which he then clothed in enigmas; cf. Jeffrey S. Rusten, "Interim Notes on the Papyrus from Derveni." In comments on the original draft of this paper, which he kindly sent to me, Denis Feeney wrote, "If it was possible in the fifth century to talk of Homer as someone who expressed truth in veiled ways, then the Stoics' later discretion in using him only as a source for early belief is even more striking." I agree. But, apart from the arguments I have advanced, it would be quite unlike their philosophy in general if the Stoics had simply appropriated an earlier, but highly contentious, approach to Homer. What I am proposing has much in common with Aristotle's view of mythically clothed truths about astronomy (see especially *Metaphysics* 12.1074b1), but a comparison with Aristotle is too large a subject to be pursued here.

[54] Until recently, the most accessible edition of this work was the Teubner edited by G. N. Bernardakis (*Plutarchus Moralia VII* [1896], which contains the Plutarchan spuria). Now, however, this has been replaced by J. F. Kindstrand's new Teubner (*[Plutarchus] De Homero*). The author of *On the Life and Poetry of Homer* sees no difficulty in making Homer the source of contradictory doctrines, for instance Stoic ἀπάθεια and Peripatetic μετριοπάθεια (cf. sections 134–35), and the inspiration of all the most famous philosophers. Thus he entirely fits Seneca's sarcastic critique (cf. n. 11 above).

CHAPTER FOUR

Hermeneutic Lines and Circles:
Aristarchus and Crates on the
Exegesis of Homer*

JAMES I. PORTER

I

ACCORDING TO the scholia to Dionysius Thrax (the learned Alexandrian grammarian of the mid-second century B.C.), the first critical editions of Homer came into existence in the following way. Homer's poems, scattered over time by floods, earthquakes, and fire, resurfaced again, but in random quantities. It fell to Peisistratus to rescue the epics from almost certain oblivion. This he did, by instituting a reward for any and all scraps of Homer, which he doled out equitably, and we might say, mechanically. Remuneration was fixed at a *per*-line rate; nobody and no lines were turned away, not even if the lines duplicated lines previously turned in, and not even if, upon inspection, the lines happened to contain plus-verses—however these may have crept into the text. Seventy-two experts (γραμματικοί) were then appointed to the task of individually (κατ᾽ ἰδίαν) reassembling Homer's poems, each according to his own lights and at a wage that befitted learned men and connoisseurs of poems (κριταῖς ποιημάτων). The results (the ἴδιαι συνθέσεις, "individual recompositions") were then judged competitively and judiciously— "with a view," writes the scholiast, "not to one-upmanship, but to the truth, as only befits the name of art." Aristarchus and Zenodotus won the

* I would like to thank the organizers of the Princeton conference for the invitation to take up so challenging a topic (Aristarchus *and* Crates; in retrospect, it would have been impossible to treat either figure separately). Thanks also go to my fellow participants and to Richard Janko, for conversations and correspondence around a number of items; to Georgia Nugent, for her thoughtful response; to various members of the audience, for their comments; and to colleagues in Ann Arbor, for helpful advice. The generous support of the National Endowment for the Humanities during 1989 is gratefully acknowledged.

first round (time appears to be no object in this version of the history of classical scholarship), and of the two, Aristarchus emerged victorious on a second vote. The story, though remarkable for its candor, has a further moral. The damage done by the plus-verses—individually contributed lines (ἰδίους στίχους) that had been introduced on the profit motive—was too great to be ignored: For "these," says the scholiast, "had already won the place of familiarity and habit among readers of Homer. None of this escaped the critics, and so, respecting the force of custom and mental habit, they let these lines stand. But to each of the lines that were suspect, foreign, or unworthy of the poet, they affixed obelisks, to express their judgment that this was the case" (29, 16 – 30, 17 Hilgard).

Contrived, and self-consciously so, this fable nonetheless gives us a valuable index to readerly perceptions from the last two centuries B.C., particularly with regard to Homer.[1] The tendency of that era, shared by specialists and lay readers of Homer alike, was towards textual conservatism. Generally speaking, the received texts of Homer were revered, whatever their imperfections. No obstacle to easy comprehension was so great that it might not, simultaneously, conceal a scrap of authentic Homer: Flaws were encased in an approving tradition like obscure flecks in prehistoric amber.[2] Scholarly practice, steeped in suspicion, only mirrored this bias. Always vulnerable to the charge of rewriting Homer's words, of practicing an ἰδίως συντιθέναι, or an idiosyncratic reconstruction of the text, the γραμματικοί of Alexandria and Pergamum had a certain line of defense in the running commentary and the monograph, where the bulk of the redaction (and justification) was done—at a safe remove from the body of the texts, which could be left for the most part intact.

It is a commonplace that the readings of the great Alexandrian librarians from Zenodotus to Aristarchus, like so much of the vast philological industry of the Hellenistic period, made little direct impact on the common reader; even then, changes wrought in the transmission of the texts of Homer were made only indirectly and by means that are still not well understood. The Museum was the seat of canonical compiling and editing (unlike Pergamum, where scholarship excelled at learned detail); its prominence seems to have helped raise general standards in the reproduc-

---

[1] On the Hellenistic sources of this anecdote, see Rudolf Pfeiffer, *History of Classical Scholarship From the Beginnings to the End of the Hellenistic Age*, 6, n. 3.

[2] Stephanie West, *The Ptolemaic Papyri of Homer*, 18: "The classics were now fossilized: even if what the author wrote appeared to be unmetrical, ungrammatical, factually incorrect, obscure, and improper, this was what must be transmitted."

tion and especially in the length of the Homeric texts, a rise that the reading public may itself have embraced. This, at least, is the inference to be drawn from the gradual consolidation of the vulgate tradition which can be detected in the Ptolemaic papyri sometime after 150 B.C. In any event, the Alexandrian "recensions" (ἐκδόσεις) of Homer were not "editions" in our sense. They were not destined for commercial circulation, nor would they have enjoyed a market.[3] Marginal critical signs, σημεῖα like the ὀβελός or διπλῆ, were in the first instance professional "readings" of Homer;[4] they had a pedagogical value, and they were used to send students to the commentaries. Hellenistic criticism and textual criticism could thus operate like transparent palimpsests on the body of the Homeric text, like so much scribbling and erasure over an impregnable and venerable surface.[5]

The technical vocabulary of textual criticism, even before Aristarchus came to epitomize it in the first half of the second century B.C., betrays this double-mindedness without a blush: γράφειν, μεταγράφειν, and ἀναγιγνώσκειν, "writing," "rewriting," and "reading" are used interchangeably in the scholia.[6] Such were the concessions of scholarship to an impalatable and unavoidable truth: to read Homer's epics was, at one level or another, to rewrite them too. These circumstances, no doubt, explain why Aristarchus could exercise so divided an influence on the popular and lay imagination. At times he appeared to be the consummate embodiment of the Museum's critical activities, ὁ γραμματικώτατος

[3] The exact relationship between "recensions" (ἔκδοσις, διόρθωσις), explanatory "commentaries" (ὑπομνήματα), and "monographs" (συγγράμματα) is a matter of some speculation. See Hartmut Erbse, "Über Aristarchs Iliasausgaben"; B. A. van Groningen, "ΕΚΔΟΣΙΣ"; R. Pfeiffer, History of Classical Scholarship From the Beginnings, 215, 221, 289 (addendum to 215); Klaus Nickau, Untersuchungen zur textkritischen Methode des Zenodotos von Ephesos, 17–18. On the "rise of the vulgate," see H. Erbse, "Über Aristarchs Iliasausgaben," 302–03, and S. West, Ptolemaic Papyri, 15–24; on the demands and needs of popular readership, see Paul Collart, "Les Papyrus de l'Iliade [2]," 40, 52; S. West, The Ptolemaic Papyri, 47–48; Kathleen McNamee, "Aristarchus and 'Everyman's' Homer."

[4] R. Schmidt, quoted in Arthur Ludwich, Aristarchs homerische Textkritik, 2, 135, n. 114: "Ipsae atheteses, quoniam nullum ex iis detrimentum capiebat Homerus . . . , non tam pro criseos sunt quam pro interpretationis documento habendae." Wilhelm Bachmann (Die ästhetischen Anschauungen Aristarchs, 1, 28) and H. Erbse ("Über Aristarchs Iliasausgaben," 303) take this line of argument to a hypothetical extreme. For an opposing viewpoint, see R. Pfeiffer, History of Classical Scholarship From the Beginnings, 215, 221, 289.

[5] A case in point is the much controverted problem of the "end" of the Odyssey. Cf. Kweku A. Garbrah, "The Scholia on the Ending of the Odyssey."

[6] See K. Nickau's "Terminologische Tabelle" (Untersuchungen, 26–30) for a concordance of such terms and their occurrences.

("the most scholarly of γραμματικοί," Athenaeus 15.671f.); at other times he was a ruthless *Phalaris grammaticus*, savagely blackening the margins of inferior lines (Cicero *In Pisonem* 73; *Fam.* ix.10.1; Horace *Ars Poetica* 447). His greatest compliment was paid by the Stoic philosopher Panaetius: He called Aristarchus a prophet, a μάντις, who could divine Homer's intended meaning (διάνοια) effortlessly (Athenaeus 14.634c). We should perhaps be wary of such praise, which is conceivably double-edged. Plato's ironies, sheathed in identical language, could never be far from mind (*Ion* 530c, 531b; *Hippias minor* 365d), and Panaetius, after all, proclaimed himself to be a pupil of Aristarchus's foremost contemporary rival, Crates of Mallos at Pergamum (Strabo 14.5.16; 1.2.24). Although Aristarchus would have declined the epithet—his piety was rather of a rationalistic cast—he would have assented, with one qualification, to the reasons tendered for it: Aristarchus did after all stand in the long line of Homeric interpreters who sought "to understand Homer's meaning (διάνοιαν), that is, what the poet said (τὰ λεγόμενα ὑπὸ τοῦ ποιητοῦ), and not just his words (μὴ μόνον τὰ ἔπη)," as Plato puts it in the *Ion* (530b–c). But whereas Plato goes on to drive a wedge into this fatal disjunction, by reducing poetry to its intelligibility as an idea and that idea to nothing (534b), Aristarchus would seek to heal the wound thus created. Homer's thought or meaning, if it was to be located at all, had to be sought, precisely, in his very words. It is to this grounding principle of all of Aristarchus's reading and rewriting of Homer that we should turn. Its meaning and implications are anything but self-evident.

A D-scholium (at *Il.* 5.385) preserves the Aristarchan principle elsewhere known, from Porphyry, as "elucidate Homer from Homer" ("Ομηρον ἐξ 'Ομήρου σαφηνίζειν, *Quaest. Hom. Il.* 297, 16 Schrader): "Aristarchus felt that interpreters ought to take what Homer said (τὰ φραζόμενα ὑπὸ τοῦ ποιητοῦ) more poetically (μυθικώτερον ἐκδέχεσθαι), not wasting their time on anything not said by the poet (μηδὲν ἔξω τῶν φραζομένων ὑπὸ τοῦ ποιητοῦ περιεργαζομένους)." In question here, in *Iliad* 5, is the myth of Otus and Ephialtes from the Gigantomachy, and Aristarchus's advice is to take the myth at face value—to concede to the poet, in other words, his constitutional right, his ποιητικὴ ἐξουσία or "licence," to use an inherited story as part of his poetic material. Aristarchus's advice has no sense at all unless it is directed against allegorizing interpretations of the passage. Allusions to the Gigantomachy were ripe for apologetics from the very beginnings of Homeric interpretation, ever since Theagenes (Porphyry *Quaest. Hom. Il.* 241, 11 Schrader); and the comments of Eustathius on this passage, and the rest of the D-scholium, only bear out that allegorism had been attempted even here. Eustathius makes explicit the contrast that Aristarchus must have had in mind: "It *is* an allegory, even if Aristarchus thought it inappropriate to waste time on any of the mythical elements in the poetry (τὶ τῶν παρὰ τῇ ποιήσει μυθικῶν) by interpreting them allegorically, [and thus to go] beyond what the poet said (ἔξω τῶν φραζομένων)" (Eustathius ad loc., 561, 29). We might call the Aristarchan alternative to physical and moral allegory a λύσις ἐκ τῆς ποιητικῆς, or a poetic solution to an interpretive scandal. In this, Aristarchus is following good, chiefly Aristotelian precedents, not inventing a new mode of interpretive analysis. So, one should think, the so-called "Aristarchan maxim," if it is tied in any way to the D-scholium, does no more than express a traditional way of finding and justifying a specifically aesthetic dimension within a poetic text through a procedure that is, moreover, patently *self*-justifying. Instead, the maxim has been subject to an altogether different sort of controversy, one that is bound up with the way in which the nature of literary, and especially Homeric, scholarship in antiquity has been viewed by modern scholars.

Surely no assessment of this topic has exerted greater authority during the past several decades than Rudolf Pfeiffer's magisterial *History of Classical Scholarship From the Beginnings to the End of the Hellenistic Age*. Pfeiffer doubted whether Aristarchus would have ventured so blanket a maxim as "elucidate Homer from Homer," even if Aristarchus's thoughts (Pfeiffer allows) tended that way: It is not Aristarchus's wont to take strong theoretical stands, because his perspective is that of a philologist, not of a philosopher. Pfeiffer can make this kind of claim, because for him Aristarchus epitomizes the tradition of *philologia perennis*, a scientific enterprise of "pure learning" first undertaken in the third century B.C. (when the discipline attained "self-conscious" reflexivity) and reaching continuously into the present. The object of classical scholarship is the recovery of past meaning through a process of subtraction; obstacles to the clear view of meaning, accreted over time, must be removed, by layers. Philology must itself be transparent, like the meanings it apprehends. Thus Aristarchus had no "theory of poetics," no theory of interpretation, and no philosophical principles either.[7] As it happens, this picture of interpretive lucidity is in fact supplied by a particular reading, and affirmation, of the Aristarchan maxim.

It is essential to the validity and continuity of *philologia perennis* that

---

[7] R. Pfeiffer, *History of Classical Scholarship from the Beginnings*, 231.

"Homer must be his own interpreter."[8] Homer was, in some sense, a proto-philologist (less a practitioner of exegesis than of "epexegesis"). Because the earliest Greek poetry ostensibly contained a "philological element," it can be said that poetry "paved the way to its understanding"—by a self-conscious philology. Scholarship, the crowning jewel of this historical process, is the final, genuine apprehension of poetry.[9] In such a setting, the rivalry between Aristarchus and Crates becomes meaningfully symbolic of the larger forces driving the history of philology. Whereas Aristarchus embodies "the art of interpretation," Crates, his Pergamene contemporary under Eumenes II, embodies an unstable fusion of "scholarship and philosophy." Not content with "sober" elucidation, Crates is led to discover Stoic principles in the poems of Homer, which can now be read as cosmic allegories and, if need be, modified—by deletion, emendation, or even interpolation—in order to bring out more fully their underlying sense (e.g., Plutarch, *De facie* 938d = Crates fr. 33 Mette). With Crates, *philosophia perennis* reads its own image through the lens of a violently allegorized Homeric text.

Although so much of Pfeiffer's analysis is admirably lucid in its details, several of his assumptions simply do not hold up. In many respects, Aristarchus's critical activities indeed do look forward to modern textual critical methods. They involved some kind of systematization of the manuscript evidence into preferential classes, they wrought transpositions of text, advanced conjectures and emendations, and they deployed the famous atheteses ("rejections" of spurious text). They may even mark an advance over the less systematic methods of his predecessor at the Library in the early third century B.C., Zenodotus of Ephesus, against whom Aristarchus devised a special critical symbol, a διπλῆ περιεστιγμένη (a fortified διπλῆ, as it were), by which Zenodotean readings could be noted and opposed. It was an honor shared by only one other rival, Crates of Mallos.[10]

But as we saw above in the fable from the later grammatical scholia, the anxieties of reading which a Crates could spectrally embody were harbored within the Museum itself. And so too, Crates and Aristarchus are—in at least one important sense—driven by the same legitimating purpose. Both fundamentally presume, as they must, that Homer clari-

[8] Ibid., 8.

[9] Ibid., 3.

[10] R. Pfeiffer, *History of Classical Scholarship From the Beginnings*, 240, has doubts on this head, but they are not well founded. Aristarchus is often responding to Cratetean readings (see below and n. 79).

fies his own meanings: Only so could Homer certify the validity of any interpretation. But each critic would justify this purpose in his own way. It is here, in their justifications, that we encounter some surprises: Crates' alleged Stoic motivations turn out, upon closer scrutiny, to have been literary and critical ones; on the other hand, Aristarchus's practice is more philosophically indebted than is readily admitted. In the end, it will be difficult to pigeonhole either figure. Both critics must be allowed to speak in their own distinctive voices, however unfamiliar these may sound to us today.

Pfeiffer doubted the Aristarchan provenance of the maxim "Elucidate Homer from Homer" on the grounds of its generality; and yet the second version of that maxim (as preserved in the scholia), Pfeiffer surprisingly concedes, is incontestably general: "According to Schol. D Aristarchus's sentence was more general, not particularly against allegory." Eustathius's mention of allegory, in his version of the scholium, is best explained as a willful "interpolation." The argument seems to be going in circles and to be steered, moreover, by a reluctance to allow self-conscious principles to impinge on scholarly practice. The justification offered looks weak (and is strangely self-refuting): "Scholars are not inclined to pronounce general principles, but philosophers are, and Porphyry was always . . . of a philosophical bent." The only real argument against the Aristarchan provenance of the maxim is this maxim by Pfeiffer.[11] Just how universal and how "philosophical" is Aristarchus's maxim, and what is its actual extension? Subsequent attempts to document a pre-Porphyrian source for *Homerum ex Homero*, based on the old assumption that at stake in this issue is Homer's "intentionality" (what he "meant," his διάνοια), have turned up good parallels for this in the medical and juridical traditions, without casting any light, however, on the specific motives of Aristarchus. I will cite just three of the proposed candidates:[12]

1. Galen: "One must conduct an exegesis of the [medical] term (τῆς λέξεως) *from Hippocrates himself* (ἐξ Ἱπποκράτους αὐτοῦ), so that we not only will be able to say that our explanation is plausible (ὅτι πιθανῶς εἴρηται), but that it also reflects Hippoc-

---

[11] R. Pfeiffer, *History of Classical Scholarship From the Beginnings*, 226–27; cf. his "general statement" (88, recapitulating 3). Pfeiffer's suspicions run deep. See his Festrede, *Philologia Perennis*, 3.

[12] Cf. Christoph Schäublin, "*Homerum ex Homero.*"

rates' own position (κατὰ τὴν ἐκείνου γνώμην)" (De comate sec. Hipp. 1, 5).

2. Aristotle: "One must look not to the letter (τὸν λόγον), but to the spirit (the "intention," τὴν διάνοιαν) of the lawgiver" (Rhetoric 1374b11).

3. Cicero: "The reader who interprets [the intention of, e.g., the testator] from his own written words (ex ipsius . . . litteris) comes much closer to the author's intention (voluntas) than does the reader who does not apprehend the writer's meaning (sententiam) from the author's own writing (ex ipsius scripto) . . . , but relies instead on his own inferences (suspicionibus)" (De inventione 2.128).

Although these examples do illustrate a position regularly taken by the ancients on the relationship of ipsissima verba to the recovery of meaning, one is left feeling that the goal of the search has been both too remote from literary meaning and, in another sense, too narrowly conceived. Paradoxically, the focus of the "intentionalist" view has been trained, we might say, on Aristarchus's words, not on his intention. What is more, the problem is no longer just one of authenticity; the very meaning of the maxim is now at stake. Rather than concede all our ground to Plato and reduce Homer's poems to their intelligibility as διάνοια, it might be better to redefine the issue and ask instead, What were the relevant theoretical justifications that made the statements in Porphyry and the scholia possible in the first place? And here we must turn to critical precedents that are specifically literary. In what follows, I will argue that the maxim "Elucidate Homer from Homer" could have easily originated with Aristarchus. In one sense, it would have been a critical banality for him; it was certainly within his expressive reach (this can be directly shown); but it also would have been strongly colored by the language and ideas of Aristotle's poetics (this can only be shown by a more circuitous route).

Aristarchus's view of Homer as a master of his craft and of his materials—as a connoisseur of poetic intricacies (a φιλότεχνος) operating in a technical tradition (Schol. A B 681a, γ 400)—is expressed in terms that are eminently indebted to Aristotle (cf. Poetics 60a5–6, 48b28–29).[13] The same holds for his notions about internal consistency, poetic unity (guaranteed by Homer's presiding presence), linearity of action, and even the

---

[13] With Schol. A Y 40b[1] and Y 147a[1] compare Poetics 14, esp. 53b25 (on poetic tradition and inherited materials). With Schol. A E 60a compare Poetics 51b20–25 (invention). The parallels and phraseology are exact.

problem of ἀδύνατα or ἄλογα (implausibilities and illogicalities),[14] all of which are traceable to the *Poetics* and many of which closely reflect Aristotelian terminology (as does, inevitably, so much in Alexandrian scholarship) and especially the tragic vocabulary of the *Poetics*. Much of this has been well established,[15] although Aristarchus's debt to the *Poetics* perhaps runs deeper than is suspected. The language of so many of his formulations, for instance, suggests that Aristarchus had a direct acquaintance not just with chapter 25 of the *Poetics* (on "problems" and their "solutions"), but with the whole of that work and its underlying principles (and not just the popular dialogue *On Poets*). Thus, Aristarchus's defense of mythical ἀδύνατα is intelligible in Aristotelian terms: "Plausible impossibility" or even supernatural events (ἄτοπα) are excusable πρὸς τὴν ποίησιν, which is to say, in light of the only criterion that matters, the poet's needs (*Poetics* 61b11).[16] This is not a mere matter of poetic "licence" or critical indulgence. At stake in this definition of the poet and this defense of myth, as much for Aristotle as for Aristarchus, was in the first instance a category of the "poetic" (e.g., Schol. T Δ 491b; Aristotle fr. 142 Rose). It was closely and implicitly allied with a conception of what we might call aesthetic autonomy, or better yet poetic specificity. It is here that Aristarchus's maxim and Aristotle's poetics resonate in an unexpected unison.

Aristotle felt that he could isolate, almost as a theoretical entity, the aesthetic character of literary compositions, and—although this is rarely acknowledged—his answer is invariably expressed in an abstractly reflexive language, suggesting a proper domain "within," one constituting an intrinsic feature or set of features of a work (or kind of work), and at the same time exposing a domain "without" (53b32): Poetics concerns "the

[14] See Schol. A Z 248b, H 79b, Θ 562, R. Pfeiffer, *History of Classical Scholarship From the Beginnings*, 230, Aristotle quoted by Porphyry on *Il.* 10.153: ἀεί (unity); Schol. A A 504a, B 724a, Λ 604b (linearity); Schol. θ 557, W. Bachmann, *Die ästhetischen Anschauungen Aristarchs*, 1, 35, Schol. A Θ 230a with *Poetics* 51a36, Porphyry *Quaest. Hom. Il.* [Schrader] 30, 13, Schol. A B 212–16, Z 433–39 (narrative logic).

[15] Adolf Trendelenburg, *Grammaticorum Graecorum . . . reliquiae*; Carlo Gallavotti, "Tracce della Poetica di Aristotele negli scolii omerici"; H. Erbse, *Beiträge zum Verständnis der Odyssee*, 166–77; N. J. Richardson, "Literary Criticism in the Exegetical Scholia" and "Recognition Scenes in the *Odyssey* and Ancient Literary Criticism"; and Roos Meijering, *Literary and Rhetorical Theories in Greek Scholia*.

[16] Aristotle also has in mind the supernatural; cf. *Poetics* 60a36 (the Phaeacians). Here too, the verbal echoes of Aristotle in the Aristarchan scholia are precise: "Let us grant this to the poets" (Schol. γ 71 [Aristarchus], *Poetics* 60b13). Isocrates could say similar things (9.9–10) but on different grounds.

75

poetic art itself" (47a1), qua its own technicalities, καθ᾽ ἑαυτήν, "in and of itself" (60b21, 23); a work of art is to be judged by itself alone (αὐτό τε καθ᾽ αὑτὸ κρῖναι, 49a8) and as exemplary of its internal functioning (τὸ αὑτῆς, 62a11); solutions (λύσεις) are to occur "from [within] the plot itself" (ἐξ αὐτοῦ τοῦ μύθου) and not through contrivances imported from outside the logic of the action (54a37, cf. 53b2), etc. The "in and of itself" of a text (that which one "judges" in a work) entails a specifically Aristotelian and essentialist view of what *defines* aesthetic intelligibility, and any espousal of Aristotelian critical logic is in a profound way committed to this view. Aristotle's "poetic essence" is very much on a par with his deliverances on essences and formal causes in other parts of his corpus (e.g., *De anima* 412a6–9; *Metaphysics* 1032b13–14), but it is intelligible even without these background assumptions and is perhaps best understood as a reaction against Plato's strictures on poetry's intrinsic worth. A work's aesthetic intelligibility just is, we might say, the formal concept of the identity of a given work, that is, of a work's identity with itself. If Aristotle, in this daring attempt at conceptual isolation, nowhere fully spells out what he means by "the in and of itself" of a work, he may be forgiven: The only statement that could exhaustively define this concept would in the end have to be identical with the work itself.[17]

It is this sense of formal self-identity which motivates the "tautology" of Aristarchus's maxim Ὅμηρον ἐξ Ὁμήρου, I believe, and which informs the criterion of what counts as "extrinsic" in the scholium version as well.[18] Porphyry's exact words, to the extent that they are expressive of Aristarchus at all, will not contradict this basic principle of coherence: "Thinking it right (ἀξιῶν) to *elucidate Homer from Homer* (Ὅμηρον ἐξ Ὁμήρου σαφηνίζειν), I have indicated how *Homer interprets himself* (αὐτὸν ἐξηγούμενον ἑαυτόν), sometimes in adjacent passages, sometimes in remoter passages." The maxim, even qualified as it is by Porphyry, needn't be restricted to a mere epexegetical "glossing" function or

[17] Thomas G. Rosenmeyer, "Design and Execution in Aristotle," 236, labels this isolation of an aesthetic aspect "τέχνηᵖ" (i.e., the τέχνη of the poet). Implied is literally a χωρισμός, or "separation" in theory. The μῦθος is the "soul" of tragedy; more rigorously, it is the formal aspect or "cause" of tragedy. See James I. Porter, "Content and Form in Philodemus: The History of an Evasion," forthcoming in a collection of essays on Philodemus edited by Dirk Obbink.

[18] T. G. Rosenmeyer, *DEINA TA POLLA*, 42, calls this feature of ancient criticism "traditional immanentism" ("the idea that a literary text carries its secret and its power exclusively *within itself*") and accordingly renders the maxim as being aimed at "recovering Homer from *within* Homer" (my emphases).

to simple questions of usage, although this is how its meaning is too often narrowed down, as for instance by Pfeiffer: "Aristarchus's main object was to discover the Homeric usage."[19] This is surely not how the notion of self-clarification was understood in the parallels adduced above,[20] nor do parallels from Aristarchus himself, to be discussed presently, reveal anything less complex than the fullest reach of Aristarchus's interpretive activities, which extended to the largest patterns of coherence that he felt he could discover in the Homeric poems. The act of interpretive "clarification" ($\sigma\alpha\varphi\eta\nu\iota\zeta\epsilon\iota\nu$), as we saw, must be transparent, virtually redundant. It is tautologous only in the sense that in theory interpretation "adds" nothing to the text; it is just the laying bare of the formal, unifying properties in a work in the way that the work lays them bare (or instances them) itself. Those properties may have less easily dissolved into pure abstraction for Aristarchus than they did for Aristotle, but they were no less discernible and no less worthy of defense.

For a comparison, we may look again to Aristotle, who was possibly the first to sponsor the idea of the internal "clarification" ($\tau\grave{o}\ \delta\eta\lambda\tilde{\omega}\sigma\alpha\iota$) of structured wholes, be they speeches or dramas (cf. *Rhetoric* 1415a22–24, on proems).[21] $\Lambda\acute{v}\sigma\iota\varsigma$, as in "[internal] solutions to the plot" above (*Poetics* 54a37), is a case in point. There $\lambda\acute{v}\sigma\iota\varsigma$, remarkably, has a double function: It is being used both in the technical sense, with reference to the end (dénouement) of the *Medea* (54b1), and in the more general sense of "solution" to a "problem" ($\pi\rho\acute{o}\beta\lambda\eta\mu\alpha$, an interpretive stumbling block), with reference to the *Peira* of *Iliad* 2 (Agamemnon's "testing" of his armies' resolve through his proposal to sail home, 54b2). In his *Problemata*, Aristotle solved the problem of Athena's divine intervention by viewing it as an internal $\lambda\acute{v}\sigma\iota\varsigma$: It is "probable," "poetic" ($\pi\omega\eta\tau\iota\kappa\acute{o}\nu$), and it occurs immanently, "as a result of what lies within the plot itself" ($\grave{\epsilon}\xi\ \alpha\grave{v}\tau o\tilde{v}\ \tau o\tilde{v}\ \mu\acute{v}\theta o\nu$) and not as a contrivance *ex machina*, which would be alien to the plot's inner logic (fr. 142 Rose).[22] Aristarchus, emphatically in agreement, defended the same episode as genuinely "Homeric"

[19] R. Pfeiffer, *History of Classical Scholarship From the Beginnings*, 227.

[20] Pp. 73–74, above.

[21] This is well brought out in Alexander of Aphrodisias, CAG 21.2, 231, 17 (cited in R. Meijering, *Literary and Rhetorical Theories*, 108). Cf. Anaximenes of Lampsacus (*Ars Rhet.* 29, 1 Fuhrmann, cited in R. Meijering, *Literary and Rhetorical Theories*, 107).

[22] Cf. D. W. Lucas on *Poetics* 54b1 and 2. Aristotle fr. 142 Rose = Porphyry on *Il.* 273 (mistakenly given by D. W. Lucas, *Aristotle, Poetics*, 163, as Schol. B 144). The fragment from the *Problemata* duplicates exactly the wording of the *Poetics*. Cf. Schol. bT B 144d ("ex machina"), Schol. A bT B 73a, Schol. bT Υ 25, and esp. Θ 429.

(Ὁμηρικῶς ἔχοντα), which is to say, as in keeping with Homer's narrative protocols (Schol. A B 156–69, against Zenodotus's doubts). Porphyry, revealingly, will call the *Peira*-action tragic (τραγικόν).[23] All of this suggests that there is a fundamental link between natural "resolution" within a unified action and the interpretive "solution" of a coherent aesthetic object, and that in Aristotelian-based criticism the line between these two kinds of λύσεις, not to say between tragedy and epic, is more easily crossed than even standard readings of Aristotle's *Poetics* suggest.[24]

Let us consider another instance of this methodological principle of aesthetic coherence (defining what is certifiably "Homeric" in Homer), this time as applied to apparent contradictions in Homer, which could be addressed as an interpretive issue (πρόβλημα). In *Iliad* 6.264 Hector refuses wine as debilitating before battle, thus contradicting his mother who has just (6.261) praised its strength-giving qualities. The A-scholium observes, "This line is marked with a διπλῆ because of an apparent contradiction (πρὸς τὸ δοκοῦν μάχεσθαι). . . . But the speakers [in each case] are different [viz., Hector and Hecuba], and each statement is addressed to a different circumstance" (Schol. A Z 265). Porphyry echoes the scholium but changes the perspective by addressing the problem in terms of the poet's relation to himself (the poet's *self*-contradictions): "The problem is posed: How is it that the poet sometimes *gainsays himself*?" (πῶς ποτε ἐναντία ἑαυτῷ ὁ ποιητὴς λέγει, *Quaest. Hom. Il.* 99, 22 Schrader, on *Il.* 6.265).[25] One solution, which Aristarchus knew how to exploit, was sought in the disparity of "narrative voices." Although characters could be allowed degrees of inconsistency (with themselves or with the narrator), Porphyry writes, in paraphrase of both Aristarchus and Aristotle,[26] "such things as Homer said himself (αὐτός ἀφ᾽ ἑαυ-

---

[23] Porphyry *Quaest. Hom. Il.* 25, 14 Schrader. The exegetical scholium at *Il.* 2.156 labels the moment a περιπέτεια.

[24] Significantly, *problemata* were not a genre restricted to Homeric criticism. Hephaestion, according to the *Suda*, wrote two volumes of dramatic λύσεις, comic and tragic (κωμικῶν ἀπορημάτων λύσεις and τραγικαὶ λύσεις). Here one could expect to see a convergence between the two kinds of λύσις (dramatic and epic). There was more than synonymy at stake.

[25] See generally, Mitchell Carroll, *Aristotle's Poetics, c. xxv*, 38; A. Römer, *Die Homerexegese Aristarchs*, 253–56; Hans Dachs, "Die Λύσις ἐκ τοῦ προσώπου," 68.

[26] See H. Schrader (in Porphyry *Quaest. Hom. Od.* [Schrader] 191), where the Porphyrean solution to *Il.* 6.265 is taken to be of Peripatetic derivation. It is of course in line with Aristarchus's assumptions. Compare Aristotle quoted in Porphyry on *Il.* 2.649 (= fr. 146 Rose) with Aristarchus (Schol. A B 649). Cf. A. Römer, *Die Homerexegese Aristarchs*, 223; H. Erbse, *Beiträge zur Überlieferung der Ilias-Scholien*, 62–77.

τοῦ; lit. *himself from himself*) *ex propria persona* (ἐξ ἰδίου προσώπου) must be consistent (ἀκόλουθα) and not in mutual contradiction" (*Quaest. Hom. in Il.* 100, 5–7 Schrader). This is what is referred to as a λύσις ἐκ τοῦ ποιητοῦ, a solution derived "from the poet" (Porphyry, on *Il.* 4.2; cf. Eustathius 1877, 23). What it signifies, however, is not "first-person" utterances (which Aristotle limits, at *Poetics* 60a7, to an optimal bare minimum) but "narratorial" control over unity and consistency.[27] With so firm a postulate of narrative coherence, elucidation of Homer from Homer is practically a foregone conclusion.[28]

There is, however, a further twist. In Greek, as in English, "the poet" stands ambivalently for his "poems"; and in scholiastic parlance, the poet stands for the narrative plane within those poems.[29] "Homer" can be expanded in both ways (as shown by the two perspectives taken by Porphyry and the A scholium on *Il.* 6.265 above), which points to tacit aesthetic underpinnings and gives content to the maxim *Homerum ex Homero*. Looking back, we can say that the two versions of the maxim, as given by Porphyry and the D-scholium, form a neat contrast and are in fact logically wedded: Aristarchus's conception of what falls *outside* Homer's words and thoughts simultaneously defines for him what falls legitimately *under* τὸ μυθικόν (poetic fiction); and this is deducible from Homer and the properties of his *mythos*, for which "Homer" is arguably no less than a metonymy. It doesn't really matter that for Aristarchus the "unity" of Homer was predicated in some way upon *both* epics (cf. Schol. A Δ 354a). The notion of unified coherence here could never hope to match the rigor of the tragic formula, except by approximation; but then this was what Aristotle had held too (*Poetics* 62b3–11; cf. 59b3). However unity is construed, together the criteria of the intrinsic and the extrinsic determine the scope of the critic's domain. Most importantly, they vali-

---

[27] Cf. Eustathius 1947, 16 (on *Od.* 23.243): ἐξ ἰδίου προσώπου (*in propria persona*) = καθ' αὑτόν φησι, "speaks according to himself," that is, according to the logic governing his narrative.

[28] Cf. Porphyry *Quaest. Hom. Il.* 281, 2 Schrader: "Because Homer himself interprets himself in the majority of cases (ὡς αὐτὸς μὲν ἑαυτὸν τὰ πολλὰ Ὅμηρος ἐξηγεῖται)." This corresponds with Aristarchus's criterion of ἐπὶ τὸ πολύ and διὰ παντός (procedural uniformity), e.g., Schol. A Ξ 32a, Θ 562.

[29] Plutarch explicitly discusses the idiom ("buying Plato" and "acting Menander"), *De Is. et Os.* 379a. Cf. Schol. A K 299a: The organization of Homer's verses (his words) and that of the contents (the actions) are isomorphic: ὡς ἡ τῶν ἐπῶν ἔχει τάξις, οὕτω καὶ τὰ πράγματα—just as for Aristotle μῦθος is ideally the coincidence, along a consistent plot line, of language, event, and structure. The principle is commandeered by Heraclitus *Quaest. Hom.* 6.1–2.

date method in the name of an internal "elucidation" (δήλωσις, *Rhetoric* 1415a19, b5–6, *Poetics* 51a35; σαφηνίζειν, Aristarchus). In this way, method is rendered internal to its objects.[30]

I hope it is obvious that Aristarchus's language is far from being innocent of implicit assumptions. Thus, poetic "licence" is never totally "free" or permissive; it is tightly defined and closely circumscribed by poetic "rules" and theoretical constraints (not to mention moral strictures), however tacitly these are acknowledged. Second, as Aristotle shows, how one "reads" is dictated by what one reads (or thinks one is reading). Thus, Aristarchus's exegetical maxim simultaneously involves a preconception of what counts as a proper *object* of exegesis. Incidentally, the one feature that Aristarchus's aesthetics notably lacks is, precisely, a separate concept of the poet's "intentionality" (nor does Aristotle know any such category). The reason? Such a notion is too impoverished to account for the complex "poetic" intention of a work like the *Iliad*, which is embodied in its formal and structural integrity. After all, it was the integrity of Homer's text, not just Homer's "intention," that Aristarchus was seeking to preserve in the end. Panaetius's compliment only counts for so much.

II

Aristarchus's maxim could be honored in unexpected ways, and even in the breach (we might call this Aristarchus's interpretive licence,[31] but as we saw, license implies obedience). Moreover, *pace* Pfeiffer, σαφηνίζειν ("clarify" or "elucidate") *is* "used for the activity of the interpreter," which effectively removes one more obstacle to Aristarchus's authorship of the maxim. We shall be misled, however, if we assume that the principle was narrowly restricted to questions of "usage." Aristarchan practice suggests that it wasn't even restricted to Homer. By way of qualifying and enriching our view of Aristarchus's exegetical techniques, we may consider the following two examples.

At *Iliad* 1.349a, a scholium ascribed by Erbse to Nicanor, who generally

---

[30] With the D-scholium expansion of the maxim, compare the injunction, at *Rhetoric* 1354a14–28, not to busy oneself with what is extraneous to the rhetorical τέχνη (ἔξω τοῦ πράγματος . . . πραγματεύεσθαι).

[31] Ἐξουσία is actually used in this sense, in Philodemus *On Poems* V, col. XVII, 15 (Jensen).

represents Aristarchus's notes on punctuation,[32] states that a "short punctuating pause" is to be read into the text (διασταλτέον) at the word δακρύσας ("weeping") in the verse pair αὐτὰρ Ἀχιλλεὺς/δακρύσας ἑτάρων ἄφαρ ἕζετο νόσφι λιασθείς, "But Achilles weeping went and sat in sorrow apart from his companions" (Lattimore, tr.), with the explanation, "For this *clarifies* the situation better" (μᾶλλον γὰρ σαφηνίζει τὰ πράγματα).[33] The point, so delicate as to be almost imperceptible, is an example of Aristarchus's acutest attention to the surface of the Homeric text, which he scanned for its deeper logical, or just aesthetic, flows. Movements of the breath, also a function of reading Homer, were accomplices of meaning and tonality, and so too they could serve "interpretation" in the widest sense. In the present instance, the principle of σαφηνίζειν has been pushed almost to the point of insignificance. But it is firmly in place nonetheless. One wonders whether this isn't a case of detecting what Roland Barthes calls "the grain of the [written] voice": a reading of Homer's "écriture vocale,"[34] in a zone of significance revelatory not of "the theater of emotions" nor of any signifying code, but of something else: Homer's voice, its material texture. But even so, such delicacies of style could go hand in hand with the dictates of aesthetic teleology. Thus (the technical scholia to Dionysius Thrax can claim), the "emphatic" expiration of breath at the end of the colon Διὸς δ᾽ ἐτελείετο βουλή, "and the will of Zeus was accomplished" (*Il.* 1.5), makes the voice "hunger" after the words that follow (ζητητικὴν αὐτὴν κατασκευάζουσιν τῶν ἑξῆς);[35] ζητητικήν ("searching") here brings to mind, of course, the image of a prospective λύσις.[36] Traditional

[32] Though differences could intervene, as is stressed by David Blank in "Remarks on Nicanor, the Stoics, and the Ancient Theory of Punctuation."

[33] Schol. A A 349a; cf. Schol. A Λ 4. Clarity had been linked to intelligibility also by Aristotle: as a stylistic virtue (*Poetics* 58a18) and as the aim of punctuation (a potential source of λύσις; 61a23); cf. *Rhetoric* 1407b13; *Soph. Elench.* 166a35.

[34] Roland Barthes, *The Pleasure of the Text*, 66–67.

[35] *Schol. in Dion. Thrac.* 178, 9ff. These Byzantine scholia are an invaluable source for reconstructing earlier grammatical speculation (cf. H. Erbse, *Scholia Graeca*, 1, lxiii; D. Blank, "Remarks on Nicanor," passim). Contrast Heraclitus's quite different "thirst," 1.6–7.

[36] Λυτικοί is the name given to experts in λύσεις; A. Gudeman, "Λύσεις," e.g., 2513, 7–8; H. Erbse, *Beiträge zur Überlieferung*, 59–77; problems are commonly set with the phrase "The reason is sought (ζητεῖται)," as in Porphyry on *Il.* 6.265, above; cf. Schol. bT A 1a–b. Aristarchus had anticipations of his own; cf. Schol. A Λ 604b (with reference to *Il.* 1.5). His comment at Schol. A A 5–6 is by no means uninformed by Peripatetic tastes: It restricts Zeus's "plan" to an event *internal* to the *Iliad*, thus marking a clear ἀρχή for the plot's unfolding (in contradistinction to the epics of the Cycle).

grammar accorded reading aloud a primacy of place: In the words of Dionysius Thrax, Aristarchus's distinguished pupil, "Reading aloud, which is versed in modulations of the voice (ἐντριβὴς κατὰ προσῳδίαν), is the first of the six parts of γραμματική" (*Ars Grammatica* 1 Uhlig); it was the first rung on the technical ladder leading to the crowning achievement of the art, the discriminating evaluation of poems (κρίσις ποιημάτων; cf. *Schol. in Dion. Thrac.* 306, 1; 177, 3 Hilgard). "Reading," in this logical and physiological sense, was a matter of interpretation too.

A second example, which ought to lay to rest any doubts about "the rare word σαφηνίζειν" (Pfeiffer),[37] is given by the A scholium to *Iliad* 23.638–41. The context is furnished by Nestor's still puzzling remarks, at the funeral games, about his solitary defeat at the hands of the sons of Aktor: "It was only in the chariot-race that the sons of Aktor/ defeated me, crossing me in the crowd (πλήθει πρόσθε βαλόντες). . . . / Now these sons of Aktor were twins; one held the reins at his leisure, / . . . while the other lashed on the horses." The question here became, how many hands, and indeed how many bodies, did it take to fell the single, incomparable (23.632) Nestor, πλήθει πρόσθε βαλόντες, whatever this phrase meant.[38] The Actoriones, it seems, were "twins" (641), but they also appear to have been more, or rather less, than mere twins. Aristarchus's solution, the A scholium tells us, was to "understand 'twins' not in the way we are accustomed to think of the word, such as the Dioscuri were, but rather as *biformis* (διφυεῖς), that is, as having two bodies [in one], fused together (συμπεφυκότας ἀλλήλοις); and he invokes Hesiod (fr. 18 Merklebach-West) as a witness." No wonder Nestor lost the chariot race against such formidable opponents, because however we imagine them, whether they each had two bodies or they were a species of Siamese twins,[39] they had a far greater manpower than poor Nestor could single-handedly match.[40]

What is remarkable about this reading from our perspective is, first, the verb that is used by the scholiast to describe it: "In this way what is

[37] R. Pfeiffer, *History of Classical Scholarship From the Beginnings*, 227, n.3.

[38] Lattimore renders it "crossing me in the crowd"; van der Valk, "surpassing me in number" (*Researches on the Text and Scholia of the Iliad*, 2, 255); for Leaf, "this phrase defies interpretation."

[39] A. Römer, *Die Homerexegese Aristarchs*, 131–32, 157–58; M. van der Valk, *Researches*, 2, 253–54.

[40] A similar crux exercised the wits of Asclepiades of Myrlea, Athenaeus 11.488e, 491f. (συμφυής: Nestor's cup and its elaborate handles). Crates was his immediate inspiration; cf. Crates quoted in Eustathius 829, 10 on *Il.* 11.39, and below.

said about them (τὸ λεγόμενον) is *clarified* [by Aristarchus] most satis-fyingly (σαφηνίζεσθαι ἄριστα)." A second remarkable fact is that here Aristarchus is elucidating Homer's words, not through Homer but through Hesiod. Elsewhere, Aristarchus isn't averse to drawing confirm-ing parallels, whether mythological or philological, from Hesiod, and on occasion even from the tragedians.[41] In the case before us, it will not do to argue, as Aristarchus could have argued on his own assumptions, that because Homer *wrote*, and because Hesiod *read* Homer (Schol. A P 719; M 22a), Hesiod therefore gives us a legitimate "reading" of Homer where Homer's text is its own unique witness. You cannot escape a vicious her-meneutic circle merely by extending its perimeter, and it is doubtful that having enjoined his opponents not to look beyond Homer's words Aris-tarchus was guilty of so simple a fallacy on the present occasion. Com-mon sense would have instructed him otherwise. Nor is "usage" the an-swer.[42] The crux from the funeral games Aristarchus "solved," such as he did, through a mythological parallel.[43] And as Adolph Römer inadver-tently showed (*Die Homerexegese Aristarchs*), "Mythenforschung" (132), "Mythenexegese" (133), and "Wortforschung" (133) are inseparable ac-tivities, not reducible to the establishment of usage. Aristarchus is again following Aristotle's advice, namely that in retracing a poet's steps we should "resolve" the myths from their own materials when it is reason-able to do so (*Poetics* 53b22), and otherwise make allowances for invention (51b23). Seeing that here Homer and Hesiod are drawing from the same pool of materials,[44] it is fair to say that Aristarchus's maxim is at work on this showing, but in silhouette.[45]

Let us take stock momentarily. Aristarchus's reading of Homer flowed from his overt purpose, which was dictated by the exigencies of textual criticism: namely, to isolate what was specifically Homeric in Homer. That this not only included but presupposed a conception of what was

[41] A. Römer, *Die Homerexegese Aristarchs*, 132 (Hesiod); Schol. A B 649 (Sophocles; against the Chorizontes); A B 45a (Euripides); o 74 (Hesiod, as a contrast).

[42] R. Pfeiffer, *History of Classical Scholarship from the Beginnings*, 227; A. Römer, *Die Ho-merexegese Aristarchs*, 133.

[43] M. van der Valk accepts the scholium as Aristarchan and applauds it: "Aristarchus has this time offered a correct interpretation of the Homeric text" (*Researches*, 2, 255). Cf. H. Erbse ad loc.; Schol. T Ψ 641a[1].

[44] The assumption that the Homeric and Hesiodic traditions were "one" was widespread even among allegorists; cf. J. Tate, "On the History of Allegorism," 105.

[45] Eustathius 3, 18 ("clipping Homer's wings"); 40, 28; and 614, 4 (primacy of the con-tents of μῦθος, for Aristarchus) all play into this complex of μῦθος as representing the fic-tional and poetic "world" of Homer's plot, and its self-consistency.

specifically *poetic* about Homer's epics emerges from those relatively rare moments when his aesthetic views have been preserved, but especially from his repeated skirmishes with the allegorists. And here Aristarchus's principled position could not have been clearer or more firmly put than in the contrast, now made reductively explicit for him, between two kinds of intelligibility, κατὰ μὲν Ὅμηρον . . . κατὰ δὲ ἀλληγορίαν, "according to Homer, on the one hand, . . . and allegorically, on the other" (Schol. D A 18). The lines, thus drawn, are not, as one might expect, between literal and metaphorical meaning. Aristarchus recognized that if Olympus could be read, perversely, as an "allegory" for the heavens (οὐρανός), Homerically (καθ' Ὅμηρον), which is to say in a way consistent with the inner fictional frames, logic, and even metaphors of the Homeric μῦθος, Olympus just was the loftiest mountain in Macedonia (cf. Schol. A Π 364a); it was "the mountain that is named in this way," τὸ καλούμενον οὕτως ὄρος (Schol. ζ 42), certified by tradition, by poetic exigencies, or by both.[46] For Aristarchus, as for Aristotle, truth under any description is only contingently a part of fiction, never constitutively so.

On the allegorical view, by contrast, the question of truth is always threatening, always pressing, precisely because it is a constitutive factor of poetic language in the harness of philosophical meaning. Hence, "Olympus" contains within itself its own etymon, pointing, however clumsily and poetically, towards a truer level of meaning: It is "all-lighting" (ὀλολαμπής), like the sky itself. As a protection, the allegorists could ascribe this knowledge to Homer, after the fashion of a Heraclitus (author of the *Homeric Problems*) or a Cornutus; or else (as perhaps here) they could leave the question of Homer's knowledge open or override him altogether, with the confidence that truth guarantees itself, as the nature of language shows; Homer is merely its instrument. On either view, it is a sheer contingent fact that any truths found in Homer are expressed in the form of epic poems: Truths and poetic textures contribute nothing to each other; they are not even in communication at all. Whether or not the Stoics can be held responsible for the allegorical (strictly, etymological) reading of Olympus as "all-lighting," they nonetheless would frequently be taken to task for embracing this sort of contingency in so patent a fashion.[47] They could no doubt throw up a defense

[46] Cf. Schol. A T 114; Schol. υ 103; Schol. A H 422; Karl Lehrs, *De Aristarchi studiis homericis*, "De aëre, aethere, Olympo," 164–75; Martin Schmidt, *Die Erklärungen zum Weltbild Homers und zur Kultur der Heroenzeit in den bT-Scholien zur Ilias*, 81–87.

[47] M. Schmidt, *Erklärungen*, 86, feels that Chrysippus is the likely author of the "allego-

against having "accomodated" Homer to their philosophy; but that defense would not be on literary or aesthetic grounds. This is where a contrast sets in, not between Crates and Aristarchus, but first between Crates and the Stoics.

III

Crates of Mallos, Aristarchus's contemporary and rival who practiced in Pergamum and may have supervised its earliest library collection,[48] is one of those puzzling figures who seem to have been dreamt up by antiquity just to remind us of how little of the past we truly fathom. He is universally held to have been an exponent of the Stoic theory and method of Homeric exegesis, but this is a mere convenience.[49] The *Suda* calls him a "Stoic philosopher" (the attribution is unique),[50] but then acknowledges that the label is insufficiently large to encompass Crates' achievements: He was also nicknamed Ὁμηρικός (a Homerist par excellence) and a κριτικός ("critic"), because of the attentions he paid to grammatical and poetic theory. Apart from the fact that Crates argued vigorously against grammatical analogy, perhaps in the way that Chrysippus had,[51] the only other hard evidence in favor of Crates' Stoicism has been, traditionally, the very fact of his allegorical interpretation itself. But as the *Suda* and other of our sources reveal, there was a kind of determination with which

rization"; but nothing here or in its parallels points exclusively to Chrysippus or any other Stoic (cf., e.g., ibid., n. 60 [Parmenides and Philolaus]). The date and source of this allegorization must remain uncertain. The two positions on etymology sketched here correspond in principle to what A. A. Long calls "strong" and "weak" allegory, respectively (above, 43).

[48] W. Kroll, "Krates," 1636, 28 allows this to be a probability only. The evidence is indeed thin.

[49] R. Pfeiffer's arguments, *History of Classical Scholarship From the Beginnings*, 238 and 241 ("as a Stoic cosmologist"), are typical and without support.

[50] The *Suda* is followed by R. Pfeiffer, *History of Classical Scholarship From the Beginnings*, 235. Phillip De Lacey, "Stoic Views of Poetry," 252, hedges: Crates is "not central" in the Stoic school but "closely allied to it." Sliding to conclusions from here ("therefore"), De Lacey saddles the mainstream Stoics with a full-blown theory of poetics. The clues to Crates' Stoicism are less than just tenuous, as Schrader's honest statement of the evidence shows (in Porphyry *Quaest. Hom. Il.* [Schrader] 393).

[51] Crates' role in the anomaly/analogy debate is not much clearer than the debate itself. Cf. Hans Joachim Mette, *Parateresis*; H. Erbse, "Zur normativen Grammatik der Alexandriner"; Wolfram Ax, "Aristarch und die 'Grammatik' "; and Michael Frede, "Principles of Stoic Grammar" and "The Origins of Traditional Grammar."

Crates pursued these literary interests and which fell beyond the bounds of Stoicism (and in fact, Stoic interest in literary criticism for its own sake is nowhere attested).[52]

By contrast, elsewhere Crates is known without exception as "the scholar" (ὁ γραμματικός) or "the critic" (ὁ κριτικός).[53] The same contrast is found in a remark by Geminus, when he names "Cleanthes, the Stoic philosopher" and then "Crates, the γραμματικός" (Elem. astron. 16. 21 = Crates fr. 34a Mette). The notice, which probably stems from Posidonius,[54] the influential Stoic philosopher from the last century B.C., merits inspection. Crates is said to be following certain of the ancients (τινὲς τῶν ἀρχαίων), one of whom happens to be Cleanthes, in the view that Ocean covers the uninhabited torrid zone between the tropics, a view that later geography learned to reject (Elem. Astron. 16.25, 16.31). Crates went further than this, however. Odysseus's wanderings could be mapped, with the aid of a visual demonstration of the earth's spherical surface-structure and with a mathematical postulate that entailed a rigid symmetry, whatever else the postulate may have been used for. Here it is certain μαθηματικοί, probably Eudoxan mathematicians, that Crates claims to be following. The notice concludes by stating that Crates' results were "unparalleled" by either the mathematical or the physical theories and that his findings are recorded by none of the ancient mathematicians, as Crates claims. Crates clearly felt himself to be an innovator,[55]

---

[52] I am wholeheartedly in agreement with A. A. Long in his critique of the assumption, which has gone unquestioned for too long, that the Stoics were interested in allegory as a form of literary interpretation. The Stoics, I believe, had no active literary interests and only indirectly and accidentally contributed to developments in literary criticism; see J. I. Porter, "Philodemus on Material Difference," esp. 150, n. 8 (with bibliography), and n. 50 above. On allegory, see further Peter Steinmetz, "Allegorische Deutung und allegorische Dichtung in der alten Stoa," and Glenn W. Most, "Cornutus and Stoic Allegoresis."

[53] γραμματικός (often in rivalry with Aristarchus): e.g., Strabo 14.5.16; Schol. λ 14; Tzetzes 12.346; κριτικός: e.g., Schol. μ 62; Athenaeus 11.490e; cf. Aelian Hist. An. 10.42. In sorting out the ten notable men named Crates known to him, Diogenes Laertius (4.23) designates our man (no. 8) as Μαλλώτης γραμματικός. Two philosophers with school affiliations feature in the same list.

[54] W. Kroll, "Krates," 1638; cf. I. G. Kidd, Posidonius II: The Commentary, 458–60.

[55] As elsewhere. Cf. the charge, laid by Asclepiades (Athenaeus 11.490e = Crates fr. 26a Mette), that "Crates the κριτικός" claimed as his own (σφετερισάμενος . . . ὡς ἴδιον) a reading of Homer by the Hellenistic poetess Moero of Byzantium (the etymologizing of the Pleiades as Πέλειαι, doves bringing nourishment to the heavens). Crates' claims to original insight and his appropriations in the name of cosmic grandeur have nothing to do with the Stoic practice of "accommodation" (accommodare, Cicero De Nat. Deor. 1.41; συνοικ-

not just by virtue of the eclecticism of his sources[56] but in the idiosyncratic picture that resulted. Just to prove the power of his point, he emended a verse from the *Odyssey* (1.24), to ensure that the Aethiopians, living on the furthest extremes of the inhabited world (οἰκουμένη), would be "divided in twain" in the sense that they lived north and south of the equatorial tropics, as mirror images of each other (Strabo 1.2.24). The result is, of course, a violent distortion of fact and of Homer, as Posidonius objected, long after Aristarchus had. It enslaves geography to a mathematical hypothesis; it entailed the introduction of "a second οἰκουμένη"; it ran counter to Homer's own assumptions of a flat earth (a fact Aristarchus was the first to point out); and it required a drastic revision of Homer's text (Posidonius apparently deemed his own emendation of the line to be less drastic; Strabo 2.3.7). In revenge, Strabo would side with the Stoic Posidonius and "our Zeno," leaving Crates to wander aimlessly with Odysseus in the Outer Ocean (1.2.34–35).

Crates' eclecticism is not only breathtaking in its range; it is highly selective. Nowhere do we hear of Crates' having adopted the characteristically Stoic teachings that accompanied Cleanthes' physical view about the tropics—for instance, the vitalism and cosmobiology that this view, I suspect, was intended to motivate—or the notion that the sun is the hegemonic principle of the cosmos, or the concept of divine πνεῦμα (cf. SVF 1.504, 499; 2.605). Crates' silence on these and other philosophical doctrines so central to the Stoa is of the first importance; if Crates was not principally documenting Stoic teaching, we are inevitably led to wonder just what he was doing. The answer given by Geminus is not wholly satisfying, but it is at least a beginning: "Fabulously distorting (παραδοξολογῶν) what Homer said in his archaic and peculiar fashion, Crates reads (μετάγει) what Homer said into *sphairopoiia*, which is modelled after truth" (*Elem. astron.* 16.27). The juxtaposition, "what Homer said" (τὰ ὑφ᾽ Ὁμήρου εἰρημένα)/ "*sphairopoiia* and its truth" (τὴν κατ᾽ ἀλήθειαν σφαιροποιίαν) is Aristarchan, but the term σφαιροποιία here is uniquely Cratetean; it is as distinctive a label as the name he

---

ειοῦν, Philodemus, SVF 2.1078 = *De pietate* col. vi, 24 (ed. in Albert Henrichs, "Die Kritik der Stoischen Theologie in PHerc. 1428," 17).

[56] These were various, and overlaps with Stoics are fortuitous, a mere convenience (although this is not the *communis opinio*). For useful summaries of Crates' cosmology, see Alois Schlachter, *Der Globus, seine Entstehung und Verwendung in der Antike*, 54; H. J. Mette's collection of fragments and testimony on Crates, *Sphairopoiia* ("Einleitung"); F. Gisinger, "Oikumene," 2143; W. Kroll, "Krates," 1637; cf. Schol. Gen. Φ 195, Crates fr. 32a Mette; Plutarch, *De fac. in orbe lun.* 938d.

adopted to announce his superiority to the microphilology of the Alexandrian grammarians: κριτικός. We will return to the meaning of this label below. The meaning of σφαιροποιία immediately raises questions.

The postulation of a spherical earth and universe was nothing new in itself; this had been the premise of cosmological thinking even prior to Plato.[57] In the wake of Archimedes' armillary sphere and his monograph on the same,[58] σφαιροποιία can refer to the "construction" of a terrestial globe that Crates is generally credited with having designed, presumably as a visual analogue to his Homeric exegeses[59] (although the actual evidence is not wholly conclusive, and the details are suspiciously lacking). But σφαιροποιία can also have a more abstract meaning, by which it denotes the "spherical structure" of the cosmos or earth as visualized in the imagination, not of any particular model in however many dimensions.[60] Whether or not Crates can be held accountable for a *sphairopoiia* in the first sense, he clearly embraced the second dimension of the term in his so-called σφαιρικὸς λόγος, his "theory of the sphere" (Geminus *Elem. Astron.* 6.12), and this will have direct consequences for his exegesis of Homer (cf. Heraclitus *Quaest. Hom.* 43). In fact, the theory and the exegesis have inseparable fates, for there is no evidence that Crates—the

[57] There are hints of a spherical earth in Parmenides (fr. A44 D-K). The Pythagoreans launched a spherical cosmology (a centrifocal universe), Aetius *Placita* 2.7.7. See H. J. Mette, *Sphairopoiia* (esp. x, n. 3), and David Furley, *The Greek Cosmologists*, vol. 1, 54–57, 193–200, and passim.

[58] Pappus, *Synagoge* 8.3, 1026, 9 Hultsch; Proclus, *In Euc.* 41, 10 Friedlein (σφαιροποιία is in imitation, κατὰ μίμησιν, of the celestial orbits); cf. Cicero *Rep.* 22.1 (Archimedes), Diogenes Laertius 2.2 (Anaximander). There is the offbeat notice on Gorgias (fr. A17 D-K). On planetaria and σφαιροποιία generally, see A. Schlachter, *Der Globus*, 46–54. See further O. Brendel, *Symbolism of the Sphere*.

[59] See W. Kroll, "Krates," 1636; Hugo Berger, *Geschichte der wissenschaftlichen Erdkunde der Griechen*, 454–58; H. J. Mette, *Sphairopoiia*, 60; Richard Uhden, "Die Weltkarte des Martianus Capella," 106–13; and Philip R. Hardie, *Virgil's Aeneid: Cosmos and Imperium*, 28. Partly because Crates was given to visual analogues of his theory, it has become fashionable to claim him as "author" of the so-called "Great Altar of Zeus" friezes at Pergamum, but there is not a shred of evidence for this (nor does the iconography reflect Stoic philosophy; see Andrew F. Stewart, "Narration and Illusion in the Hellenistic Baroque," forthcoming). Neither is Crates' political ideology deducible from anything that has survived of him.

[60] Geminus 16.19, 16.27; A. Schlachter, *Der Globus*, 49 with n. 1; H. J. Mette, *Sphairopoiia*, ix; P. R. Hardie, "*Imago Mundi*," 14 with n. 20 for further references. Cf. the terms for "spherical layout," "structure," or "assignment" found in *Schol. in Arat.*, σφαιροθεσία (150, 13 Martin), σφαιροειδεῖς θέσεις (150, 9), σφαιροθετεῖν (98, 8; not in LSJ; Crates is named in the next line). At another degree of abstraction, H. J. Mette, *Sphairopoiia*, viii almost suggests "Kugellehre."

obsessive Homerist (ὁ Ὁμηρικός)—pursued the one without simultaneously pursuing the other. Consequently, one of the questions we shall
have to face is whether Crates' exegesis of Homer existed mainly for the
sake of illustrating his theory of the sphere (σφαιρικὸς λόγος) or whether
the theory existed mainly for the sake of illustrating Homer's poetry. If
the latter turns out to have been the case, then we may wonder whether
we shouldn't begin to regard Crates' σφαιρικὸς λόγος as a theory of
reading.

Philodemus, writing towards the middle of the first century B.C.,
brings us closer to the problem and reinforces Crates' heterodoxy. In a
fragmentary column from the treatise *On Poems*, Philodemus levels criticism at an anonymous group. "These," he writes, "frequently are agreed
that the σημαίνοντα, the signifying words [or the σημαινόμενα, their
meanings; the text is uncertain], start right from the first word of the
poem, 'Wrath' (Μῆνιν), but they want the poet to mean other things
(παριστάνειν ἄλλα), just as Crates imputes to him τὰ περὶ τῆς
σφαιροποιίας," that is, a σφαιρικὸς λόγος.[61] From the context, which
can be only roughly recovered, Philodemus's overriding concern is with
schools of critics who variously sought to disjoin the contents of poems
from their signifying material, by demoting the discursive elements of
poetry (plot, clarity, etc.) to a secondary status. Here, Crates has virtually
been thrown into the camp of the "deranged" fifth-century allegorist,
Metrodorus of Lampsacus (the grouping is significant, and an index of
filiations). As with the other critics (who include an earlier generation of
Hellenistic κριτικοί), the disjunction that Crates and company effected
through exegesis precipitates a crisis of meaning, the end of signification
as we know it. Philodemus's treatment of the problem is correspondingly
laden with anxiety. For here, with Homer's *Iliad*, the question is no
longer where signification ends but *where does it begin*. From the very first
word, Crates and others cheerfully concede. But as soon as this conces-
sion is made, the grip on meaning is effectively lost, forever, and we tum-
ble headlong into the depths of hidden, allosemic meaning (ὑπόνοια).

Philodemus goes on to talk about plots, proems, ὑποθέσεις (gists),

---

[61] Philodemus, *On Poems*, lib. incert. = *PHerc.* 1676 fr. ii (Francesco Sbordone, *Philodemi
de poematis*, 223). The papyrus yields a slightly different text, but the sense arguably follows
the lines of the printed versions. There is a complication: Crates' apparent endorsement, in
his *"Diorthotica,"* of the so-called Apellicon proem to the *Iliad* (Schol. D A 1a = Erbse test.),
which Philodemus may have ignored; or perhaps Crates took the poem proper to start at
the first mention of its narrative theme, "wrath."

λύσεις (resolutions), and πλοκή (complication)[62]—in other words, the discursive contents of poems. The evidence for Crates' views of plot, which would take us beyond the limits of this paper, is sparse and at first glance conflicting. At the very least, Crates' position was that Homeric allegory is coextensive with the Homeric text; in other respects, allegory for Crates all but effaces the plot. In this he could not have been farther away from the Alexandrian mainstream of criticism.[63] Aristarchus was always keenly aware of narrative tensions (foreshadowing, climax, temporal relation). To the essential linearity of the Homeric *mythos* (e.g., Schol. D A 5–6 test.), Aristarchus, in classically Aristotelian fashion, opposed the episodic structure of the non-Homeric Cycle. This "geometry" carries over into other areas as well: The label most frequently used by Aristarchus to stigmatize deficient lines in Homer on any grounds at all, including Homer's own stylistic deficiencies, is derived from this initial premise, so thoroughgoing is its field of application: κυκλικῶς or κυκλικώτερον ("cyclic," "vulgar").

It is hard to imagine how Crates, by contrast, could have sought a total reading of Homer through his σφαιρικὸς λόγος in the way that, perhaps, Metrodorus had. No doubt, Crates had to leave large stretches of Homer uncommented on, and in a pinch he could always invoke the excuse that Homer, after all, was not an Aratus.[64] He may even on occasion have gone in for plot analysis of the conventional kind. But allegory and narrative are by no means exclusive, any more than allegorism and literalism are. For someone like Crates, who increasingly appears to frustrate these categories, each "level" of his reading (the narrative and beyond) presupposes the other; and there can be little doubt that Crates did intend his *sphairopoiia* to yield, at least in principle, a total interpretation of Homer.[65]

---

[62] E.g., *PHerc.* 1676, fr. 4 (ὑποθέσεις; F. Sbordone, *Philodemi de poematis*, 227) and fr. 5 (229: Achilles' "wrath," Odysseus's "πολυτροπία"). The context (and the joins proposed by Sbordone) deserve much more attention than they have received.

[63] Cf. W. Bachmann, *Die ästhetischen Anschauungen Aristarchs*, 1, 17 and 37; George E. Duckworth, "ΠΡΟΑΝΑΦΩΝΗΣΙΣ in the Scholia to Homer" and *Foreshadowing and Suspense in the Epics of Homer, Apollonius and Vergil*; James V. Morrison, *Homeric Misdirections: False Predictions in the Iliad*.

[64] The ascription of this sentiment to Crates (H. J. Mette, *Sphairopoiia*, 48; M. Schmidt, *Erklärungen*, 150, with n. 65) is an inference from a medley of sources that, however, give quite different justifications for it.

[65] This, without the apologetics of a Heraclitus, whose acceptance of the premise that "everything in Homer is blasphemous if nothing is allegory" (*Quaest. Hom.* 1.1) bound him rhetorically to its converse (everything is allegory if nothing is blasphemous). Cf. Heraclitus

Nor is this contradicted by the bulk of the evidence, which suggests that it was his *physica ratio* that he most fondly elaborated and for which he was least fondly remembered. In Aristarchus's eyes, at any rate, the spherical hypothesis must have seemed like a static imposition, viciously circular, if not vulgar (κυκλικώτερον). It lacked even the forward motion of a cosmogony. And indeed, as we shall see, Crates' vision of Homer is primarily a spatial as opposed to a temporal one. It was no less literary a conception for that.

IV

Crates' most renowned allegorical readings were of the shields of Agamemnon and Achilles, two ecphrastic moments when the narrative stops unfolding and is flooded with spatial coordinates. These arresting images could not help but remind Crates that Homer was indeed attuned to the spherical structure, the σφαιροποιία, of the earth and the cosmos. In fact the latter scene gave new meaning to the term: Here, through the eyes of the reader, one could see the cosmos *in* its very construction, at the hands of Hephaestus (this is, after all, the Ὁπλοποιία, or "the making of [Achilles'] weapons"); hence Eustathius's equivalent, which undoubtedly stems from Crates: κοσμοποιία[66] ("the making of the cosmos"). We should bear in mind, however, that "construction" here is not quite cosmogonic for Crates; rather, it is an intensified glimpse into "structure" and σφαιροποιία:

> There were five folds composing the shield itself, and upon it
> he elaborated many things (δαίδαλα πολλά) in his skill and
>   craftsmanship.
> He made the earth upon it, and the sky, and the sea's water,

---

Quaest. Hom. 60.1 ("through the whole of the *Iliad*") and 75.12. Porphyry's holism is another story; see R. Lamberton's contribution to the present volume.

[66] Eustathius 1167, 39, on *Il.* 18.607. Where Eustathius has κοσμοποιία, Strabo 1.1.7 has ὁπλοποιία. Cf. Heraclitus *Quaest. Hom.* 43.1, which contains both ideas. The parallel of the two "makings" clearly goes back to Crates (cf. *Schol. in Arat.* 26; R. Pfeiffer, *History of Classical Scholarship From the Beginnings*, 240; Eustathius 1154, 41 and 62 etc.; and on *Od.* 12.62 [ἀσπιδοποιία]; Athenaeus 11.489e–492d). This may reflect the fact that Crates had to defend the authenticity of the Shield scene against Zenodotus's athetization, not of the ὁπλοποιία per se, but (possibly) of the ecphrastic Shield (cf. K. Nickau, *Untersuchungen*, 236–40). The parallel subsequently found its way into the scholia and later tradition ([Plutarch] *De vit. Hom.* 176, not in Mette).

and the tireless sun, and the moon waxing into her fullness,
and on it all the constellations that festoon the heavens (ἐν δὲ τὰ
τείρεα πάντα, τά τ᾽οὐρανὸς ἐστεφάνωται),
the Pleiades and the Hyades and the strength of Orion
and the Bear, whom men give also the name of the Wagon,
who turns about in his fixed place (στρέφεται) and looks at Orion
and she alone is never plunged in the wash of the Ocean
(*Iliad* 18.481–89, Lattimore, tr.).

Crates famously called this scene a μίμημα τοῦ κόσμου (an *imago mundi*);
and he gave it a detailed analysis, in terms of zodiacal, climatic, and other
heavenly identifications, the common coin of Hellenistic cosmology, and
of all cosmology since Eudoxus (the hallmark of Eudoxan cosmology
being its rigorous geometrical schematization and its Chinese-box arrangement of concentric spheres).[67] The ancient lore that informs the details of Crates' reading would carry us far beyond the topic at hand; in
what follows, the details will matter less than the modalities of his readings and the ensuing debates with the Alexandrian camp. At any rate, in
Iliad 18 Crates is no longer performing allegorical exegesis. It is Homer
who is describing the cosmos; Crates is merely the faithful and painstak-
ingly literal transcriber of a self-evident scene (cf. Heraclitus *Quaest.
Hom.* 26.11).

Aristarchus would of course deny all of this: not that Homer had produced a μίμημα of the cosmos, but that Homer's cosmos was spherical
in shape (cf. Schol. Σ 607–08). His response is instructive: Wherever possible, he would attempt to minimize the textual supports for the competing view, which meant, significantly enough, the thematizations of circularity, when these lent themselves to a proof of *sphairopoiia*. At 18.485,
if the reports of the scholia are to be trusted, Aristarchus forcibly altered
the παράδοσις (the "tradition" or "received text") of the manuscripts, so
as to block the possibility that heaven "has the astral bodies set round it
as a crown" (τά τ᾽οὐρανὸς ἐστεφάνωται, mss.), framing them with
its sphere. Our evidence that Aristarchus dug in his heels on this, though
the notice is anything but helpful, comes from the A-scholium ad loc.; its
logic can be supplemented from the context: "Zenodotus reads, '[the
stars stand] *fixed in the heavens* (οὐρανὸν ἐστήρικται)'; Aristarchus,

[67] Eudoxus is named by Heraclitus (49.1), implicitly as one of Crates' sources of inspiration. Cf. H. J. Mette, *Sphairopoiia*, xiii and 34 for details, and F. Gisinger, "Oikumene,"
2143. Further, G. E. R. Lloyd, *Magic, Reason and Experience: Studies in the Origins and Development of Greek Science*, 119, 173–79, 181–82.

'[the stars] *garland the heavens* (οὐρανὸν ἐστεφάνωκε; cf. Lattimore's "festoons"),' " perhaps horizontally overhead, but not as a "crown" shaped by the vault of heaven and circling above and below the horizon, which was forbidden on the flat-earth view. That this inference is just what he could have feared is clear from an exegetical scholium to verse 488, which implicitly rejects Aristarchus's emendation and draws the natural connection between ἐστεφάνωται, στρέφεται ("turns," 18.488), and κυκλοτερής ("circular"): "That heaven (Οὐρανός) is *shaped as a circle* (κυκλοτερής) is shown by the verbs *turns about* and *is crowned*."[68] Crates' hand can be felt here (as in the next line, which he emended to his own liking; Strabo 1.1.6). Aristarchus's objections would moreover be in vain. Heraclitus, in a chapter of his *Homeric Problems*, would repeat Crates' arguments all over again, including his interpretation of the "circular crown" (στέφανος κυκλοτερής) of the παράδοσις: "For just as a *crown* is a *circular* adornment (κόσμος) for the head, so too it is apt that the celestial bodies girdling the heavenly vault, being dispersed *in the shape of a sphere* (κατὰ σφαιροειδοῦς σχήματος), be named the '*crown of heaven*' " (48.8).[69] Thus, Heraclitus reasons, with *Iliad* 18.485 Homer has given us a demonstration of the spherical worldview (48.7).

Circular motifs could be construed as corroborating evidence that Homer had indeed embraced a σφαιρικὸς λόγος. No other explanation can account for Crates' fixation on the shield of Agamemnon. It displays no overtly cosmological signs (apart from a comparison of the inlaid serpents to rainbows amid clouds), but only σημαίνοντα, signifiers, which recall Hephaestus's intricate labor of book 18:

And Agamemnon took up the man-enclosing elaborate stark shield,
a thing of splendour (πολυδαίδαλον). There were ten *circles*
    (κύκλοι) of bronze upon it,
and set about it were twenty *knobs* (ὀμφαλοί) of tin, pale-shining,
and in the very *centre* another knob of dark cobalt.

[68] Cf. Schol. A N 736b; and e.g. Crates fr. 24v Mette. The background is complex; see M. Schmidt, *Erklärungen*, 125–26, 215–18 (to which add Schol. A Σ 597–98 and T Σ 597 [Aristarchus athetized this too, clearly for reasons other than those alleged by the scholiasts], Athenaeus 15.672a, and especially Parmenides frs. A37, B12 D-K).

[69] διεζωκότα ("girdling") recalls the "zones" or intervallic spaces (διαστήματα) between the cosmic rings (κύκλοι); cf. Achilles *Comm. in Aratum* 62, 20 Maass, and Heraclitus *Quaest. Hom.* 50.1. Cf. Schol. Σ 488b (citing Aratus *Phaenomena* 226–27); ἄστρων στεφανούντων τὸ πᾶν, [Plutarch] *De vit. Hom.* 216 (460, 19 Bernardakis). Spheres and circles are not always neatly distinct in this literature (Heraclitus *Quaest. Hom.* 43.14).

And *circled* in the midst of all (ἐστεφάνωτο, again) was the blank-
   eyed face of the Gorgon
with her stare of horror, and Fear was inscribed upon it, and
   Terror. . . . [A]nd there also on it
was *coiled* a cobalt snake, and there were three heads upon him
twisted to look backward (ἀμφιστρεφέες) and grown from a
   single neck, all three.

(Iliad 11.32–40, Lattimore, tr.).

And yet Agamemnon's shield, with its neatly concentric layers, its constellations of bosses, and its other circular motifs, was likewise considered
by Crates to be a μίμημα of the cosmos.[70]

Aristarchus and Crates clashed over this too. All that remains of their
battle is a dispute over a word, ἀμφιστρεφέες (ἀμφιστεφέες, vulg.
and Crates), which not so surprisingly happens to be tied to the verb
στεφανόω ("crown");[71] but at stake was nothing less than the concept
and range of mimesis itself. Crates was implicitly testing not just the Aristotelian but also the Platonic conceptions of imitation. His reading extended the meaning of the term far beyond what prior critical tradition
would permit.[72] And in allowing greater scope to the object of mimesis
(which was nothing less than the cosmos), Crates was also asking that we
reevaluate the modalities of imitation at the artist's disposal, along with
the critical modes of grasping them. Some of this is directed against Aristotle, who in the *Poetics* had effectively dismissed natural philosophy
from aesthetic consideration, in the unfavorable contrast between Homer's and Empedocles' hexameters, for these have "nothing in common":

[70] In book 18, in the description of the shield itself and within the next one hundred odd
lines, circling images and motions abound (e.g., the holy circle of the elders' benches, the
dancing floor, the potter's wheel, Ocean rimming the whole). Cratetean activity is detect-
able between the lines of the scholia here, which deserve to be investigated (e.g., the scholia
to *Il.* 484b, 570c¹, 591–92, and 607–08). For a similar focus, see on Asclepiades, below. In
this reclamation of material from the silences of our sources, M. Schmidt's admirable methods should be followed (*Erklärungen*), in close counsel with A. Ludwich's "ars nesciendi"
(*Aristarchs homerische Textkritik*, 2.103).

[71] At 11.40, in reading ἀμφιστρεφέες ("twined round") in place of the vulgate reading
ἀμφιστεφέες ("crowned round"), Aristarchus was again warding off a "confusion" with
11.36, ἐστεφάνωτο ("has as its crown"), which is to say that he was eager to avoid any
further connotations of (Cratetean) circularity; cf. the "h" scholium, given in Erbse's test.
ad loc.; Eustathius ad loc.; Crates quoted in *Schol. in Arat.* 62 (98, 9 Martin).

[72] On the Platonic and Aristotelian notions as these applied to Homer, see especially
N. J. Richardson's contribution to the present volume. Crates' "μίμημα" is meant to clash
with critical orthodoxy on mimesis.

"It is right to call the former a poet, but the latter a natural scientist (φυ-σιολόγον) rather than a poet."[73] Presumably, this was partially aimed at preempting the claims of allegoresis, just as the *Poetics* as a whole is resistant to anything resembling allegorical interpretation. In any case, in later centuries Aristotle's judgment was no longer quite tenable. Dionysius of Halicarnassus, 'Longinus,' and Menander Rhetor learned to value the poetic possibilities of φυσιολογία (natural inquiry) and τὰ φυσικά (physical phenomena), as did the self-conscious poets of the Augustan age (Vergil and Ovid, to name just two).[74] And Crates did much to efface the boundaries for them.

In what follows, I will focus on what I have found to be the most surprising and striking instance of Crates' profound impact on later developments in criticism. The example, transmitted by Heraclitus, is one of Crates' more fanciful readings of the *Iliad*, pertaining to the description of Hephaestus's literal ejection from Olympus at the end of book 1. The passage in question reads,

> There was a time once before now I was minded to help you [Hera]
> and he caught me by the foot and threw me from the magic
> threshold,
> and all day long I dropped helpless, and at sunset
> I landed in Lemnos, and there was not much life left in me.
> (Iliad 1.590–93, Lattimore, tr., modified).

The maiming of divinity borders on impiety, Heraclitus argues (*Quaest. Hom.* 26.1), unless one discovers Homer's hidden philosophical intention (νοῦς) and reads the episode as a Stoicizing allegory of "god-sent fire" (26.3; 26.15). Heraclitus then passes a quick, disparaging glance at Crates' interpretation of the event, which he calls "baroque" (a τερατεία; Buffière's rendering). It is a bizarre piece of theorizing which argues, Heraclitus writes,

> that when Zeus was interested in *taking the measure of the universe* (ἀναμέτρησιν τοῦ παντός) using two beacons traveling *at an equal speed* (ἰσοδρομοῦσιν)—Hephaestus and Helios— he marked out *the distances of the cosmos* (διετεκμήρατο τοῦ κόσμου τὰ διαστή-

---

[73] 1447b17 (Janko, tr.). *On Poets* (fr. 70, Rose) makes amends, but it does not alter the underlying assumptions; cf. D. W. Lucas and R. Janko, ad loc.

[74] Dionysius of Halicarnassus *De comp. verb.* 98, 9 Usener-Radermacher; ['Longinus'] 12.5, 35.4; Menander Rhetor, 336–37 ("Scientific Hymns"). In general, see D. C. Innes, "Gigantomachy and Natural Philosophy," and P. R. Hardie, *Virgil's Aeneid*.

μᾰτᾰ), hurling the one from on high, from the so-called "threshold" (βηλοῦ) [of heaven],[75] and permitting the other to take its course from its rising to its setting. As it turned out, the two bodies were in perfect synchrony, for Hephaestus "landed in Lemnos at sunset."[76] Whether this is some kind of *cosmic measurement* (κοσμική τις ἀναμέτρησις)[77] [as Crates claims] or, what has more truth on its side, an allegorical teaching (ἀλληγορικὴ παράδοσις) concerning man's reception of fire as we know it [as Heraclitus himself argued, 26.15], Homer has uttered no impieties about Hephaestus (*Quaest. Hom.* 27).

Crates' reading, so far from being Stoical, is not even legitimately "allegorical" in Heraclitus's eyes. What is more, in opposing "cosmic" to "allegorical," Heraclitus seems to have got it right. Crates is practicing some third kind of reading that is spectacularly hyperbolic.

Wolf, following Heraclitus, could scoff at this reduction of a myth to "an experiment in physics,"[78] but this is to miss the point. Crates' reading does more than "prove" that the two diameters of the cosmos are of equal length. He has taken the measure of Homer's mind. Aristarchus, typically, will react by reading distances "Homerically"; hence, Olympus is emphatically *not* identical with the heavens: It merely marks the point of ἴσον διάστημα, or equal distance, between heaven and earth.[79] But this sober response likewise goes wide of the mark. The only fair reading of Crates was given not by Aristarchus, Heraclitus, or Wolf, but by the far more appreciative 'Longinus,' who I wish to argue devoted the ninth chapter of his treatise *On the Sublime* to a reinterpretation of this very passage (or its source). As the dates of Longinus and Heraclitus are un-

---

[75] "So-called," because Crates infamously read βῆλος for the Homeric βηλός ("threshold") and argued that the word was of Chaldaean origin, signifying "heaven" (Schol. A 591c [and test.] = Crates fr. 22b Mette). Cf. M. Schmidt, *Erklärungen*, 86 (with n. 62) and 94. Aristarchus took issue with this (Schol. D A 591; Schol. A A 593a¹; M. Schmidt, *Erklärungen*, 87, n. 64), and with Crates' views on the semantics of "all day long" (Schol. A 472, Schol. bT A 601; cf. Schol. bT A 592 and Porphyry ad loc.).

[76] κάππεσον (cf. πεσόντα, *Il.* 1.594). Crates' reading makes a little more sense if we compare *Il.* 8.485 ("the shining light of the sun fell into [ἐν δ᾽ ἔπεσε] Ocean"). Crates, of course, saw cosmology in this (cf. Schol. bT Θ 485b).

[77] For similar terms and concepts, cf. Geminus 16.5–6; Heraclitus *Quaest. Hom.* 36.8.

[78] F. A. Wolf, *Prolegomena to Homer [1795]*, 218.

[79] Cf. Schol. A Ξ 174a¹; K. Lehrs, *De Aristarchi studiis homericis*, 167. Yet another instance of the principle established by M. Schmidt, *Erklärungen*, 189, "dass in der Homererklärung im allgemeinen Aristarch die Erklärungen des Krates voraussetzt (und gegen sie polemisiert)."

certain, it is safest to say that Longinus is deriving his information about Crates from an independent source. But a handful of clues scattered throughout *On the Sublime* suggest that Longinus is actually referring, in oblique fashion, both to Crates' reading and to its critique by Heraclitus. There are simply too many verbal and thematic coincidences to account for in any other way, and the complication of argument all lies on the side of Longinus.

With the excerpt from Heraclitus compare the following from chapter nine. There is a suggestive lacuna in the manuscripts, and we re-join Longinus with the words: ". . . the *interval* (διάστημα) from earth to heaven. One might say that this is *the measure* (μέτρον) not so much of Eris (Strife) as *of Homer*" (9.4–5, Russell, tr., modified). Eris is described in *Iliad* 4 in colossal terms, as "striding on the earth, while her head strikes (ἐστήριξε) heaven" (*Il.* 4.443). Heraclitus had dealt with the figure of Eris allegorically within a page or two of Crates' reading of Hephaestus (29.4), so it is likely that Longinus's gaze is directed in our direction. From the Homeric scholia we know that Crates did concern himself with Eris (Schol. bT N 358–60b);[80] it is conceivable that he dealt with her appearance in another scene (*Il.* 11.5–8); all three passages would have been related, on Crates' way of thinking, to the cosmic dimensions of Homer's meaning (see below, p. 109). But even if Longinus may not be alluding to a physical reading by Crates of this giant, Longinus's cosmic measurement is surely in Crates' spirit. On the other hand, we can be certain that Longinus cannot, irrespective of dates, have derived the notion of cosmic measure—διάστημα, figuratively transposed to poetic grandeur—from Heraclitus, who is not concerned to illustrate cosmic *intervals* in his treatment of Eris and instead gives a moral palliative for the verses (with etymology—"strife"—furnishing the pretext). Longinus immediately goes on to quote, somewhat depreciatingly, from the *Shield* of Hesiod (9.5; *Shield* 267). This may be a further sign that Crates has left his imprint on these passages.[81] The two "shields" had long been connected in the critical

---

[80] Aristarchus, naturally, took an opposing view. Cf. Schol. A N 359a and A. Ludwich, *Aristarchs homerische Textkritik*, 1, 35; M. van der Valk, *Researches*, 2, 97. Curiously, it is Crates who takes a "literalist" stance, while Aristarchus, faced with an overt allegory in Homer's text, gets himself entangled in evasive maneuvers. An "exegetical" scholium on *Il.* 13.358–60a may preserve some of his students' embarrassment: μικτὴ ἡ ἀλληγορία; the allegory is "mixed," not wholly figural, viz., not quite a "complete" allegory (on which, Schol. bT T 221–24a¹). The connection between "wrath" and "strife" must have loomed large since *Il.* 1.8 (cf. Eustathius 21, 1–5 and esp. 21, 35 ["broken bonds"]).

[81] A few scraps of Crates' Hesiodic criticism are preserved. See Curt Wachsmuth, *De*

tradition, as was inevitable. Lines 156–59 of the *Shield* are, after all, identical with *Iliad* 18.535–38; and Zenodotus may have rejected the Homeric Shield scene because of its "Hesiodic character" (Schol. A Σ 39–49). Crates, moreover, could be critical of parts of the Hesiodic corpus (though no traces of his thoughts on the Hesiodic *Shield* have survived).[82] This background debate, sadly lost, might have been crucial to appreciating the way in which Longinus's "commentative" allusion played into it. The sequel, in any case, leaves little room for doubt that Crates has indeed made an impression on Longinus.

"How," Longinus asks, "does Homer magnify the divine power?" In answer, Longinus reproduces a simile from Homer, which suggests an infinite vision into and beyond the heavens, by means of a comparison with the stride of Hera's twin steeds (5.770–72) as they move "through the space between the earth and starry heaven" (5.769):

> He uses a *cosmic distance* to *measure* their *speed* (τὴν ὁρμὴν αὐτῶν κοσμικῷ διαστήματι καταμετρεῖ). This enormously impressive image (lit.: "on account of the hyperbole of its grandeur," διὰ τὴν ὑπερβολὴν τοῦ μεγέθους) would make anybody say, and with reason, that, if the horses of the gods took two more strides forward, *they would find no more room in the universe* (οὐκέθ᾽ εὑρήσουσιν ἐν κόσμῳ τόπον). (*On the Sublime* 9.5, Russell, tr.)

The final, transgressive image in Longinus completes the earlier hyperbole in Homer. It also signals that we have been broaching, unwittingly, another domain. Here Longinus is helping himself to a perplexing cosmological issue, one that dates back to Archytas's arm-reaching query (Archytus, fr. A24 D-K): If I stand on the rim of the cosmos and stretch out my arm, where will it land? The question can be asked only if we postulate a finite cosmos (as on the spherical hypothesis of Greek cosmology). Various answers could be given: It will land in nothing, in some void, or in infinite void.[83] We do not know how Crates stood on the mat-

---

Cratete Mallota, 55 and R. Pfeiffer, *History of Classical Scholarship From the Beginnings*, 241. Longinus's gesture may be a wink to the reader; or the tribute may be more direct.

[82] Crates rejected both proems to the remaining poems by Hesiod *(Life of Dionysius Periegetes* 72, 59–60 in Rudolf Kassel, "Antimachos in der Vita Chisiana des Dionysios Periegetes"). See R. Pfeiffer, *History of Classical Scholarship From the Beginnings*, 177, for a convenient synopsis of Alexandrian views on the two "Shields," and K. Nickau, *Untersuchungen*, 239. In this connection, Zenodotus's conjecture at *Il.* 18.485 (οὐρανὸν ἐστήρικται) may have been based on *Shield* 218 (ἐστήρικτο, also in final position).

[83] Cf. "they would find no more place in the cosmos" (οὐκέθ᾽ εὑρήσουσιν ἐν κόσμῳ

ter. But that is beside the point. Longinus has been quoting from the language of cosmology all along (cf. Democritus fr. A40.3 D-K, Epicurus *Epistle* 2.89). In the foregoing (9.4–6), that language matches up perfectly with what we found in the reading by Crates known to us from Heraclitus (quoted above, pp. 95f.). And as Longinus correctly places the accent, in *his* version of an exegetical *Gedankenexperiment*, the emphasis falls on intervallic διαστήματα, gaps and hiatuses, "the space between the earth and starry heaven" (*Il.* 5.769), measured distances and distanciations, all imperiling the very concept of measure, but all figures and effects that, nonetheless, are achieved through carefully measured hexameters (cf. τέτρασι καταμετρουμένου [τοῦ ῥυθμοῦ] χρόνοις, 39.4). Longinus never loses sight of the technical means of poetic production. Nor did Crates, for his part.[84]

From here it is an easy step to the Gigantomachy and the Theomachy. The cosmos at odds with itself, gaping in its dimensions, is a hypostatization of divine strife:

The imaginative pictures (φαντάσματα) in the Battle of the Gods are also very remarkable (ὑπερφυᾶ). . . . Do you see how the earth is torn from its foundations, Tartarus laid bare, and *the whole universe overthrown and broken up* (διάστασιν τοῦ κόσμου) . . . Heaven (οὐρανός) and Hell (ᾅδης), things mortal and things immortal (*On the Sublime* 9.6, Russell, tr.).

But on a sublime view of things, these images enjoy a consummating value: They "round out" the picture of the universe's fullest construction, be this physical or poetic (phantasmal). In literary terms, Longinus is probing the techniques and themes that generate comparable degrees of sublimity, at the nether ends of imagistic referents (celestial and infernal).

τόπον), as if they will have passed outside the cosmic "place" into a beyond. Longinus only *intimates* this beyond ("two strides" that the steeds haven't yet taken). Aristotle held that there was no such beyond, "neither place nor void" *(De caelo* 279a11). See Friedrich Solmsen, "Beyond the Heavens." The Stoics, possibly following Epicurus, named that nothingness beyond the cosmos "void"; see D. E. Hahm, *The Origins of Stoic Cosmology,* 103–10, esp. 104; A. A. Long and D. N. Sedley, *The Hellenistic Philosophers,* §49. Longinus is not going outside the reigning cosmologies *(pace* Winfried Bühler, *Beiträge zur Erklärung der Schrift vom Erhabenen,* 24–26).

[84] W. Bühler, *Beiträge,* 24–26, denies these parallels any meaningful connection. But his denial is impossible to sustain, in light of his important observations on Longinus's elaborate use of hidden quotation (here, 25; cf. [Longinus] 9.8). See below, section V. The fact that the connection could be made independently by Bühler and by me may strengthen its plausibility.

The sublime, after all, is nothing less (and possibly no more) than the measure of an interval. On Crates' physical hypothesis, which amounts to an aesthetic judgment of grandeur, Tartarus is just the physical extreme of the universe, all parts of which are inextricably and symmetrically (viz., indifferently) bound together by the same "figure" (nor did Gorgo's image deter Crates at *Il.* 11.36; cf. Eustathius ad loc.).[85] The cosmic spectacle extended to all sides and to both hemispheres—an extension that was technically unavoidable, mathematically calculable, and aesthetically gratifying in its own right. It is worth noting the terminological equivalent, in the cosmological tradition, for "intervals" ($\kappa\lambda\iota\mu\alpha\tau\alpha$) stretching across the world: $\kappa o\sigma\mu\iota\kappa\alpha i$ $\delta\iota\alpha\sigma\tau\alpha\sigma\epsilon\iota\varsigma$ (e.g., Schol. A M 239). Longinus's language in the two passages above is not innocent of this connotation, which gives us *his* universal measurement and technical palliative and which paves the way for the poetic acceptance of an otherwise objectionable image.

Allegory, Longinus adds at this point (9.7, again echoing, it appears, Heraclitus *Quaest. Hom.* 1.1), would be required to "save the phenomena" of Homer, were we less appreciative of their intrinsic, poetic power, which is $\dot{\upsilon}\pi\epsilon\rho\phi\upsilon\eta\varsigma$ (sublime): "But, terrifying as all this is, it is blasphemous and indecent ["if judged on moral and theological criteria," as Russell ad loc. crucially fills in the ellipsis] unless it is interpreted allegorically." Of course, Longinus's criteria are literary and sublime, and so the recourse to allegory is unnecessary. We are permitted to enjoy for its own sake the Tartarean imagery, while Longinus studiously fails to allegorize the passage—a gesture that is an avowal of indebtedness to prior critics (cf. 9.8).[86] The most outstanding of these debts here, as Longinus quietly makes plain with his equivocation on "allegory" and with his complex set of allusions, was to Crates of Mallos, who was something more than an allegorist.[87] Whether or not he was the superior critic, Longinus at

---

[85] Crates frs. 37–39 Mette; M. Schmidt, *Erklärungen*, 105–09.

[86] On the avoidance, see Russell at 9.5 and 9.7; W. Bühler, *Beiträge*, 29. Russell nicely puts his finger here on where Longinus's heart lies. Other arguments may be brought to bear (cf. 9.8, $\delta\iota\iota\sigma\tau\alpha\tau o$; 9.13, Homer as the sun; 9.14, the doves of Zeus, which Crates preferred to read "physically" [Crates fr. 26a Mette], etc.).

[87] That is, "allegorist" in the ancient sense of the term, and as it was most often put to use (apologist, accommodationist, etc.), e.g., by a Heraclitus or by an Aristarchus (in the sense of an exegete who practices nonliterary exegesis); cf. D. A. Russell, *Criticism in Antiquity*, 96–97; R. Lamberton, *Homer the Theologian*, 145, n. 3. Crates' practice exceeds all standard defintions, as H. J. Mette hints, *Sphairopoiia*, 33–34. One set of allusions which surprisingly has not been noticed: the inversion at [Longinus] 9.7 ("in Homer gods are mortal, mortals are gods"): this goes back to Heraclitus's namesake (fr. B62 D-K) and is part and parcel of

least knew how to recognize, and salvage, the most valuable insights of his predecessors.

Crates' σφαιρικὸς λόγος, I would suggest, was at least in part a way of adding new dimensions to criticism, and especially to the appreciation of latent literary possibilities. It may be to him that we owe the aesthetics of the interval or gap (which Longinus also knew how to exploit), or rather, its earliest application to literary criticism. The notion of διαστή-ματα (intervals) was already in place in the rarified aesthetics of musical criticism even before Aristoxenus. This strand, too, may have been woven into cosmic poetic thinking in, say, Eratosthenes (e.g., in his poem on ascension to heaven, *Hermes*) before finding a home in criticism with Crates; the combination of physical allegory and musical cosmology, as it appears in Heraclitus *Quaest. Hom.* 12, probably was unthinkable until after Eratosthenes and Crates. Some kind of influence may be suspected, flowing from the earliest musical theories of the ἁρμονικοί (Plato, *Rep.* 531a) to the criticism of Crates (by way of his poetics of euphony, to be discussed below), and then down to Dionysius of Halicarnassus (*On the Composition of Words*) and Longinus (39, on σύνθεσις). With διαστή-ματα so usefully broadened, the question naturally arises, Was Crates locating "intervals" and "spaces" that show up in a text like Homer, or those which open up dimensions of signification of a different sort, as only disclosed in exegesis—gaps, as it were, between signifiers and signifieds, to call again upon Philodemus's terms? That he was searching for a way to nominate these discrepancies too—discrepancies that are as much constitutive of the text as they are disruptive of it ([Longinus] 40.4)—would seem to follow from the very exorbitancy of Crates' readings (as Heraclitus remarked), and from their internal logic as well.

Paradoxes ensue, which Crates must have sensed: the incongruity of two "infinities," brought into collision (the miniature of the shield, the universe that it reached out to embrace); or the paradox of a Hephaestus, now creating the cosmos, now falling more or less victim to it. The two dimensions, already figured by text and cosmos, could converge dramatically in a single line: "*Homer measured* for us (ἐμέτρησε) the spherical shape of the cosmos (τὸ σφαιρικὸν τοῦ κόσμου σχῆμα) *through a single line* (δι' ἑνὸς στίχου)" (Heraclitus *Quaest. Hom.* 36.4; cf. 46.7, 47.1–6); compare Longinus: "Sublimity exists often *in a single thought*" (12.1). That line, which Heraclitus fortunately reproduces for us, reads: "*as far*

Heraclitus's policy to put right side up: in *Quaest. Hom.* 24.4, where the fragment of Heraclitus is cited, and, e.g., in ibid. 56.

101

(τόσσον) beneath the house of Hades *as from* (ὅσον) earth the sky (οὐρα-νός) lies" (*Il.* 8.16). Eris took up precisely half of that magnitude; and Longinus, in his "commentary" on Crates (9.5), quotes a parallel passage about magnitudes that are commensurable perhaps only in the imagination: "*As far as* (ὅσον) a man can peer through the mist, sitting on watch, looking over the wine-dark sea, *so long* (τόσσον) is the stride of the gods' thundering horses" (*Il.* 5.770–72). Such were the velocities and the vertigoes that Crates' confronting of Homer and a "γεωμετρικὴ θεωρία" or σφαιρικὸς λόγος could provoke. "That is why *Homer took the measure* of the spherical shape [of the universe] (τὸ σφαιρικὸν σχῆμα διεμέ-τρησεν), *more geometrico* (γεωμετρικῇ θεωρίᾳ), when he wrote: [*Il.* 8.16]" (Heraclitus *Quaest. Hom.* 36.8).[88] Spheres, after all, are paradox incarnate: They are both bounded by a horizon and without limit (Heraclitus, *Quaest. Hom.* 47.5).[89]

In general, though, Crates' tendency was toward expansiveness and exorbitancy, not miniatures or the subtler forms of paradox.[90] His embracing of exoceanism, that is, his locating the wanderings of Odysseus in the Great Sea beyond the Mediterranean basin, had the same effect of enlarging the scope of Homer's epic, not of his plots per se, but to borrow a phrase from Democritus, of Homer's κόσμος ἐπέων, his "cosmos of words."[91] If any of this can be believed, Crates was not just a precursor to the theory of the sublime, but one of its first critical practitioners.[92] Again, Crates' achievement can only be measured against the then-current traditions in literary criticism (of which we know too little) and against our modern accounts of those traditions (which pay too little heed to Crates).

[88] Cf. the dissonant hermeneutics of the scholia ad loc.; Heraclitus *Quaest. Hom.* 36.5; M. Schmidt, *Erklärungen*, 107 with n. 18.

[89] Hence spheres offer a distinctively Cratetean, non-Aristarchan λύσις (*Schol. in Arat.* 98, 9 Martin) to apparent contradictions in Homer. Cf. Heraclitus *Quaest. Hom.* 47.5: Homer's paradox just is internal to, and the condition of, a certain geometry (an aesthetics of measure). For the Aristotelian line on circles, see *Metaphysics* 1016b17.

[90] Cf. [Longinus] 12.1–2 (on αὔξησις). At 12.3 the "open sea of grandeur" that "spreads out richly in many directions" hits the nail on the head. See section V below.

[91] Dio Chrysostom, *Or.* 53.1 (1.163, 7 Dindorf). The conceit has several survivals ([Plutarch] *De vit. Hom.* 216), most strikingly, however, in Neoplatonic writings, where the Platonic dialogue as a whole is likened to a κόσμος (*Anonymous Prolegomena*, 15–16, p. 29 Westerink). Cf. James A. Coulter, *The Literary Microcosm*, 102.

[92] Ὕψος and related words enter the standard critical vocabulary late (with Dionysius of Halicarnassus), but there are some notable exceptions (Dioscorides, *Anth. Pal.* 7.411 [3d c. B.C.]) and some clear precedents in fifth-century criticism; the term ὑφηγορία is of course familiar to epic (D. A. Russell, *'Longinus' On the Sublime*, xxx).

Reinserting Crates back into the sublime tradition would mean, first, reevaluating the place that physics and φυσιολογία could occupy in literature and especially in criticism in antiquity (cf. [Longinus] 12.5). Second, it would call for a reevaluation of the very concept of the sublime, which in modernity has come under the sway of a romanticized "sublimity," but which in some ancient circles sprang from very different impulses and sensibilities—and these, as we have begun to see, could be at once scientific, rhetorical and "technological" (cf. τεχνολογία [Longinus] 1.1).[93] The sublime (ὕψος), which perhaps has some claim to being called a "material sublime," exceeds so many of our current formulations, precisely by its being born of an uncomfortable enjambement, or crisis (κρίσις): of poetry and φυσιολογία; of formalist and materialist tendencies; of idylls of the mind confronted with the materiality (or exorbitations) of another, richer epistemology. Physical division, technical measurement, and the interval or hiatus are its most unfamiliar coordinates. But Crates' σφαιρικὸς λόγος had a possible further critical effect, which so far as I know was without precedent, and without successors until much later in the history of criticism. It will suffice to draw attention to two final examples of this curious use to which Crates' σφαιρικὸς λόγος could be put—a use that, as we shall see, is also emphatically literary and "critical."

V

The "Shieldlike Plain" of Iliad 11.754

At Iliad 11.754 Nestor relates how he pursued the hostile Pylians either διὰ σπιδέος πεδίοιο (so Zenodotus, followed by modern editions) or δι᾽ ἀσπιδέος πεδίοιο (possibly the vulgate reading). The meaning of either alternative remains unclear today. Aristarchus (Schol. A Λ 754a [Herodian]) reports (ἀποφαίνεται) that some preferred a punctuating pause (διαστολή) before ἀσπιδέος,

> on the grounds that Homer was making the image more vivid (εἰκαστικώτερον) by calling the plain "shield-like," because long and broad plains *appear to be round in shape* (περιφερῆ φαίνεσθαι), *there being no other limit in sight but the horizon provided by the open air* (τοῦ ὁρίζοντος ἀέρος). Others (he continues) construe ἀσπιδέος as a

---

[93] D. C. Innes, "Gigantomachy and Natural Philosophy," has done much to relocate some of the coordinates of the ancient traditions of the sublime.

plain strewn with shields, with the line that follows it as proof: "picking up their magnificent armor" (11.755). Others say that σπιδέος is from "full" (ἐκ πλήρους), viz., "vast and long." And indeed Aeschylus frequently uses the term in this way (fr. 378 Nauck), as does Antimachus (fr. 114 Wyss).

Caught between impalatable alternatives, Aristarchus left the question open.[94] Where the parallel within Homer was uncompelling, and the recourse to outside Homer inconclusive, the first option was the least gripping. It smacked too much of Crates. Compare the *grammaticus* Achilles, in his *Commentary on Aratus* (51, 27–28 Maass): " 'Horizon' derives its name from the fact that it defines (ὁρίζει) the *hemispheres* which lie above and below the earth." This view is more than simply compatible with Crates' own, as the sequel reinforces: Ocean defines the limit of the earth's sphere (51, 28–29); and as a scholium on Aratus clinches: "Aratus calls the horizon 'Ocean.' *Poetically* speaking (ποιητικῶς), ⟨Ocean⟩ is the horizon, *beyond which there is nothing else* (μεθ᾽ ὃν οὐδὲν ἔτι ἐστίν). . . . For it *encircles* (κύκλῳ περίκειται) our inhabited world, the οἰκουμένη, just as in Homer. . . ." Naturally, the example taken from Homer to illustrate this point is the shield of Achilles, which "Hephaestus conceived as a μίμημα of the cosmos" when he rimmed it with Ocean (*Schol. in Aratum* 70, 17 – 71, 9 Martin). The analogies between Ocean, horizon, (cosmic) limit, and shield thus merge in a powerful nexus. And that nexus derives from Crates.[95]

Crates' reading (ἀσπιδέος ["shield"], it goes without saying) is given immediately after Aristarchus's indecision (same scholium) but with no argument for it; that argument, I suspect, is self-evident from Aristarchus's words: The phrase in question vividly recalls the circular "horizon" and perhaps the "empty" measure of a diastem.[96] An exegetical scholium, however, picks up the thread for us: "δι᾽ ἀσπιδέος ("through the shieldlike [plain]"): viz., *in the shape of a circle* (κυκλοτεροῦς), for

[94] K. Lehrs, *De Aristarchi studiis homericis*, 153, and Johannes Helck, *De Cratetis Mallotae studiis criticis, quae ad Iliadem spectant*, 18. M. van der Valk, *Researches* 1.230, n. 146 must be wrong.

[95] Cf. Carl Reinhardt, *De Graecorum Theologia*, 62; H. J. Mette, *Sphairopoiia*, 35; M. Schmidt, *Erklärungen*, 129 (with generous discussion, 127–32, on "horizon"). None of these accounts includes the scholia to *Il.* 11.754.

[96] Cf. κένος, narrative "gap" (Schol. bT Z 119b; Aristophanes of Byzantium quoted in *Schol. in Eur.* 1, 243, 8–12 Dindorf), which is often "filled" by a diversion (ἀνάπαυσις); cf. Schol. bT Π 431–61: διάστημα = narrative "relief." For Crates' cosmic alternative to narrative relief, see below, nn. 113 and 121.

whenever we are in an open place (ἐν ἀναπεπταμένῳ τόπῳ), *we view it in the shape of a circle*" (Schol. Λ 754c; cf. Schol. Θ 485b). A sublime response. It is only a short remove from Longinus, who will write, in one of his hyperbolically physical readings of the universe:

> The *cosmos, taken whole, is not wide enough* (οὐδ᾽ ὁ σύμπας κόσμος ἀρκεῖ) for the range of human speculation and intellect. Our thoughts often travel *beyond the boundaries* of our surroundings (τοὺς τοῦ περιέχοντος ὅρους ἐκβαίνουσιν).[97] If anyone wants to know what we were born for, let him look *round* at life (lit., "*in a circle,*" ἐν κύκλῳ) and contemplate the splendour, grandeur, and beauty in which it everywhere abounds (τὸ περιττὸν ἐν πᾶσι [lit., "*the extraordinary/excessive in everything*"] 35.3, Russell, tr., modified).

Longinus goes on to mention natural attractions (phenomena by which we are φυσικῶς πως ἀγόμενοι): the Nile, the Ister, the Rhine, "*and above all, Ocean*" (πολὺ δὲ μᾶλλον τὸν Ὠκεανόν). An earlier remark from 12.3 has a place here as well: "[And Plato's style] spreads out richly in many directions, like a sea, into an *open* grandeur" (καθάπερ τι πέλαγος, εἰς ἀναπεπταμένον κέχυται πολλαχῇ μέγεθος).

Clearly, this is not nature without artifice. We are still in the ambit of citations, and within Crates' nexus of physical and poetic analogies. The next images follow the bipolar schema noted above for Crates (Heaven/ Hades), to which they supply the missing complement (the upper hemisphere having, as it were, been accounted for already, and now again by the "fires of heaven" [τῶν οὐρανίων], 35.4): eruptions out of the depths of earth, around "the craters of Etna," are effluvia of "earth-born, spontaneous fire"; they are, in other words, chthonic, Titanic, and Tartarean (cf. Pindar *Pythian* 1, Hesiod *Theogony* *860, Lucretius 6.639, 647–51; etc.). Remarkably, Longinus is again paralleled by Heraclitus ("earthborn, spontaneous fire," [Longinus] 35.5; Heraclitus *Quaest. Hom.* 26.15).[98] But as before, Longinus's practice is complex; for although his overt reference names "Etna," his allusive language, if it is lifted verbatim from Heraclitus, but possibly even if it is taken from Crates by way of

[97] Cf. 9.6: "the [horses of Hera] will find *no more place in the cosmos*"; the allusion to the earlier section is deliberate.

[98] See D. A. Russell ad loc. on the text (the texts of Heraclitus and Longinus have been emended in light of each other, on the basis of this parallel); and W. Bühler, *Beiträge*, 141. Lucretius 6.639–54 is remarkably close in tone (and to be taken with the conflicting emotions of the "physiologist" at 3.14–30: *voluptas . . . atque horror*).

some other source, names the volcanic "Lemnos" (the explicit topic of *Quaest. Hom.* 26.15). Is Longinus paying another tribute to Crates (via his reading of Hephaestus's ejection at *Il.* 1.590–93), whose presence we have already detected behind the scenes of *On the Sublime* 35 above? Was the conflation already anticipated by Crates himself? If so, he could have drawn it in turn from preexisting tradition. Pherecydes (fr. B5 D-K) appears to have read *Iliad* 1.590 (Hephaestus's rejection) as an allusion to Tartarus and to Zeus's banishment of refractory gods.[99] It is an inference that any Greek could have made. *Iliad* 15.18 (Hera's dangling from heaven) and 1.590 had been thrown together for perhaps entirely different reasons by Plato, *Rep.* 378d (but cf. *Il.* 15.22–24 and 8.19–27); but the connection has some logic, and it could have stuck or been made independently again. Heraclitus draws the connection at 26.12–15, in allegorizing Hephaestus's rejection as volcanic eruption. Celsus (quoted in Origen, *Contra Celsum* 6.42) will draw it again, if he is not in fact citing from Pherecydes, as the passage suggests.[100] Crates would have, and just may have, gladly seized upon the structural implications—the physical polarities, or rather tensions—of a conflation like this. It is in any case this major juxtaposition of polarities and the earlier train of lesser juxtapositions that give content to Longinus's concluding summation: The source of all wonder is "paradox" (τὸ παράδοξον, 35.5), which is nothing beyond the measure of an interval. Its emotional counterpart is equally paradoxical: a mixture of *horror* and *voluptas*. Crates, παραδοξολογῶν, would have been the first to admit as much.

Longinus calls us back to an immanent grandeur ("Look round at life and contemplate the splendor, grandeur, and beauty in which it everywhere abounds"), one that is, in the end, a literary grandeur (as his bountiful allusions imply). Does not Crates do the same, in referring us to properties that are always, ultimately, of Homer's poems? We might compare a remark that has some chance of stemming from Crates: "It was befitting for a great poet (Homer) to talk about great things (περὶ μεγάλων)" (Achilles, *Comm. in Arat.* 29, 24 Maass = Crates fr. 24a Mette); or Heraclitus *Quaest. Hom.* 43.1, where a contrast is drawn between the smaller-scale proofs (ἐλάττω τεκμήρια) of Homer's allegori-

<hr>

[99] Félix Buffière, *Les Mythes d'Homère et la pensée grecque*, 98, n. 65 usefully sums up the teachings of Pherecydes' *Heptamychos*; see also now, Hermann S. Schibli, *Pherekydes of Syros*, 99, n. 54.

[100] And as J. Tate once assumed, "The Beginnings of Greek Allegory," 215. On the mythological parallels between *Il.* 15.18, 1.596, and 8.19, cf. further Cedric H. Whitman, "Hera's Anvils."

zations presented so far, and the Shield to come: "But in the *Hoplopoiia*, Homer has compressed [or "surveyed"] the genesis of the universe (τῶν ὅλων), by means of a magnificent and cosmogonic meaning (μεγάλῃ καὶ κοσμοτόκῳ διανοίᾳ)." It is as if in his fixation on shields and oceans, and especially on circular shapes and images that open for him a visual field larger than life, Crates has been led to invest Homer's poetry, at every conceivable opportunity, with their connotative power. The connections that Crates seems to have discovered are by no means self-evident. A last example will provide another instance of Crates' successful quest for "evidence" of the *sphairopoiic* thesis.

Aristarchus and Crates on the "Geography" of the Ships (Il. 14.31–36)

Early in *Iliad* 14 the Greeks beach their ships and begin constructing their defensive wall. The text reads:

> They had hauled up the first ones
> on the plain, and by the sterns of these (ἐπὶ πρύμνῃσιν) had built
>   their defences;
> for, wide as it was, the sea-shore *was not big enough to make room*
> *for all the ships*, and the people also were straitened; and therefore
> they had hauled them up in depth (προκρόσσας), and filled up the
>   long edge
> of the *whole sea-coast, all that the two capes compassed between them.*
>   (14.31–36, Lattimore, tr.)

While the Greeks assumed one battle formation, another was forming between Alexandria and Pergamum. An interpretive dispute in Alexandria and Pergamum arose round the "geography" of the Greek ships in their encampment and in physical relation to the wall. So consumed was Aristarchus by the question, he devoted a separate monograph to it (Περὶ τοῦ ναυστάθμου, Schol. A M 258a), complete with visual map (διάγραμμα, Schol. A Λ 807a). Even so he revised his opinions throughout his career.[101] Needless to say, at issue here were, again, circles and lines.

In Homer's text the wall was said to have been built ἐπὶ πρύμνῃσιν, by the sterns or ends of the "first" ships. This is where the agreement ended. Into how many rows were the ships crowded? An exegetical scholium asserts flatly, "The ships were not in two rows (ἐν διστιχίᾳ), as

---

[101] Schol. A O 449–51a; K. Lehrs, *De Aristarchi studiis homericis*, 226.

Crates says" (Schol. bT Ξ 31–32). Herodian (one of Aristarchus's contin-uators) counters Crates' logic (and reading, πρύμνῃσιν) with an Aristar-chan objection. He reports, frowningly, that Crates construed πρύμνῃσιν as a form of the adjective πρυμνός, "understanding by this '*at the ends*' (ἐπὶ ταῖς ἐσχάταις) rather than at the 'sterns.' " But the evidence tells against Crates. For the poet "in general" (ἐπὶ τὸ πολύ) uses the adjective not to signify the end of a separate body (ἐπὶ διεστῶτος σώματος) but the end of a given body (like the end of your finger).[102]

Since Herodian, scholars have unanimously followed the exegetical scholium; Crates obviously must have said that the ships were in two rows, and naturally Aristarchus took the opposing view, or as Karl Lehrs put it, and as has been unquestioningly repeated since, "Aristarchus rightly rejected [Crates' reading], on the assumption that the ships were arranged *in a single, semicircular* row."[103] Lehrs was no doubt encouraged by the fact that Aristarchus had deduced, from a careful study, that the encampment was formed round a θεατροειδῆ τόπον, a space shaped after a theater, in which the assemblies were held (Schol. A Λ 807a); and that the beaching of the ships gave the same appearance itself (ὥστε θεα-τροειδὲς φαίνεσθαι τὸ νεώλκιον, Schol. A Ξ 35a). We see some of this theatricality hinted at in 14.37: "These lords walked in a group, each leaning on his spear, [desirous] *to look at the clamorous battle*," τῷ ῥ᾽ οἵ γ᾽ ὀψείοντες, a reading Aristarchus made a point of defending against Ze-nodotus, by taking the phrase as emphatically equivalent to ὀπτικῶς ἔχοντες, "viewing," and not to "hearing" (Zenodotus: ὀψαίοντες; Schol. A D Ξ 37a[1], c).[104] If Lehrs is right, then Aristarchus seems to be beating Crates at his own game, by offering up a counter-λόγος, as it were, a "theatropoiia." The evidence suggests, however, that Lehrs is wrong, and that there is more at stake in the ancient dispute than meets the eye at first.

Lehrs and others can only have reached this conclusion by ignoring certain ambiguities. θεατροειδής ("shaped after a theater") is a case in point. This word Aristarchus "glossed" with "[14.35]: *because the ships are ranged in a ladder-like fashion, in steps, one before the other* (ὅτι προκρόσσας τὰς κλιμακηδὸν νενεωλκημένας ἑτέρας πρὸ(ς) ἑτέρων; Lehrs's own

---

[102] Schol. A Ξ 32a. For a similar conflict, apparently, over "ends," see the scholia to *Il.* 13.358–60, where Aristarchus's and Crates' positions on allegory are effectively reversed (above, n. 80).

[103] K. Lehrs, *De Aristarchi studiis homericis*, 225.

[104] Cf. Walter Leaf, ad loc. and M. van der Valk, *Researches*, 2, 42 for different punctua-tions (and constructions) of Zenodotus's reading.

emendation!), so that the beached ships *gave the appearance of a theater,* for stepped copings of parapets (κρόσσαι) are ladders [for scaling them]" (Schol. A Ξ 35a).[105] The ships were apparently staggered in tiers, as in a theater, but hardly in a single semicircle.[106] Neither are the words "The ships were not in two rows (ἐν διστιχίᾳ), *as Crates claims*" unambiguous. And a glance at Eustathius shows why. Eustathius writes, "But Crates claims that the ships were *not* in two rows [lit.: "lines"] (ὁ μέντοι Κράτης οὐκ ἐν διστίχῳ φησὶν εἶναι τὰς ναῦς): To explain how he contrives this reading would be a waste of time" (965, 36). As Eustathius's commentary in context suggests,[107] Crates may well have argued— impossibly, for Eustathius—that the ships were arranged καθ᾽ ἕνα στίχον, "in a single row," following the contours of the bay.[108] One could make good sense of the scholia on this interpretation.[109] And if this is right, then it is Crates, not Aristarchus, who held that the ships were arranged in a semicircle (following the contours of the bay).[110]

This is another instance of Crates peforming a measurement (καταμέτρησις, based on inference, though now one that is no longer quite "cosmic" (nor is his fascination with measure in general unique to this

---

[105] See H. Erbse, ad loc. It is astonishing that Lehrs could have argued for a *single* semicircle, but this appears to be what he meant and how he was understood (J. Helck, *De Cratetis Mallotae studiis criticis*, 23: "serie semicirculata *una*" [italics in original]); Eustathius 965, 39 (ἄλλας ἐπ᾽ ἄλλαις) superficially resembles Lehrs's reading.

[106] In conformity to the topographical rise on the land. Κλιμακηδόν ("ladder-like," "stepped") reflects Aristarchus's revised opinion, from κεφάλιδες (probably straight rows, "headed" by a ship: *Suda* κ 2473, under κρόσσας); Porphyry on *Il.* 12.258 *(Quaest. Hom. Il.* [Schrader] 179, 20), who is critical of Aristarchus's "ladder" solution, also suggests an alternative that may have contributed to the confusion (μὴ ἐπ᾽ ἴσου στίχου, 180, 11).

[107] Eustathius gives us at least a control on the Greek, hence an option. But he can also be an independent source of information, esp. for lost T-scholia; see H. Erbse, *Beiträge zur Überlieferung*, 123–73, esp. 153 with n. 1.

[108] The arguments of Eustathius (965, 25) are too absorbing to enter into here. Briefly, he feels that the beach was too constricted to permit a single file of ships (καθ᾽ ἕνα στίχον), and so he opts for a solution of "no less than two rows" (τὸ ἐλάχιστον δύο στίχους). "But Crates says that the ships were not in two rows. To explain how he contrives this would be a waste of time (περιττόν, "redundant")," because the grounds for Eustathius's own conclusion have already ruled out Crates' alternative without naming Crates.

[109] This also follows from Autochthon's report and counter–factual (Schol. bT Ξ 31–32), which could give Crates' reason. Autochthon rightly objects that this is sheer hair-splitting: πρώτας implies comparativeness in itself.

[110] H. Erbse, on *Il.* 15.656, briefly suggests that Crates may have held the two-row theory, while Aristarchus held a many-rowed theory (thus perpetuating half of Lehrs's error) at *Il.* 14.31–32. I am grateful to Richard Janko for calling this reference to my attention and for confirming, from his own notes, the direction of the hypothesis put forward here.

passage).[111] Or is this possibly a cosmic reading too? "*Coronal* rims of parapets" (τὰς τῶν ἐπάλξεων στεφάνας), suggesting *crowns*, seem to have been roped into this same complex of issues at *Iliad* 12.258 and in Aristarchus's specialized monograph as well.[112] Eris could have found her cosmic place in this too, for at *Iliad* 11.6–8 we read that "she took her place . . . *in the middle* [between those who] had hauled their . . . ships up *at the ends* (ἔσχατα)." The "topological" information contained in those lines Aristarchus found singularly illuminating (Schol. A Λ 6). Crates would have found them no less revealing. The centrality of earth is crucial to the spherical hypothesis (Heraclitus *Quaest. Hom.* 36.5, glossing *Il.* 8.16; Schol. b Θ 16b²); and Eris conveniently measures half a cosmic diameter.[113] Did Crates find a further, confirming echo in what was known at the time as the "Trojan διάκοσμος" ("the arrangement of the Trojan forces")?[114] Whatever the case may have been, again we note, with some astonishment, the way in which Crates has clung to his σφαιρικὸς λόγος; and, in passing, the way in which Aristarchus with his *theatropoiia* has replicated, perhaps unconsciously, Aristotle's wisdom on the mutualities between tragedy and epic (*Poetics* 49b18f., and ch. 26). As always, the two views are *toto caelo* different. At any event, reading Homer meant taking a critical stand on issues like these too.

Here we have seen two instances that confirm what earlier examples suggested as well, namely that Crates was finding so to speak more circles in Homer than he needed to find in order to demonstrate his *sphairopoiic* thesis. Earlier, we saw how Crates' *sphairopoiia* lent itself to an appreciation of Homer's "sublimity." Now it would seem that in his fixation on circles and spheres Crates has transformed his *sphairopoiic* thesis into a "theme."[115] Has Crates all along been conducting something akin to the-

[111] Cf. Schol. D ad loc. and Leaf ad loc., who adopts Crates' reading and believes he has adopted Crates' explanation as well. One wonders, though, how Crates defended προκρόσσας. It is also unclear whether the "first" ships were thus for Crates at the "ends" of this single file; but Homer's syntax is unclear on this too (cf. Schol. A Ξ 75–76).

[112] *Suda* κ 2473; Apollonius Sophistes *Lex. Hom.* 104, 14 (Bekker). See H. Erbse, test. on *Il.* 12.258. Cf. Eris at *Il.* 4.770–72, coupled with the Cratetean reading quoted in Heraclitus *Quaest. Hom.* 36.4–5.

[113] Cf. also Parmenides fr. A 44 D-K. Needless to say, the Alexandrians read "intervals" here as non-cosmic; cf. Schol. Y 213a, c–e; Aristotle fr. 162 Rose.

[114] Strabo 13.1.55; cf. Athenaeus 4.141e (Demetrius's "version" of μιμήματα). Cf. Metrodorus of Lampsacus, fr. A3 D-K, where διακόσμησις is used in connection with the allegorical practice of Metrodorus ("hypostases of nature, and *arrangements* of elements"), possibly by Metrodorus himself.

[115] H. J. Mette, *Sphairopoiia*, viii, plausibly calls σφαιροποιία "das Stichwort" of Crates' Homeric interpretation.

matic criticism? (Modern avatars such as Gaston Bachelard and Georges Poulet come to mind.) A treatise by Asclepiades of Myrlea *On Nestor's Cup*, some of which is preserved in Athenaeus (11.488–93 = Crates fr. 26a Mette), suggests that he indeed has. Asclepiades follows Crates on the spherical hypothesis, views the cup as a "*μίμημα* of the cosmos" (489c–d) and, most notably of all, foregrounds circular motifs. At 489d, tables and chairs are called to witness—this sounds like a philospher's lingo. But then, cakes, loaves, and cups are quintessentially circular too (ibid.). If so, then Crates not only deserves to be resituated in the sublime tradition of criticism. He may be the first instance of a thematic critic in the history of literary criticism.[116]

It only remains to decide whether Crates' "theme" points fully to meaning or to its open construction (as written and as read). If the latter is indeed the case, then Crates has bequeathed us a disquieting hermeneutic project.

VI

If Crates' inheritance was pluralistic and culled from every imaginable discipline, the legacy he left was in the field of letters. Our treatment of him has suffered an inevitable foreshortening; on the other hand, the scholia have little to say about Crates' stylistic theories, even though these must have been central to his conception of poetics. Like any critic of his day, Crates ransacked the toolbox of philology; his writings ranged freely over lexical, glossographical, and prosodic items, in addition to attempting humbly to "get the facts straight" (to establish the literal meaning and facts of the text). The relics of his philological criticism, and rarely a stylistic comment, are preserved in the scholia (e.g., at *Od.* 9.60), but there is no telling what their original form was or in what context they appeared. Pfeiffer boils down Crates' critical output to two compact volumes, a *Diorthotica* of textual criticism (in nine books) and a *Homerica* of interpretive readings, but this is a mere expedient. Crates' critical activity extended to Hesiod, the tragedians, Aristophanes, and Aratus.[117] Pfeiffer's lament that a complete *Cratetis Mallotae fragmenta* still does not exist bears repeating. Equally lamentable is the paucity of our sources.

Suetonius records Crates' impact on Roman criticism; he does not

---

[116] See, for example Gaston Bachelard's chapters "Maison et univers" and "La Phénoménologie du rond" in *La Poétique de l'espace*; and Georges Poulet, *Metamorphoses du cercle*.

[117] Cf. C. Wachsmuth, *De Cratete Mallota*, 55–62; R. Pfeiffer, *History of Classical Scholarship From the Beginnings*, 241–42.

breathe a word about allegory but only about the diligent interpretation and commentary of poems which Crates inspired (*De grammaticis* 1–4). Crates' extended sojourn in Rome, occasioned by an accident that is tactfully euphemized in the handbooks, also seems to have given rise to a surge of interest in uncanonized literature ("carmina parum adhuc divolgata"). Naevius, Ennius, and Lucilius are named as beneficiaries; sphairopoiic criticism may have played a part, but it cannot have been the primary attraction. Crates, after all, redefined himself as a κριτικός, in pointed opposition to the Alexandrian style of philology.[118] His first allegiance was to letters and to the critical evaluation of poems.

From Philodemus we learn how Crates fell in with a theory about euphony that had been espoused by earlier generations of κριτικοί.[119] For them, the prime criterion of a poem lay not in its contents, but in its physical, empirically determinable sound quality, which is epiphanic and evanescent, and productive of unrivaled aesthetic pleasure (ἡδονή, which is ἐπιτερπής). Following their lead, Crates located the discriminating judgment (κρίσις) of a poem's qualities in the very quantitative "differences," the φυσικαὶ διαφοραί, that obtain among the letters or "elements" (στοιχεῖα) in combination (σύνθεσις); and these, they claimed, are the constitutive ingredients (or "causes") of sound, euphony, rhythm, and other poetic "epiphenomena."[120] The model he adopted here was from yet another branch of physics, only this time the approximation is to the arrangements of physical elements (atoms) and their interstitial spaces (intervals); and that is the inheritance of a long tradition of speculation about the language of poetry viewed as a discontinuous array of material parts in σύνθεσις. At this level of poetic analysis and technique, one can expect to find Crates' thoughts on στιχοποιία (versification, Schol. A Λ 130a)—a striking but ultimately intelligible contrast to his exploitation, on the level of meaning and thematics, of *sphairopoiia*.

How did these fit together? How did Crates get from the circle to the line? One intimation that these levels ought in principle to cohere is found in Crates' doctrine, from the same source, that what one judges in a poem

---

[118] Suetonius *De grammaticis* 4; and cf. the derisive epigram by Herodicus of Babylon, the Cratetean ("Flee, you Aristarchans, . . . buzzing in dark corners, you monosyllabics," Athenaeus 5.222a). Generally, K. Lehrs, *Herodiani scripta tria emendatiora*, "De vocabulis φιλόλογος, γραμματικός, κριτικός," 379–401; A. Gudeman, "Κριτικός."

[119] *On Poems*, Bk. V (cols. 22–26, Jensen). See J. I. Porter, "Philodemus on Material Difference."

[120] Studies *de letteris syllabisque* and *de metris*, attributed to a *posterior Ennius*, immediately precede the first mention of Crates in Suetonius *De grammaticis* 1 and may have been brought to mind by Crates' theory of euphony and composition.

is "*not without the thoughts, but [it is] not the thoughts themselves either*" (καὶ
οὐ|κ ἄνευ τῶν [νοο]υμένων, | οὐ μέντοι τὰ νοούμε|να; Philodemus,
On Poems V, col. xxv, 26–29). A mystifying phrase. Yet, on reflection,
one could not imagine a better description of Crates' exegetical method,
or a more pointed reversal of Plato's condemnation of allegorical meaning (ὑπόνοια) in the *Republic*. There Plato had decreed that such stories
as pertain to Hera's dangling from heaven, Hephaestus's free fall, and
theomachies, etc. (and we are to understand, inter alia, specifically *Homeric* stories—that is Plato's ὑπόνοια) are to be denied admission into the
state, *whether they are composed with concealed underlying thoughts or without
them* (οὔτ᾽ ἐν ὑπονοίαις πεποιημένας οὔτε ἄνευ ὑπονοιῶν, 378d5).
Nor was Crates' brand of allegory itself divorced from pleasurable ends.
Here I can only cite the likelihood, which a string of comparisons would
greatly strengthen, that Crates is the source for the following remark
from the Homeric scholia: "At the same time Homer gives the reader a
rest (ἀνάπαυσις) and brings in the *Hoplopoiia* (the fashioning of
Achilles' armour), which is also a delightful (ἐπιτερπής) κοσμοποιία
(fashioning of the cosmos)" (Schol. bT Π 793–804a).[121] Finally, if Jensen's
instincts are right, according to Philodemus, "Crates declared that [in po-
etry] primacy (ἡγεμονίαν) is conferred on the *words*."[122] Crates, it seems
clear, was an eminently literary critic.[123]

Pleasure, perception, lines, and circles seem to have come together for
Crates in a way that we can only dimly make out. Whatever else we can
say, his worldview begins in the realm of nature and physics (τὰ φυσικά).
It finds a sublimation in that of poetics (τὰ ποιητικά).[124] And there, poetry enjoys as much a claim to autonomy and "poeticity" (or ἡγε-

[121] Here we find yet another contrast with Heraclitus *Quaest. Hom.* 26.4: Homer "wasn't
delighting (οὐ τέρπων) his audience with poetic fictions, when he presented us, for example, with a lame Hephaestus." Other supporting evidence in favor of Crates' distinctive view
(and authorship of the remark quoted in the text) is found in Eustathius, Heraclitus, and
Athenaeus, all in contexts that point to the fusion of "nature" (φύσις) and poetic style.

[122] *PHerc.* 1073, fr. 1, 18–21 = Jensen 152 = F. Sbordone, *Philodemi de poematis*, 165. See
M. L. Nardelli, *Due trattati filodemei "Sulla poetica,"* xxviii, n. 54 a.

[123] The idea that follows ("and poetry uses the emotions as allies") is Longinian (17.1).
The term ἡγεμονία appears elsewhere in the papyri from *On Poems* and is distinctively
Cratetean. Note, incidentally, that ἡγεμονία carries none of the connotations of the Stoic
ἡγεμονικόν, and if anything Crates' use of the term is opposed to that strain of rational
teleology.

[124] Cf. Eustathius on *Il.* 18.607f. (1167, 30), a wonderful observation that probably derives from Crates too: καὶ ὅρα φυσικὰ ποιητικὰ πάρισα κτλ., "and note how the natural
and the 'poetic' are balanced," etc. Cf. [Plutarch] *De vit. Hom.* 216, with which contrast
ibid. 6.

μονία) as it did in the Aristotelian view of aesthetics to which it is opposed. Aristarchus chafed against this translation, but not as much as one imagines—not, that is, from the larger perspective of the history of criticism. For, ultimately, Crates and Aristarchus were making common cause against Plato.[125]

[125] G. M. A. Grube's opinion was overly pessimistic: "Our information is too scanty to make any real valuation of the contribution of Crates, and of the Pergamum school generally, to literary theory and criticism. . . . The evidence, such as it is, will be found in the study of H. J. Mette: *Parateresis*" (*The Greek and Roman Critics*, 132 and n. 1).

CHAPTER FIVE

The Neoplatonists and the Spiritualization
of Homer

ROBERT LAMBERTON

U P TO THIS POINT, the papers in this volume have dealt with readings of the *Iliad* and *Odyssey* in the major philosophical traditions of antiquity. Plato and the early Academy were conspicuously absent, for two reasons. First, although there is a great deal about Homer to be found in the dialogues of Plato, there is not what we could call a reading of the *Iliad* and *Odyssey*. The second reason illuminates the first. The stance of the Socrates of the dialogues toward Homer is unrelentingly hostile—backhanded references to the "divine" Homer aside—and the reading and interpretation of poetic texts, and specifically of the *Iliad* and *Odyssey*, are repeatedly and explicitly rejected as means of reaching the truth. Given this orientation of the fundamental texts of the Platonic tradition—an orientation that constitutes the Platonic extension of the Presocratics' reaction against the Homeric encyclopedia—it is indeed surprising that the later pagan Platonists should have so blatantly violated the founding principles of their school as to embrace the poetry of Homer, along with other early hexameter poetry, as texts of extraordinary authority.

That the later pagan Platonists should have a place here alongside the Peripatos and the Stoa is in itself something of a paradox. By contrast with those schools, they have suffered from the sort of opprobrium that breeds neglect. This was not true during the Renaissance, of course; and from the perspective of Ficino at the end of the fifteenth century, the extraordinarily well preserved writings of the Platonists of the Roman Empire, from Plotinus in the third century to Proclus in the fifth, and beyond, were essential keys to the meaning of the dialogues of Plato and to the secret doctrine they concealed. But the Enlightenment discredited those keys, exposed anachronisms, and surgically removed the accretions on the Platonic corpus with the goal of isolating and restoring the true thought of Plato, and putting Platonism (as distinct from Plato) in perspective.[1] Since the Enlightenment, later pagan Platonism has found its

---

[1] This process is documented in E. N. Tigerstedt, *The Decline and Fall of the Neoplatonic Interpretation of Homer.*

champions at the margins of the European intellectual community—colorful but decidedly odd figures such as Thomas Taylor and Stephen MacKenna. It is probably safe to say that during the past three centuries more poets than philosophers have read Plotinus, Porphyry, Iamblichus, and even Proclus.

The later pagan Platonists' commitment to theurgy as a complement to philosophy, their acceptance of a substantial body of metaphysical dogma that was simply postulated and never meaningfully tested, and finally their willingness to settle philosophical problems by appeal to authority, whether that authority was Plato or the Chaldaean Oracles—all these elements have severely limited the attractiveness of the writings of the later Platonists for most modern students of ancient thought.[2]

There are, however, a few areas in which these shortcomings translate into strengths. Specifically, the appeal to authorities from the past—so alien to the spirit of Plato and Aristotle—engendered an intellectual seriousness about issues of interpretation on a grand scale, about hermeneutics, that is a genuinely new departure. There are multiple sides to this issue, and we would look in vain for a global theory of interpretation in later pagan Platonism—indeed, in ancient philosophy generally—that might provide a basis for reading *any* text, for reading Plato, Homer, *and* the Chaldaean Oracles. Of these various foci of hermeneutic attention, the reading of Plato has attracted the most interest among modern scholars.[3] The organization of the meaning of each dialogue around a single topic, or more specifically, a single "end" or "target" ($\sigma\kappa o\pi\acute{o}\varsigma$)—the contribution of Iamblichus[4]—was an extraordinarily powerful move, and

---

[2] Augustine's treatment of the *platonici* lies in the background of this development. The main lines of his discussion are familiar: Of thinkers in harmony with Plato (whatever their origin or school), Augustine writes, "We place all of them above the others and declare them to be closer to ourselves" ("eos omnes ceteris anteponimus eosque nobis propinquiores fatemur," *Civ. Dei* 8.9). Finally, though, all pagan philosophy is declared inadequate—for all Plato's insights, the platonici remain polytheists (8.12). And Platonist demonology and theurgy, attacked by way of Apuleius (8.16–22), is dangerous and misleading. Augustine's exposure of the Platonists' weaknesses, their inadequacy, may ultimately have exerted more influence than did his praise.

[3] See James A. Coulter, *The Literary Microcosm: Theories of Interpretation of the Later Neoplatonists.*

[4] The principal text is the introduction to Hermeias's *Commentary on the Phaedrus*: ἕνα δὲ πανταχοῦ χρὴ εἶναι τὸν σκοπὸν καὶ αὐτοῦ ἕνεκα ⟨πάντα⟩ παρειλῆφθαι, ἵνα ὡς ἐν ζῴῳ πάντα τῷ ἑνὶ συνάπτηται. διὸ περὶ τοῦ παντοδαποῦ καλοῦ φησιν ὁ Ἰάμβλιχος εἶναι τὸν σκοπόν, ὡς ἐφεξῆς ἐροῦμεν. See John Dillon, ed., *Iamblichi Chalcidensis in Platonis dialogos commentariorum fragmenta*, 92, 2–5.

116

one echoed repeatedly down to present-day commentaries on the dialogues. The evidence suggests, however, that this principle was not extended to problems of interpretation beyond the one for which it was developed. Iamblichus gave high priority to defining the single σκοπός of the *Phaedrus*, but Proclus in hundreds of pages of discussion of the *Iliad* is not concerned with defining a single focus for the epic.

Like so much of the intellectual content of later Platonism, the interpretive theory and practice of these thinkers have principally Stoic precedents. Zeno and Chrysippus took archaic Greek poetry seriously, and numerous examples of their interpretive practice have reached us. Moreover, certain principles of interpretation can be derived from those instances. But what we lack in the period before the Neoplatonists is a coherent body of interpretive theory and practice in the reading of archaic poetry. If their account of the meaning of the *Iliad* and *Odyssey* is incomplete as it reaches us, it is nevertheless vastly better preserved and vastly more comprehensive than any other ancient reading, and even if we set aside for present purposes its very considerable influence and historical importance, this quality alone makes it stand out among ancient interpretive efforts.

I address two very broad questions here: first, "What did the Neoplatonists draw from earlier interpretive traditions?" and second, "What was unique to the Neoplatonists' reading of the *Iliad* and *Odyssey*?"

To the first of these questions, the apparent answer is that they took pretty much everything that came to hand. Neoplatonist interpretation as a whole is extraordinarily eclectic, and what is surprising is the ease with which interpretive material from other philosophical traditions seems to have been absorbed by readers like Porphyry and Proclus.

Of particular interest here is the relationship between the Stoa and the later Platonists, and although much remains to be learned about the interpretive theory and practice of Stoic interpreters, I would like to propose a general model for the relationship of Stoic to Platonic exegesis. Stoic exegesis, Stoic commitment to the meaningfulness of myth and of at least some poetry and cultic art, would seem to be related in a fundamental way to Stoic determinism. In a world where only bodies could act upon bodies, and where that interaction took place in such an inevitable manner that it determined the position of everything in the universe with mathematical precision, what would we expect the status of *cultural* artifacts to be? The question has been answered in various ways by various materialist traditions, but the only generalized solution known to me is the Marxist one, in which cultural phenomena become epiphenomena,

117

comprehensible only in terms of the relations of production and consumption that underlie them. This model has been extraordinarily productive, but whatever the Stoic solution may have been, it was clearly something quite different. What, then, might this have been? I think the answer can be glimpsed in the Stoic interpretive activities described by A. A. Long in his paper in this collection.[5]

The single tool, the single technique of Stoic interpretation that is most characteristic and most highly developed, is etymology. For both of our major anthologies of Stoic allegoresis, Heraclitus's *Homeric Allegories* and Cornutus's *Epidrome*, it is central and pervasive. Both of these collections of interpretive material are secondary, harnessing the interpretive theory and practice of earlier thinkers to specific goals—an introduction to the reading of Homer on the one hand, and an introduction to theology, or perhaps (as Glenn Most has called it) a "first textbook in philosophy,"[6] on the other. Thus, it is not surprising that neither work offers any theoretical justification of its methods. More discouraging still, however, both Heraclitus and Cornutus use etymology so freely and are so willing to bring forward and display contradictory evidence in a manner an unsympathetic observer might well qualify as fatuous, that any hope of recovering an underlying methodological coherence seems, on the face of it, futile. If we look back further into the more fragmentary evidence for the role of etymology in the early Stoa, however, the picture is not so bleak.[7] It would seem that, for Zeno and Chrysippus, language was composed of a series of primary particles with knowable characteristics, whose interaction throughout the history of articulate humanity produced the vast proliferation of words they observed. This implied physics of language is reflected by Philo (*De op. mundi* 148), who associates it with the naming activity of Adam (Genesis 2.19), and seems to be echoed by the Platonist Numenius in the second century CE (fr. 31.1–7).[8] If language itself has a structure of this sort, then early Stoic etymology must have taken as one of its tasks, one of its methodological mandates, the recovery of those primitive elements of meaning, whose scattered decay particles have arranged themselves in the world of human discourse just as inevitably as the lightest bits of matter have found their way to the top of the κόσμος and the heaviest have gone to the bottom.

---

[5] See above, 52–57.

[6] Glenn W. Most, "Cornutus and Stoic Allegoresis: A Preliminary Report," 2031.

[7] See Phillip De Lacy, "Stoic Views of Poetry," and most recently a lucid overview in G. Most, "Cornutus and Stoic Allegoresis."

[8] Cf. my *Homer the Theologian*, 46–47 (Philo) and 76–77 (Numenius).

This model gives us, of course, only a very rudimentary account of how the Stoa might have accommodated cultural artifacts in a worldview that was both materialistic and deterministic. That more complex utterances—say, the *Iliad* and *Odyssey*—should also come into being according to analogous processes is not, to my knowledge, explicitly claimed. But this sketch should suffice to help us realize the deep contradictions involved when Plotinus, Porphyry, or Proclus appear to take seriously etymological and other interpretations of Stoic origin. That a hermeneutics is inseparable from a metaphysics—if not from a psychology and a politics as well—is a principle central to much of modern thought on interpretation. How, then, did later Platonism, engaged polemically with Stoic and other "materialisms," find value in Stoic hermeneutics and exegesis? To answer this question, I would suggest, we need first to remove the emphasis from the problem of "materialism"—a polemic that often obscures the issues and masks deeper affinities—and look more closely at the relationship of Stoic determinism and Platonist providence (πρό-νοια). Given that the evidence permits us to formulate such generalities only with the greatest caution, it would seem that the status of cultural artifacts in the physically determined universe of the Stoa was not really so very different from their status in the Platonists' very different κόσμος, contained and structured as it was by the constant activity of divine πρό-νοια. In the "materialist" system as in the one that never tired of asserting its antimaterialist stance, phenomena were endowed with meaning by virtue of their position in a net of necessity, in a web of relationships that constituted the order of the universe. Viewed in this perspective, the Platonists' appropriation of Stoic materialist hermeneutics finds a belated echo in the activity of Walter Benjamin, the theological Marxist critic, who envisioned the "Angel of History" plummeting backward through time and watching the debris accumulate before him.[9]

This is not the place to begin the exploration of the (perhaps unrecoverable) process by which Stoic interpretive theory and practice were translated into Platonist terms, but there is one phenomenon that should be mentioned for the light it throws on the very large questions just raised. When in the fifth century Proclus formulated an account of poetry that postulated a triadal hierarchy of modes of poetic discourse, classified according to the relationship of sign and referent (*In Rep.* 1.177–99), he was clearly integrating an account of cultural artifacts into a broader on-

---

[9] Walter Benjamin, "Über den Begriff der Geschichte [ix]," in *Illuminationen: Ausgewählte Schriften*, 255.

tology.[10] For at least two centuries, the orthodoxy of the three Plotinian hypostases, The One, Mind, and Soul, had prevailed in Platonist circles. Something of the mystery of the relationships of these three levels of being—the true reality, to which the world of matter stands in the relationship of the limiting darkness to the radiating light—seems gradually to penetrate into every mode of inquiry, every question of meaning. The three modes of poetry are modes of experience, the poet's experience, transmitted to the audience in different ways. The lowest mode is the one that is mimetic (and hence the true target of Socrates' attack on Homer in the *Republic*) and is further subdivided into an accurately mimetic submode and an illusionistic one. In the psychological hierarchy, we are at the lowest levels of soul, in the realm of φαντασία. The next level is the one on which the poet's soul (drawing that of his audience along) turns inside itself, away from the envisioning of the material world, and focuses its attention on Mind. The resultant category seems to be, roughly speaking, that of didactic poetry. It is not mimetic, though its actual mode of representation is not clearly defined; it seems to be presided over, in any case, by Wisdom (ἐπιστήμη). Finally, the third and highest mode of poetry is characterized by the union of "the most unified part" of the poet's soul with "the One beyond all being." This, Proclus argues, is the characteristic mode of Homeric poetry, working through symbols (σύμβολα or συνθήματα) rather than images or imitations, and so immune to all criticisms of mimesis. And thus, such a passage as the deception of Zeus (*Il.* 14.153–351), whose impropriety, indeed obscenity, was an embarrassment, is discovered to be poetry of the highest mode, in which nonmimetic symbols "represent" their true referents in obscure ways—often, as here, by their opposites.

This very beautiful formulation represents an apparent revolution in poetics. Nowhere else in preserved ancient literature is such a semiotics of the literary artifact attempted. At the same time, Proclus is hardly to be expected to offer us original formulations. Much of what he has to say about Homer he attributes to his teacher Syrianus—indeed, the closing words of the sixth book of the *Republic* commentary identify the whole of Proclus's treatment of Homer as a dedication to the memory of his conversations with his master—and the debts, in turn, of Syrianus cannot easily be reconstructed.[11] The problem of the antecedents of this appar-

---

[10] R. Lamberton, *Homer the Theologian*, 188–95. See Table 1.

[11] See Anne D. R. Sheppard, *Studies on the 5th and 6th Essays of Proclus' Commentary on the Republic.*

TABLE 1

The Three Levels of Poetry ($\pi o\iota\eta\tau\iota\kappa\dot\eta$) and the Three Lives or Conditions ($\zeta\omega\alpha\dot\iota$ / $\xi\xi\epsilon\iota\varsigma$) of the Soul, According to Proclus

Soul	Poetry
First: Soul on the level of the gods, transcending individual mind ($\nu o\tilde{\upsilon}\varsigma$) and attaching "its light to the transcendent light and the most unified element of its own being to the One that is beyond all being and life" (*In Rep.* 1, 177.20–23)	*nature*: Absolute fusion of subject and object; inspiration, possession by the Muses; divine madness ($\mu\alpha\nu\dot\iota\alpha$) filling the soul with symmetry
	means: Symbols ($\sigma\dot\upsilon\mu\beta o\lambda\alpha$), which are non-mimetic [though Proclus is not consistent and sometimes seems to say that images ($\epsilon\dot\iota\kappa\dot o\nu\epsilon\varsigma$) of transcendent patterns ($\pi\alpha\rho\alpha\delta\epsilon\dot\iota\gamma\mu\alpha\tau\alpha$) may also occur in this, the highest poetry]
	examples: The Song of Ares and Aphrodite (*Od.* 8.266–366) and the Deception of Zeus (*Il.* 14.153–351)
	represented in Homer by: Demodocus
Second: Soul turns within itself and focuses on mind ($\nu o\tilde{\upsilon}\varsigma$) and wisdom ($\dot\epsilon\pi\iota\sigma\tau\dot\eta\mu\eta$)	*nature*: Again, fusion of knower and known—this poetry knows the essential truth and loves to contemplate beautiful actions and accounts of things ($\lambda\dot o\gamma o\iota$); It is "full of advice and the best counsel . . . offering prudence and the other virtues"
	means: Nonmimetic (as above)—based on wisdom ($\dot\epsilon\pi\iota\sigma\tau\dot\eta\mu\eta$)
	examples: The description of Herakles in the $\nu\dot\epsilon\kappa\upsilon\iota\alpha$ (*Od.* 11.601ff.) and unspecified Homeric passages on the parts of the soul and the arrangement of the elements of the universe
	represented in Homer by: Phemius
Third: The lowest life of the soul, based on imagining ($\varphi\alpha\nu\tau\alpha\sigma\dot\iota\alpha$) and irrational sense perceptions ($\dot\alpha\lambda o\gamma o\iota$ $\alpha\dot\iota\sigma\theta\dot\eta\sigma\epsilon\iota\varsigma$)	*nature*: This poetry is full of opinions ($\delta\dot o\xi\alpha\iota$) and imaginings ($\varphi\alpha\nu\tau\alpha\sigma\dot\iota\alpha\iota$); it shocks and manipulates the audience and projects a false image of reality; it is a shadow painting ($\sigma\kappa\iota\alpha\gamma\rho\alpha\varphi\dot\iota\alpha$), appealing to the emotions. This lowest level of poetry is further divided into: a) accurately mimetic ($\epsilon\dot\iota\kappa\alpha\sigma\tau\iota\kappa\dot o\nu$) b) illusionistic ($\varphi\alpha\nu\tau\alpha\sigma\tau\iota\kappa\dot o\nu$)
	means: Mimetic (using resembling images [$\epsilon\dot\iota\kappa\dot o\nu\epsilon\varsigma$])
	examples: a) Heroes fighting or portrayed in character performing other activities b) Descriptions of what *appears* to be, for example, the sun rising "out of a lake" in *Od.* 3.1 [rare in Homer]
	represented in Homer by: a) The bard ($\dot\alpha o\iota\delta\dot o\varsigma$ $\dot\alpha\nu\dot\eta\rho$) left to look after Clytemnestra (*Od.* 3.267f.) b) Thamyris (*Il.* 2.595)

ently innovative approach to the classification of poetry thus becomes very obscure, but there is one thing we can say with certainty. Among the ancient philosophical schools, down to the time of Augustine (who was about 55 when Proclus was born), it is only in the Stoa—and, on more recent and fragmentary evidence, among the Epicureans—that an explicit concern with signs can be found.[12] At roughly the same time, we see this concern with signs emerge in two related but contrasting contexts, in Augustine and in Proclus. All I wish to suggest here is that the dim prehistory of Proclus's classification of the modes of Homeric poetry may well include a Stoic formulation of just the sort we have been speculating about—one in which the relationship of this particular sort of cultural artifact to a materialist cosmology was explicit and developed along similar lines. Echoes of a hierarchical classification of etymological interpretations of individual words can be found in Varro (*De ling. lat.* 5.7–8).[13] The question with which we are left is simply whether the integration of the complex cultural artifact into a generalized account of reality was completed among the Stoics and left ready to be translated into the terms of a nonmaterialist cosmology by the later Platonists, or, on the other hand, whether Proclus's predecessors, working from a Stoic account that had carried that integration only to the level of language, should themselves get the credit for the step of showing how the poem fits into the κόσμος.

Something that is more certain is that the Stoic "theory of cultural transmission, degeneration, and modification" that A. A. Long identifies as the theoretical substructure of Stoic interest in myth was taken over by the later Platonists, but with significant modifications.[14] The primitive intuition lying at the source of correct theological knowledge—already a dubious postulate—comes increasingly, in the Platonic version, to resemble a revelation. It was, in any case, shared among a number of peoples—the Brahmans, the Jews, the Magi, and the Egyptians—and the proximal end of the chain, and simultaneously the touchstone by which all those exotic formulations were to be tested, was Plato, the successor of Pythagoras.[15] This formulation of the matter belongs to the second century CE, and it seems that already at that time archaic Greek poetry had come to have a place among the authoritative texts that were the bearers of those

[12] For an overview from Augustine's perspective, see Ralph A. Markus, "St. Augustine on Signs."

[13] R. Lamberton, *Homer the Theologian*, 46.

[14] Above, 52–53.

[15] See Numenius, fr. 1, des Places, and above, xx, with n. 40.

accurate theological intuitions. Later, in the third century, the process was certainly complete when "the Theologian"—a term that, without further qualification, generally referred to Orpheus in later Greek—could be used without ambiguity to refer to the author of the *Iliad* and *Odyssey*.[16]

The influence of the Stoa on Platonist interpreters from Porphyry to Proclus, difficult as it is to reconstruct in detail, is nevertheless pervasive and evident. Porphyry, at any rate, also knew and respected the interpretive theory and practice of Aristarchus, but that influence is to be found primarily in his *Homeric Questions*, from which the "larger treatises (or matters)—πραγματεῖαι" are explicitly excluded (Porphyry *Quaest. hom. Il.* 281, 8–10 Schrader). And although it is fascinating that the same Porphyry found no contradiction in writing as an Aristarchan in the *Homeric Questions* and as an allegorist in the *Essay on the Cave of the Nymphs*, which must surely be one of those "larger πραγματεῖαι," we must look to the latter work and the tradition it represents for the distinctively Neoplatonist reading of the *Iliad* and *Odyssey*. Here we find one more influence evoked, one that deserves mention before we move on to the problem of characterizing the original contribution of these readers to the understanding of the *Iliad* and *Odyssey*. Unfortunately, it is an influence even more obscure than those already discussed, concerning which any historical certainty is quite elusive.

Most of the interpretive ideas that Porphyry puts forward in the essay on *Odyssey* 13.96–112 are explicitly attributed to two shadowy figures of the second century, Numenius and Cronius, both of whom are characterized here and elsewhere as "Pythagoreans" (Πυθαγόρειοι). The fragments of Numenius, who is far better represented in the literature than his friend (ἑταῖρος) Cronius, make it clear that the most appropriate category in which to place his philosophical activity would be "Platonism," yet to the ancients he was unambiguously a "Pythagorean." It is by no means clear just what this means. It is tempting to go to Philostratus's richly imaginative description of a Pythagorean of the previous century, Apollonius of Tyana, for illumination, but unfortunately Philostratus's biographical novel is more concerned to define a style of life than any specific philosophical content. There is the further question whether these "Pythagoreans" of the first centuries of the Roman empire represented any sort of continuous tradition going back to the Pythagoreanism evoked in the dialogues of Plato, the tradition that flourished from the latter part of the sixth century until sometime in the fourth but then

---

[16] Porphyry, *De antro nympharum* 32. R. Lamberton, *Homer the Theologian*, 22.

largely disappeared from the record. To summarize a matter that yields reluctantly to such treatment, we can say first that there is some slight evidence for a concern with the interpretation of Homer among pre-Platonic Pythagoreans, and second, that it is not impossible that some thread of this tradition of interpretation survived to reach Numenius and Cronius in the second century. But even if this is the case, they represent a "Pythagoreanism" deeply permeated with Platonism, a tradition that appears to draw much of its "Pythagorean" content from the dialogues of Plato themselves, and for which those dialogues constitute authoritative evidence for the thought of "Pythagoras." It may in fact be no exaggeration to say that these "Pythagoreans" could more appropriately be labeled simply "dogmatic Platonists" or "esoteric Platonists" committed to the existence of a largely Pythagorean "secret doctrine" obscurely communicated by the dialogues of Plato.

The reason why these so-called Pythagoreans, alternately praised and undermined by Porphyry, are so imprtant is that they are the primary identifiable source for much of what is most distinctive in the later Platonist reading of Homer. The bulk of the Numenian material in Porphyry's *Essay on the Cave of the Nymphs* is made up, not surprisingly, of specific interpretive claims. The passage describes a cave with two gates (*Od.* 13.109–11). Numenius asserted that these were to be understood as the "same" as 1) the two chasms in the other world, as seen and described by Er in the myth in the final book of the *Republic*; 2) the astrological signs Cancer and Capricorn; and 3) the "gates of the sun" of *Odyssey* 24.12. Similarly, the "people of dreams" (δῆμος ὀνείρων) of *Odyssey* 13.112 were to be identified with 1) disembodied souls, 2) the Milky Way, and 3) "the light that binds heaven" of *Republic* 10 (616c). More claims of this sort could be cited, but these will serve to make the point that Numenius "interpreted" the myths of Homer by way of the myths of Plato, and moreover that he and the tradition he represented had before them an *Iliad* and an *Odyssey* that richly deserved the epithet "spiritualized" that I have used to characterize the Neoplatonists' reading of the poems. To these Pythagoreans, or esoteric Platonists, if you will, of the second century, we owe both the first evidence for an *Iliad* and *Odyssey* read as tales of the fate of souls *and* the first evidence for any reading of the poems that was holistic in the sense of reaching beyond specifics and interrogating the meaning of the whole poem, the whole story.

There had, of course, been earlier readings of the epics that stressed their unity. This formal concept is central to Aristotle's treatment of epic and drama, and from at least the time of Plato the claim that a text should in some sense possess unity is heard repeatedly.[17] But both the organic unity called for in the *Phaedrus* (264c2–5) and the peripatetic notions of the limits of the coherent plot are concepts largely unrelated to problems of interpretation. In both cases, we are dealing rather with descriptions— or prescriptions—that bear on formal characteristics of the text, not on its referents, whether διάνοιαι (Aristotle's usual word for "meanings") or ὑπόνοιαι ("sub-meanings" or "allegories"). The two interpreters of Homer for whom we have any evidence who *might* have attempted readings that were holistic in the sense that the Neoplatonic readings demonstrably were, are the eccentric Metrodorus of Lampsacus and Crates of Mallos. As for the latter, James Porter's paper in this collection now makes it clear that his well-documented obsession with spheres carried over into his hermeneutics. We can certainly say that variegated round objects in the poems—specifically, the two shields—under his glance leapt from the page to become cosmic symbols. But what we do not have, unfortunately, is evidence to confirm that Crates took the further step of relating either Homeric epic—as a totality—to the cosmos or to any other single referent. We are left with the scanty but tantalizing evidence that Metrodorus may have taken the elements of the *Iliad*—specifically, the *characters*, divine and human—and made of them allegorical representations of the constituent parts of the cosmos (fr. A4 D-K). Tatian says he turned "everything" into allegory (Metrodorus fr. A3 D-K); the list given by Philodemus (Metrodorus fr. A4 D-K) indicates that the mortal characters constituted an allegory of the physical cosmos (Achilles = the sun, Helen = the earth, Paris = the air (ἀήρ), and Hector = the moon), while the immortals, for their part, constituted a bizarre representation of the constituent parts of the human body or at least of the organs associated with the humors (Demeter = the liver, Dionysus = the spleen, and Apollo = the bile).[18] Realized or not, the impulse was there to organize the representational system of the poems on a very grand scale. We can only wonder whether in fact it had the coherence to provide a true precedent for the Neoplatonic hermeneutic program, which by comparison appears staid and sober.

At this point, without stating it in so many words, we have passed over into consideration of my second question: "What is unique to the Neo-

[17] See on this general theme most recently Malcolm Heath, *Unity in Greek Poetics*, and my review in *Ancient Philosophy*, forthcoming.

[18] The passage is mentioned by several of the contributors to this volume (3, 44, cf. 89–90). It was discussed by N. J. Richardson, "Homeric Professors in the Age of the Sophists," 68–69.

platonists' reading of the *Iliad* and *Odyssey*?" What stands out most conspicuously here is the *scope* of that reading. As we have seen, the philological tradition tended (as do its modern heirs) to reduce problems of meaning to two categories, lexical and syntactical. If the reader knows the meaning of the individual words (no small task, considering the idiosyncrasies of epic dialect) and understands the archaic, poetic syntax, then the reader knows what the text means. The more adventurous hermeneutic enterprises of the Stoics, and perhaps of the Pythagoreans, seem to postulate a vastly broader understanding of "the meaning of meaning," but as preserved they have in common with the philological tradition a tendency to look only at specific *elements* of a myth or text, in isolation. For the Stoics, the issue may well be that they simply had no concept of the poem—the *Iliad* or *Odyssey*—as the unit of meaning. That Homeric words and Homeric myths were of interest to them and fit into a larger hermeneutic enterprise seems undeniable, but that they posed the question of the meaning of the *Iliad* and the meaning of the *Odyssey* is far from proved. Their exercise seems *not* to have been one of textual interpretation.

Porphyry's *Essay on the Cave of the Nymphs* sets out to explain approximately fifteen lines of the *Odyssey*—a unique undertaking in the preserved literature, in that a detailed exegesis of a passage of some substance is offered. But Porphyry does not stop there. He examines the passage in considerable detail, exploring the significance of each element and its place in a larger encyclopedia of symbols. This cave at the center of the poem, described in curious detail and endowed with cultic significance, turns out to be a symbol of the world, the material cosmos. All its many other resonances either confirm or embellish this central meaning. But the conclusion sets Porphyry's essay apart from all earlier preserved Homer interpretation, and these generalizations deserve to be cited at length. Notice that, in an essay that has confined itself rigorously to the explication of a dozen lines, Porphyry now starts to reach out for context. The dramatic function of the cave within the *Odyssey* is on the surface relatively simple. The Phaeacians have left Odysseus on his own shore with a considerable treasure, incompatible with the beggar's role he has to play to regain his position. Athena tells him to put these gifts in the cave and provides him with the disguise of an elderly beggar. This immediate context is first evoked to indicate the status and significance of the cave:

Homer says that all outward possessions must be deposited in this cave and that one must be stripped naked and take on the attire of a beggar and, having withered the body away and cast aside all that is superfluous and turned away from the senses, take counsel with Athena, sitting with her beneath the olive, to learn how he might cut away all the destructive passions of his soul.[19]

That, then, is the "meaning" of the cave in its immediate context in the *Odyssey*. Next, Porphyry leaps to a much higher context, and here again Numenius is his guide:

No, I do not think that Numenius and his friends were off the track in thinking that, for Homer, Odysseus in the *Odyssey* was the symbol of man passing through the successive stages of *genesis* and so being restored to his place among those beyond all wavecrash and "ignorant of the sea"—[quoting Teiresias, from *Od.* 11.122–23]: "until you reach men who do not know the sea and put no salt on their food." "Open sea" [πόντος] and "sea" [θάλασσα] and "wavecrash" [κλύδων] are words that likewise in Plato refer to the material universe.[20]

The *Odyssey*, we are being told, is a poem about the fate of souls, and more specifically, *this* epic relates the progress of one single soul through the realm of matter (γένεσις), the sublunary realm of coming to be and passing away. On the one hand, it is still Homer who explains Homer—the true meaning of the cave by the sea at the center of the poem (*Odyssey* 13.102–12) is to be found through juxtaposition with the prophecy of Tiresias about the ultimate fate of Odysseus, two books earlier. But there are other contexts that allow us to secure this reading. The first is the

[19] εἰς τοῦτο τοίνυν φησὶν Ὅμηρος δεῖν τὸ ἄντρον ἀποθέσθαι πᾶν τὸ ἔξωθεν κτῆμα, γυμνωθέντα δὲ καὶ προσαίτου σχῆμα περιθέμενον καὶ κόψαντα τὸ σῶμα καὶ πᾶν περίττωμα ἀποβαλόντα καὶ τὰς αἰσθήσεις ἀποστραφέντα βουλεύεσθαι μετὰ τῆς Ἀθηνᾶς, καθεζόμενον σὺν αὐτῇ ὑπὸ πυθμένα ἐλαίας, ὅπως τὰ ἐπίβουλα τῆς ψυχῆς αὐτοῦ πάθη πάντα περικόψῃ (79, 12–19 Nauck).

[20] οὐ γὰρ ἀπὸ σκοποῦ οἶμαι καὶ τοῖς περὶ Νουμήνιον ἐδόκει Ὀδυσσεὺς εἰκόνα φέρειν Ὁμήρῳ κατὰ τὴν Ὀδύσσειαν τοῦ διὰ τῆς ἐφεξῆς γενέσεως διερχομένου καὶ οὕτως ἀποκαθισταμένου εἰς τοὺς ἔξω παντὸς κλύδωνος καὶ θαλάσσης ἀπείρους·

εἰσόκε τοὺς ἀφίκηαι οἳ οὐκ ἴσασι θάλασσαν
ἀνέρας οὐδ᾽ ἔθ᾽ ἅλεσσι μεμιγμένον εἶδαρ ἔδουσιν.

πόντος δὲ καὶ θάλασσα, καὶ κλύδων καὶ παρὰ Πλάτωνι ἡ ὑλικὴ σύστασις (79, 19–80, 2).

vocabulary of Plato (another hint that Numenius was principally concerned not with Homer but with Plato), where the same fixed metaphors can be found. The sea *means* the flux, the instability, of the material universe, in Homer as in Plato.

The next appeal, again to the immediate context of the passage, turns on an exceptional sensitivity to Homeric prosopography. It is the only ancient reading known to me that accounts for the centrality of the Cyclops episode in the *Odyssey*, an issue that is of interest *only* if the poem as a whole is taken as the unit to be analyzed. The sea god Phorkys is mentioned in exactly two contexts in the *Odyssey*. First, in *Odyssey* 1, Zeus identifies him as the grandfather of the Cyclops, and then, with no explanation, the harbor at Ithaca in *Odyssey* 13 is twice described as belonging to him (13.96, 345). This utterly marginal phenomenon, this bit of Homeric trivia, suddenly becomes central, the thread that bears the burden of the meaning of the poem. Porphyry goes on:

> I believe he called the harbor "the harbor of Phorkys" for the following reason. Homer provided us from the beginning of the *Odyssey* with the information that Phorkys' daughter Thoosa was the mother of the Cyclops whose eye Odysseus put out, and the poet did so in order that there might be some hint of a memory of Odysseus' sins right up to his arrival home.[21]

Odysseus, Porphyry is telling us, emerges here as a suppliant to the Old Man of the Sea, to Phorkys, whom he has offended by maiming his grandson. This in itself does not get us much further than the account of the "meaning" of the enforced wanderings of Odysseus offered by Zeus in Book 1—an account that has seemed inadequate to most readers. What, after all, does it matter whether one sea god (Poseidon) or another (Phorkys) has to be appeased for Odysseus to reach home? The whole business seems from almost any perspective simply contrived, not to say hokey. But Porphyry has a solution that restores the centrality of the Polyphemus episode better than most. He explains:

> It was not in the nature of things for Odysseus to cast off this life of the senses simply by blinding it—an attempt to put an end to it

---

[21] διὰ τοῦτο, οἶμαι, καὶ τοῦ Φόρκυνος ἐπωνόμασεν τὸν λιμένα·

Φόρκυνος δέ τίς ἐστι λιμήν, ἁλίοιο γέροντος,

οὗ δὴ καὶ θυγατέρα ἐν ἀρχῇ τῆς Ὀδυσσείας τὴν Θόωσαν ἐγενεαλόγησεν, ἀφ᾽ ἧς ὁ Κύκλωψ, οὗ ὀφθαλμὸν Ὀδυσσεὺς ἀλάωσεν, ἵνα καὶ ἄχρι τῆς πατρίδος ὑπῇ τι τῶν ἁμαρτημάτων μνημόσυνον (80, 2-8).

abruptly—and the wrath of the gods of the sea and of matter came upon him as a result of his presumption in trying to do so.[22]

The claims made in this strange sentence give us a glimpse into an ancient reading of the *Odyssey* that one might have thought impossible before the age of psychoanalysis. The narrative of the blinding of the Cyclops, it seems, was the externalization of an episode that in fact occurred deep within the fabric of the experience of Odysseus, that soul traveling through matter. The Cyclops—that Stone Age *homme moyen sensuel*—was simply the narrative expression of the life of the senses, the life embedded in matter, of the soul that is Odysseus. And Odysseus tried to put a violent end to it. He tried to kill himself. And *that* is why this specific act mattered so much that it condemned him to nearly ten more years of seafaring. And who are those offended divinities, who at the contrived narrative surface "bore grudges" that resulted in the enforced wanderings? Not the highest god (the Zeus of Book 1), not Athena (who is generally identified in this literature with divine wisdom and providence), but the divinities that preside over the sea of γένεσις, those δαίμονες who enforce the claims of this world, which, once entered, must be treated with respect. Porphyry knew these demons well—he had once been close to suicide himself, and his marriage late in life was explicitly a gesture of respect toward them.[23] Here he elaborates on the obligations Odysseus the soul has incurred:

These gods must first be appeased by sacrifice and by the hard labor of the poor and by patience. He must at one moment confront and conquer the passions, then bewitch and trick them, and so totally free himself from them that, stripped of his rags, he may destroy them all—and even so, he will not be free of his labors until he has become completely free of the sea, and wiped away his very experience of the sea and of matter, so that he thinks that an oar is a winnowing fan in utter ignorance of the business of seafaring.[24]

---

[22] οὐ γὰρ ἦν ἁπλῶς τῆς αἰσθητικῆς ταύτης ἀπαλλαγῆναι ζωῆς τυφλώσαντα αὐτὴν καὶ καταργῆσαι συντόμως σπουδάσαντα, ἀλλ᾽ εἵπετο τῷ ταῦτα τολμή- σαντι μῆνις ἁλίων καὶ ὑλικῶν θεῶν . . . (80, 11–14).

[23] See the *Life of Plotinus* 11 (suicide) and the *Letter to Marcella* 2 (propitiation of the γε- νέθλιοι θεοί). Cf. R. Lamberton, tr., *Porphyry on the Cave of the Nymphs.*

[24] οὓς χρὴ πρότερον ἀπομειλίξασθαι θυσίαις τε καὶ πτωχῶν πόνοις καὶ καρτε- ρίαις, ποτὲ μὲν διαμαχόμενον τοῖς πάθεσι, ποτὲ δὲ γοητεύοντα καὶ ἀπατῶντα καὶ παντοίως πρὸς αὐτὰ μεταβαλλόμενον, ἵνα γυμνωθεὶς τῶν ῥακέων καθέλῃ πάντα καὶ οὐδ᾽ οὕτως ἀπαλλαγῇ τῶν πόνων, ἀλλ᾽ ὅταν παντελῶς ἔξαλος γένηται καὶ ἄπειρος

The principle at work here is the same internalization that transformed the Polyphemus episode. Teiresias's prophecy, again, is Homer's narrative of the culmination of the quest of Odysseus the soul. "A dry soul is best," said Heraclitus, as these interpreters love to remind us, and to Porphyry and his tradition both Heraclitus and Homer clearly meant "disembodied" when they described a soul as "dry." The problem is how to shake off all that moisture, how to get wrung out. And so it cannot possibly be a matter of the ignorance of those landlocked yokels whom Tiresias tells Odysseus he must visit. The only ignorance that matters is *his own*, and if Homer's narrative screen projects that ignorance out onto others, it is our job as readers to reflect it back where it belongs and to decipher the complex screen of the fiction by restoring the centrality of the salvation of Odysseus.

The Stoics had long been accused of being perverse and intellectually dishonest readers, of making the early poets into Stoics. From the way the criticism is stated, e.g., in Cicero's *De natura deorum*, one may infer that the Stoics did not have a ready answer to the accusation. Porphyry's arsenal, on the other hand, is considerably more sophisticated. He is prepared to defend his reading from within the poem, and he is prepared to demonstrate its coherence in terms of a variety of larger contexts. If, finally, it turns out that this ancient text rather unexpectedly organizes itself around just the paradox that most obsessed Porphyry and his philosophical tradition—the relationship of soul to body, of spirit to matter—the modern reader may well be tempted to revive against Porphyry the criticisms leveled against his Stoic predecessors. He proves, however, infinitely less vulnerable than they had been, and the peculiarities of his reading of the *Odyssey* bring us up against issues that bear on the problem of reading itself.

Porphyry marks the beginning of the preserved series of readings of Homer by late-antique Platonists. There is no reason to think of his reading of the *Odyssey* as original, and as we have seen, its explicit debts to the Platonism of the second century are substantial. In the generation after Porphyry's death—roughly speaking, the first few decades of the fourth century—the influence of Iamblichus became the dominant one in Platonist circles, and we see little direct evidence of concern with the interpretation of poetic texts (aside from the *Chaldaean Oracles*). We do, however, have a great synthesis of Platonic Homer interpretation from

θαλασσίων καὶ ἐνύλων ἔργων, ὡς πτύον ἡγεῖσθαι εἶναι τὴν κώπην διὰ τὴν τῶν ἐναλίων ὀργάνων καὶ ἔργων παντελῆ ἀπειρίαν (80, 14–81, 1).

the middle of the following century, thanks to the exceptional degree of preservation of the works of Proclus, one of the last "successors" to the chair of Platonic philosophy in Athens. It is very striking, first of all, that both of these thinkers were exceptional for their concern with literature. Indeed, if it were not for these two rather aberrant figures, we might have been left with little more evidence for late-antique Platonists' concern with the meaning of the *Iliad* and *Odyssey* than we have for such concerns in other philosophic traditions. But both Porphyry and Proclus were literary figures, scholars, at the same time they went about the business of "doing philosophy" as that activity was understood in their time.

Proclus—probably the same Proclus to whom we owe the preservation of the summaries of the Epic Cycle[25]—devoted two massive chapters of his commentary on the *Republic* to the defense of Homer against the criticisms developed by Socrates in Books 2, 3, and 10. Here his agenda is set by the Socratic attack itself, but what emerges is nevertheless an encounter with the problem of the meaning of the two epics. The bulk of the defense is concentrated on details—on specific episodes, often specific words. But if we augment these chapters with evidence gleaned elsewhere in the corpus, we find before us an account to balance the Porphyrian one, with a commitment to certain principles that inform the total organization of the epics—and even the cycle—combined with a scholar's capacious knowledge of the history of commentary on specific loci. Little that we find among the detailed interpretations can be put in the category under examination here, that is, the unique contributions of the Platonists to the reading of Homer. But Proclus's account of the Troy tale as a whole complements what we have found in Porphyry and puts it in a larger context of interpretation.

Proclus does not set out to argue this "big picture"—in fact, he mentions it almost casually, in the context of a discussion of the myth of Homer's blindness (*In Rep.* 1.175.15–21):

> The myths want to indicate, I believe, through Helen, the whole of the beauty that has to do with the sphere in which things come to be and pass away, and that is the product of the demiurge. It is over this beauty that eternal war rages among souls, until the more intellectual are victorious over the less rational forms of life and return hence to the place from which they came.[26]

---

[25] See R. Lamberton, *Homer the Theologian*, 177–78, n. 51.

[26] ἅπαν γὰρ οἶμαι τὸ περὶ τὴν γένεσιν κάλλος ἐκ τῆς δημιουργίας ὑποστὰν διὰ τῆς Ἑλένης οἱ μῦθοι σημαίνειν ἐθέλουσιν, περὶ ὃ καὶ τῶν ψυχῶν πόλεμος τὸν

That is why Homer told the tale of the most beautiful woman in the world—to project onto his screen of poetic narrative an account of what draws souls into this world—and the war itself, on the highest level of generality, is a metaphor for the state that they are drawn into. Though it is not in Proclus, we know from Hermeias, his contemporary and fellow student in Athens under Syrianus, that this reading of the epic cycle was supported by etymology, an etymology that in this instance can hardly have been Stoic. From the perspective of the thoroughly iotacized Greek of the fifth century, *Ilion* (Ἴλιον), whatever else it might be, was clearly the realm of matter, ὕλη, which in Plato's time may have been pronounced *hüle* but now had become *ili*—in the encyclopedia of symbols, the terrestrial equivalent of that sea of matter that dominated the *Odyssey*.

When we remember that Proclus and Hermeias had learned from Syrianus not only the piecemeal allegories—the "true" significance of episodes in the poems, single words, names of gods, and so forth—but this "big picture" as well, *and* that they had at their disposal the semiotic classification of levels of poetry elaborated in Proclus's *Commentary on the Republic*, it seems clear that the later pagan Neoplatonists had fully realized something that is only dimly anticipated in the earlier literature. Drawing largely on ideas of meaning and techniques of interpretation from the Stoa, they had brought to completion the project we saw foreshadowed in early Stoic etymology. They had made a place for the cultural artifact—or at least for certain privileged cultural artifacts, including the *Iliad* and *Odyssey*—in a general account of the cosmos. Now, on the surface of it, they had considerable advantages over the Stoics in undertaking this sort of integration. They were unencumbered by the Stoics' materialist commitments—their position that only bodies can act on bodies—and this would seem to change the entire picture, the entire enterprise. But as we have seen, the world of the later Platonists bore, finally, a far greater resemblance to that of the Stoics than we might think. The pervasive divine providence, the spontaneous structuring of reality and experience by the divine, overflowing from the source of being, remote from matter, was not finally so different in its workings from the Stoics' fiery λόγος that kept every particle in the universe in its place.

What does seem to be different here, though, is the level of commitment to the artifacts, the epics, themselves. What we see in the two

---

ἀεὶ χρόνον συγκεκρότηται, μέχρις ἂν αἱ νοερώτεραι τῶν ἀλογωτέρων εἰδῶν τῆς ζωῆς κρατήσασαι περιαχθῶσιν ἐντεῦθεν εἰς ἐκεῖνον τὸν τόπον, ἀφ᾽ οὗ τὴν ἀρχὴν ὡρμήθησαν (Proclus, *In Rep* 1.175,15–21 Kroll).

scholar-philosophers Porphyry and Proclus, in very different forms, is a phenomenon that may be unique. That allegories of Homer were pervasive in the education and even the philosophy of late antiquity seems clear—a German scholar once described this allegoresis as a sort of weed, an *Unkraut*, proliferating all over the intellectual life of the Roman empire. But at least in these two instances, we seem to have something more: the elevation and integration of allegorical reading to a level that makes it look very much like the beginning of what we may call literary hermeneutics. This, along with the remarkably richly articulated theoretical substructure these thinkers provided for their acts of interpretation, is what makes these late Platonists at the same time the most idiosyncratic and the most disturbing of Homer's ancient readers.

CHAPTER SIX

The Byzantines and Homer[*]

ROBERT BROWNING

B Y THE TIME Constantine inaugurated his new capital on the Bosphorus, the Homeric poems had been schoolbooks for at least eight centuries, ever since Athenian schoolboys had learnt by heart the meaning of such obscure Homeric terms as ἀμενηνὰ κάρηνα and κόρυμβα.[1] It may seem odd today that children should be taught the art of reading from poems composed in a form of language which no one actually spoke or ever had spoken, but Greek society was not the only one that taught this way. Because of the very strangeness of their language, the Homeric poems were also, and of necessity, the object of close philological study in antiquity. Democritus may (or may not) have written a treatise on Homeric glosses. And the impressive textual, grammatical, metrical, and lexicographic studies of the great Alexandrian scholars laid the foundation on which all European literary and philological studies have been built.

The *Iliad* and the *Odyssey* were the earliest texts containing information on the Greek pantheon and the rituals of its worship, and hence they enjoyed the prestige of religious authority. As Greek religion became progressively moralized, they also acquired moral authority, as guides to conduct. The response to the critique of Xenophanes and others of the moral content of Homer was to see in the Homeric text a hidden meaning—an ἀλληγορία—that comprised either appropriate moral precepts, or a description of the workings of the physical universe, or an allusion to historical events. The great Alexandrian scholars on the whole despised allegorical explanation of textual difficulties—it was all too easy. But the Stoic philosophers, who saw all things as interconnected, imposed their own doctrines on Homer by wholesale allegorical interpretations—or so we have been led to believe, both by their ancient critics and

---

[*] Some fifteen years ago I published a short article, "Homer in Byzantium," based on lectures I had given in Britain and the United States. Inevitably, I will have to touch on some points mentioned in that article. But I will do my best to avoid the besetting sin of aging academics, self-plagiarism.

[1] See Aristophanes, fr. 222 Kock.

by modern scholars.[2] The Neopythagoreans and Neoplatonists in their turn provided a thorough-going allegorical interpretation of Homer that, filtered through the *Homeric Questions* (Ὁμηρικὰ ζητήματα) of Porphyry and his later, more directly philosophical treatise on the Cave of the Nymphs in the *Odyssey*, coloured Byzantine attitudes to Homer. I shall not take the time here to review the contributions of the late-antique Neoplatonists to the interpretation of Homer,[3] but we should bear in mind that Proclus's commentary on Plato's *Republic* contains in its fifth and sixth essays—at two rather different levels—the longest piece of extant continuous commentary on Homer until we reach Eustathius in the second half of the twelfth century. Moreover, the systematic search by the Neoplatonists for a deep and hidden meaning in the poems marks the climax of a long process of elevation of Homer from the status of an inspired poet to that of an equally inspired—and infallible—prophet, a man who had privileged access not only to the secrets of the universe but to the mind of God, in the sense in which this term is used by a modern cosmologist such as Stephen Hawking. Whether Proclus actually composed a commentary on Homer, as the *Suda* asserts, remains an open question.

An aspect of this investment of authority in Homer was that rhetoricians, whose real models were the Attic orators and later the writers of the Second Sophistic, began to lay claim rather implausibly to Homer not merely as the father of tragedy but also as the father of rhetoric—the archetypal windbag. Perhaps their status dissonance prompted this claim; they hobnobbed with the men of power without possessing much power themselves. Hermogenes, whose works became canonical in the Byzantine world, says that one would not err in regarding Homer's poetry as a "metrical panegyric" and that he was "the best" not only "of poets" but also "of rhetors and prose-writers."[4] Elsewhere he says that none of the ancients attained the right mixture of forms so well as Demosthenes did, "after Homer, of course" (μετά γε Ὅμηρον, 279.25–26). A little later, Telephus of Pergamum wrote a *Rhetoric According to Homer* (Ῥητορικὴ

---

[2] A. A. Long presents a very different view of the matter in his paper included in this collection.

[3] See R. Lamberton, *Homer the Theologian. Neoplatonist Allegorical Reading and the Growth of the Epic Tradition*.

[4] "Τοῦτ᾿ ἂν Ὅμηρος εἴη κατὰ τὴν ποίησιν, ἣν δὴ πανηγυρικὸν λόγον ἐν μέτρῳ λέγων εἶναί τις οὐκ οἶμαι εἰ διαμαρτήσεται. . . . ἀρίστη τε γὰρ ποιήσεων ἡ Ὁμήρου, καὶ Ὅμηρος ποιητῶν ἄριστος, φαίην δ᾿ ἂν ὅτι καὶ ῥητόρων καὶ λογογράφων. . . ." Hermogenes *De ideis* 389, 21–27 Rabe.

καθ' Ὅμηρον), in which he declared that Homer was the father of oratory, an opinion repeated by the Late Antique author of anonymous *Prolegomena to the Staseis of Hermogenes*: "Homer sowed the seeds of art."[5] Incidentally, the nine volumes of Walz's *Rhetores Graeci* contain at least nine hundred references to or citations of Homer, in which Homer's place as the inventor of rhetoric is again and again emphasised. An example is in Maximus Planudes' scholia on Hermogenes, *De Ideis* 1: "All who have pursued the arts of language give way to Homer, inasmuch as they have received the first principles and the seeds of their undertakings from him."[6] The same Planudes appends an autograph note to the text of Nonnus's hexameter *Paraphrase of the Gospel of John* in cod. Ven. Marc. 421: "One must know, moreover, that the reading of Greek literature is always something lovely and desirable for lovers of learning, and most of all that of the writings of Homer, on account of his eloquence and variety of diction. For this reason, the present paraphrase was written in heroic verse, for the delight of lovers of learning and of language."[7]

This reminds us that underlying all the pedagogical, philosophical, rhetorical, and other specialist interest in Homer, the *Iliad* and the *Odyssey* continued to be appreciated by some as the magnificent works of literature that they are, and that a thirteenth-century monk and scholar could see in them an appropriate mode for paraphrasing one of the central documents of Christianity.

Now that we have surveyed some of the attitudes towards the Homeric poems that developed in the course of more than a thousand years of ancient culture, let us see what the Byzantines made of this complex and daunting heritage.

First of all, Homer continued to be the schoolbook par excellence for all who aspired to something more than the mere ability to read and write. We have not much direct evidence from the so-called Dark Age—which was perhaps not so dark after all. But the fact that many of the same aids to reading Homer were in use in the ninth century as in the sixth is strong evidence that they were in continuous use in the interven-

---

[5] Ὅμηρος τὰ σπέρματα τῆς τέχνης κατέβαλεν. *Rhetores Graeci* (Walz) 7, 5.

[6] Παραχωροῦσιν Ὁμήρῳ πάντες ὅσοι τὰς λογικὰς μετῆλθον τέχνας, ἅτε ἐξ αὐτοῦ τὰς ἀρχὰς εἰληφότες καὶ τὰ σπέρματα τῶν ὑποθέσεων, *Rhetores Graeci* (Walz) 5, 505.

[7] Ἰστέον δὲ ὅτι ἀεὶ προσέτι τοῖς φιλομαθέσι ποθεινὸν καὶ ἐράσιμον ἡ τῶν Ἑλληνικῶν συγγραμμάτων ἀνάγνωσις, καὶ μάλιστα ἡ τῶν Ὁμηρικῶν διὰ τὸ εὐφραδὲς καὶ ποικίλον τῶν λέξεων· οὗ ἕνεκα καὶ ἡ παροῦσα μετάφρασις ἐν ἡρωικοῖς ἐγεγράφη στίχοις, πρὸς τέρψιν φιλομαθέσι καὶ φιλολόγοις.

ing centuries, and that the practice of the secondary schoolmaster—the γραμματικός—had changed little if at all since late antiquity, even if the number of his pupils decreased. Constantine-Cyril, the future apostle to the Slavs (b. 827) who had been unable to find the kind of education he wanted in Thessaloniki—he was an avid reader of the works of Gregory of Nazianzus but found the saint's language and style rather difficult—came to the capital to study. There, we are told in the Slavonic biography written a few years after his death, he learnt the whole of "grammar"—probably he studied the *Grammar* of Dionysius Thrax with one of its numerous commentaries, perhaps that of George Choiroboskos—in three months and then went on to Homer.[8] In the same way two centuries later, Michael Psellus goes on from elementary education to the study of Homer before beginning to study rhetoric. And in the last centuries of Byzantium countless manuscripts were written—evidently intended for use in teaching—that contained the first two books of the *Iliad*, two or three plays, selections from Pindar, some Theocritus, and perhaps some poems of Gregory of Nazianzus.

If Homer was difficult for Athenian boys in the fifth century, he was much more difficult for Byzantine pupils a millennium and a half later. Reading aids were needed. Some were taken over unchanged from late antiquity, such as the *Scholia Minora* with their elementary grammatical explanations and information on mythological and other matters. The *Homeric Epimerisms*, the first volume of a critical edition of which was published a few years ago by Andrew Dyck,[9] were compiled by an unknown Byzantine scholar, probably in the ninth century. Other reading aids were the work of Byzantine teachers, in particular the line-by-line and sometimes word-by-word paraphrases of the poetic text, which are often found written interlinearly. Little work has been done on these since the Appendix to Arthur Ludwich's *Aristarchs homerische Textkritik*, volume 2. Perhaps they scarcely merit profound study. Yet they throw light on the history of the Greek language, on pedagogical methods and aims, and on much else besides. They are the kind of texts to which the concept of authorship may have little relevance, because any schoolmaster was capable of modifying or supplementing the work of his predecessors. However, several distinct varieties or recensions can be identified. The paraphrase of the *Iliad* by Procopius of Gaza, which Photius read, sur-

---

[8] F. Grivec and F. Tomšič, *Constantius et Methodius Thessalonicenses: Fontes*, 99 (iv.1–2).

[9] A. R. Dyck, ed., *Epimerismi Homerici, I: Epimerismos continens qui ad Iliadis librum A pertinent.*

vives only in meagre fragments. Then there is the so-called Psellus para-phrase—in fact only a few manuscripts seem to attribute it to Michael Psellus and it seems too humble and pedestrian to be his handiwork. It is a word-for-word paraphrase, with scarcely any explanatory additions, and appears to exist in two redactions. A paraphrase of *Iliad* books 1–2, omitting the Catalogue of Ships, is attributed, probably rightly, to Ma-nuel Moschopoulos. It is lengthier and contains more explanatory addi-tions than does the Psellus paraphrase. Codex 454 in the Marcian library in Venice—the famous Venetus A of the *Iliad*—has an interlinear para-phrase in its earlier part, written in a much later hand than the text is, perhaps in the fifteenth century, which is independent of Psellus or Mos-chopoulos. Then there is a paraphrase compiled or copied by Theodore Gazes (ca. 1400–76) and dedicated to Francesco Filelfo, which seems to be an eclectic fusion of earlier paraphrases; it may well have been written before 1427, when Filelfo returned from Constantinople to Italy.[10] The interlinear paraphrase in Vat. gr. 1315 (probably twelfth century) appears to be independent of any one of the preceding. There are several other interlinear paraphrases in fourteenth- or fifteenth-century manuscripts whose status has not been investigated. Ludwich knew of two in the Na-tional Library in Naples. And last and most intriguingly, a fragmentary manuscript discovered in 1975 in the Monastery of St. Catherine on Mt. Sinai, written in a curious pre-minuscule cursive hand that may very hes-itantly be dated to around 800, contains an interlinear paraphrase of which only a few lines have so far been published. There does seem to be work for a Ph.D. student in these curious texts, which can perhaps be compared with the surviving paraphrases of Nicander by Euteknios and similar texts (though we must bear in mind that Nicander was not a "set book" in Byzantine education).

So the Byzantine child's first introduction to literature and to much else besides was through a text of Homer accompanied by an interlinear para-phrase or glosses on hard words and by an elementary marginal commen-tary that was essentially grammatical. Of course, the schoolboy did not usually possess such a manuscript. He learnt the poetic text from dicta-tion by the teacher, who then went on to explain difficulties in the text. Michael of Ephesus speaks of thirty lines a day as the norm, with only

[10] See Nicolaos Theseus, Ὁμήρου Ἰλιὰς μετὰ παλαιᾶς παραφράσεως ἐξ ἰδιο-χείρου τοῦ Θεοδώρου Γαζῆ. Nicolaos Theseus was a wealthy Cypriot merchant estab-lished in France, who played a notable part in raising money abroad for the Greek cause during the Greek War of Independence.

the brightest students reading fifty lines a day;[11] this is what "reading" Homer implied.

For more advanced students—perhaps those who aspired to become teachers themselves—stronger meat was available. The two great Venice manuscripts of the *Iliad* (Ven. Marc. 454 and 453), the Townley Homer in the British Library (Burney 86, written in 1059), and the Geneva Homer (Genavensis 44) with their rich marginal scholia dealing with textual problems, with mythology, with allegorical interpretation, etc., were not for schoolboys. Like almost all other surviving manuscripts of Greek texts, they are but the tip of an iceberg. We can dimly discern the underwater contours of another similar collection of exegetic material on Homer in the work by "Apion and Herodorus," to which Eustathius often refers in his *Commentary* (Παρεκβολαί) and which may be the source or a source of the Venice A scholia. Whether textual, mythological, grammatical, or allegorical, this exegetic material is all salvaged from the scholarship of antiquity and probably put together in the form of marginal scholia by Byzantine scholars of the ninth or early tenth centuries. The channels by which it was transmitted from late antiquity largely escape us, in spite of the work of generations of scholars, of whom the most recent are Erbse and van der Valk. Two features mark all of these collections. First of all, they are presented as authoritative; never does the compiler say, "The ancients say so and so, but I—ἡμεῖς δέ—know better." Second, they virtually exclude all Christian points of view. In both of these respects, the eleventh and twelfth centuries see a radical change. Michael Psellus's friend and erstwhile teacher Niketas sometimes gives a Christian interpretation of Homeric passages. For instance, the "dear homeland" to which Odysseus longs to return is the "heavenly Jerusalem." And Psellus himself gives a Christian interpretation of the Golden Chain in *Iliad* 8.19–27. This is not a matter of systematic Christianisation of Homer, which never took place, but rather of a recognition that Homer in a sense belonged to the world of his Byzantine readers and could on occasion be understood in their terms. Similarly, Johannes Tzetzes in his commentary on Book I of the *Iliad*[12] sometimes argues with the authorities whom he quotes, largely from the older scholia. His com-

---

[11] CAG 20, 613, 4–7.

[12] Edited in part by G. Hermann, *Draconis Stratonicensis liber de metris poeticis, Ioannis Tzetzae Exegesis in Homeri Iliadem* (1812) and by L. Bachmann, *Scholia in Homeri Iliadem* (1835), the remaining portion edited by A. Lolos, *Der unbekannte Teil der Ilias-Exegesis des Johannes Tzetzes (A 97–609)* (1981). A new edition of the whole by Prof. Manolis Papathomopoulos is in preparation.

mentary consists mainly of elementary grammatical observations, interrupted by quite lengthy allegorical explanations, summaries of mythology, and even by thirty-three political verses on the rise of the Nile flood. His sarcastic wit and combative attitude towards his predecessors are no doubt partly a matter of personal character and resentment of the course that his life had taken, but they are also a sign of the developing self-confidence of Byzantine scholars, a prelude to the great work of his younger contemporary Eustathius and of the often highly original fourteenth-century philologists. For Tzetzes, as for Eustathius or Manuel Moschopoulos, the scholars of antiquity and indeed the writers of antiquity were their intellectual contemporaries and equals.

These were not the only changes in attitudes to Homer in the middle Byzantine period. From being the preserve of grammarians—"a veritable treasure-house of grammatical irregularities," in the words of a nineteenth-century English schoolmaster—his poems became once again literature to be read and enjoyed by adults, if not in the original, at least in epitomes, and the questions asked by readers changed. They wanted to know how the stories told in the *Iliad* and the *Odyssey* fitted into the larger pattern of the tale of Troy. And they were interested in a sub-text or super-text of meaning not evident on the surface. This development, too, is part of "contemporising" of Homer, though its effects could be pernicious in diverting the reader's attention from the problems of the text itself. The most obvious example of this trend is in the *Homeric Allegories* of Johannes Tzetzes, written in 1146 for Berta-Eirene, the consort of Manuel I, as a kind of introduction to Greek culture. In 9,741 fifteen-syllable political verses, the poem begins with a long account of the prehistory of the Trojan war, starting with the birth of Paris, and goes on to offer interpretations of successive passages of the *Iliad* and *Odyssey*, sometimes, but by no means always, by way of natural, moral, or historical allegory—e.g., Apollo is the sun—sometimes by Euhemerising demythologisation—e.g., the flashing armour of Diomedes, which struck terror among the Trojans, was really the effect of mirrors—and sometimes by straightforward factual information. One can only wonder what the eighteen-year-old German princess made of this remarkable work. Perhaps not very much, for it was not completed until Tzetzes had found a new patron, one Constantine Kotertzes.

This was not the only indication of the new interest in Homer as literature. Tzetzes himself wrote the *Carmina Homerica* covering the whole of the Trojan cycle in 1,676 hexameters and drawing material for the pre- and post-Homeric sections from Byzantine chronicles, from the poem by

Quintus of Smyrna, and from the mythological handbook of Apollo-dorus. Compulsive writer that he was, he later added scholia to his text, which have been only partly published. In his *Theogony*, too, written for another Eirene, the widow of Manuel's brother Andronicus, he devoted 340 lines to a list of Greek and Trojan heroes of the *Iliad*.

Constantine Manasses's *Chronicle* from Adam to 1081, written for the same Eirene, devotes 433 lines to the story of the Trojan war. In his hands it becomes a rather different war from that recounted by Homer. Indeed Manasses criticises Homer because he "twists and turns" (στρέφει καὶ περιστρέφει). There is no mention of the gods. Few individual heroes are named or their exploits described. Hence Achilles stands out with much greater prominence than in the *Iliad*. Yet in general the picture presented is one of a confrontation of two mighty armies rather than a series of heroic combats. To a similar popularising tendency belong the medi-ocre treatises of Isaac Porphyrogenitus, *What Homer Left Out*, his *Descrip-tions of the Greeks and Trojans at Troy*, and his *Preface to Homer*.[13] The au-thor is probably to be identified with Isaac Comnenus, younger son of Alexios I, brother of Anna Comnena, and friend or patron of Theodore Prodromos.

The major figure in Homeric studies in the twelfth century is of course Eustathius. He was much more than a scholar, as his speeches and ser-mons as Metropolitan of Thessaloniki and his moving record of the hor-rors of the Norman capture of the city in 1185 demonstrate. His is per-haps the most attractive personality among twelfth-century Byzantine scholars.[14]

His immense *Commentary* on the *Iliad* and the *Odyssey* is marked by a certain gigantism, and few today have the stamina—or the time—to read it from end to end attentively. Yet it repays study. Features of structure and form betray the teacher, e.g., the constantly repeated "One must know . . ." (ἰστέον ὅτι), the detailed attention given to orthography and orthoepy, etc. Yet this can hardly be the text of his lectures. He was "master of the rhetors" (μαῖστωρ τῶν ῥητόρων) and taught rhetoric, not grammar, before becoming a bishop, though he may well have been a γραμματικός at an earlier stage of his career. The text is far too long

---

[13] The latter was published by J. F. Kindstrand, *Isaac Porphyrogenitus. Praefatio in Ho-merum*. The Greek titles of the other treatises are Περὶ τῶν καταλειφθέντων ὑπὸ τοῦ Ὁμήρου and Περὶ ἰδιότητος καὶ χαρακτήρων τῶν ἐν Τροίᾳ Ἑλλήνων τε καὶ Τρώων.

[14] Cf. most recently A. Kazhdan and S. Franklin, *Studies in Byzantine Literature of the Eleventh and Twelfth Centuries*, 115–95.

and too full of digressions to be suitable for school use. Eustathius himself gives us a clue to the nature of his work in the preface to his commentary on the *Iliad*. "It has not been written," he says, "at the behest of a grandee" (οὐ πρὸς μεγιστάνων τινῶν ἐπετάχθημεν) but at the request of his dear pupils, who hold him in high esteem. "It was my aim," he goes on,

> to go through the *Iliad* and to provide what is useful for the reader. I do not mean for a learned man, for he is likely to know all this, but for a young man who has recently begun his studies; or perhaps one who has completed them but needs to be reminded. I do not repeat all that has been written on Homer—this would be a wasted effort— my aim is rather to furnish useful ideas for prose writers who wish to make use of appropriate rhetorical subtleties, procedures helpful to those who wish to imitate the poet and admire him for his skill, words, mostly for prose use, but sometimes hard, rugged and poetic, which call for etymological explanation, maxims, by which Homer's poetry is adorned, factual information drawn not only from Homer but from other sources, too, myths, both in their pure form and allegorically interpreted, and a myriad other things both beautiful and useful. It can be read either on its own or in conjunction with the *Iliad*. It is not a continuous and uninterrupted text which might weary the reader, but each useful item of information may be read on its own and the reader may then go on to the next. It is organised in the same way as my commentaries on Dionysius Periegetes and on the *Odyssey*.[15]

So the commentary is not a text-book but rather a companion to the *Iliad*, to be read with or without the Homeric text, by adults as well as by schoolboys, and for many different purposes. It is noteworthy that Eustathius's autograph manuscript of his commentary on the *Iliad* (Cod. Laur. gr. 59 2–3) has a marginal index, in the hand of the author, to facilitate consultation. This is something new in Byzantine literature as well as in Byzantine scholarship.

Most of what he has to say is derivative. Much of it is based on a fuller version of the Venetus A scholia, on the allegorising scholia, on the *Etymologica*, on the *Suda*, on George Choiroboskos, on Gregory of Corinth, on excerpts and epitomes of Herodian, on Strabo, and on countless other often unidentifiable sources. The admirable new edition of the *Commen-*

[15] *Comm. in Il.* 1, 3, 1 – 4, 6 van der Valk.

tary by van der Valk makes it easier than heretofore to trace the sources of Eustathius's encyclopaedic learning. But the selection (ἐκλογή) and arrangement (μέθοδος) of this vast body of information belong to Eustathius alone. Unlike an ancient scholiast, he has an editorial personality. Thus he often cites without comment allegorising explanations of this or that passage. But in his preface he delivers a stern warning. Some, he writes, have completely put in the shade (ἐσκίασαν) the poetry of Homer, as if they were ashamed that the poet spoke in human terms (ἀνθρωπίνως) and have turned everything into allegory—not only mythical elements but what are admitted to be historical personages, such as Agamemnon, Achilles, Nestor, or Odysseus, and made the poet speak to us as in dreams. Others, on the contrary, have clipped Homer's wings and not allowed him to fly on high. Obsessed by superficial appearances, they have dragged the poet down from the mystical heights and permitted no allegorical interpretations, even of mythical elements. Among these was Aristarchus, and his example was not a healthy one. The better commentators leave the historical elements as they are and expound the mythical elements first of all as they are recorded, examining their fiction (πλάσις) and the plausibility with which a certain truth can be represented in myth. And finally, because of the natural impossibility of the mythical elements, these commentators abandon the physical representation and have recourse to allegorical treatment (θεραπεία) and explain the text either physically or morally or historically.[16] This is the voice of a balanced, critical, and humane literary critic, who loves the *Iliad* as poetry but who has no clear concept of fiction. But who had in the twelfth century? For Eustathius the *Iliad* is in one sense a contemporary text. He often illustrates or explains a point by citing a word or expression from the colloquial Greek of his own time or a feature of contemporary life. Thus he observes (on *Il.* 1.52) that the ancient Greeks used to burn their dead, "a practice that persists still among some of the northern barbarians" (ὃ δὴ καὶ εἰσέτι παραμένει τισὶ τῶν βορείων βαρβάρων). When he first explains the prosodic phenomenon of synizesis he quotes Herodian and then goes on to draw attention to a similar phenomenon in popular fifteen-syllable verse "now called 'political verse'" (ἄρτι πολιτικοὶ ὀνομαζόμενοι), which οἱ πολλοί often extend to seventeen or more syllables. If these verses are properly pronounced, "the fact that they have excess syllables is not noticed on account of the rapid running-together

---

[16] *Comm. in Il.* 1, 4, 11 – 5, 8 van der Valk.

of the vowels and the trochaic rhythm is preserved."[17] Yet viewed from another standpoint, the *Iliad* belongs to a remote past. Words have changed their meanings, and the reader must be alert to these semantic changes. He goes on (commentary on *Il.* 1.25) to give a list of words whose meanings have changed since Homer's time.[18]

Eustathius is a prolix and discursive writer, and to read long sections of his *Commentary* is a laborious undertaking. But he reveals better than any other writer the richness of Byzantine attitudes to Homer and to the whole of traditional Hellenic culture in a period of experiment, innovation, and reassessment. He is also the only Homeric scholar to have been recognised as a saint. He is depicted in fresco on the north wall of the church of the Serbian royal monastery of Gračanica, decorated in 1321–22, in episcopal vestments and with the halo of sanctity and the legend ὁ ἅγιος Εὐστάθιος Θεσσαλονίκης (St. Eustathius of Thessaloniki). The other saints portrayed in the church have legends in Slavonic.

The late Byzantine period saw more systematic and intense study of some classical texts than there had been in the twelfth century, but with little evidence of sophisticated scholarship devoted to Homer. He continued to be a schoolbook, read in extracts accompanied by elementary explanation and paraphrase. But the great textual scholars of the fourteenth century concentrated their attention on Attic drama and on Pindar, which offered a greater challenge to their ingenuity than Homer did. However Michael Senacherim, statesman and soldier in the Nicaean Empire, composed a commentary on the *Iliad* or part of it, which still remains unpublished and which probably survives only in fragments;[19] John Pediasimos, polymath, "chief of the philosophers" (ὕπατος τῶν φιλοσόφων), and Chartophylax of the Bulgarian church at the end of the thirteenth century, wrote an allegorising paraphrase of *Iliad* 1–4; Manuel Gabalas, *alias* Matthew of Ephesus, in the first half of the fourteenth century wrote several treatises on the *Odyssey*, some of which interpret the text allegorically.[20] Curiously enough, though a clergyman himself, he seeks to draw moral lessons from Homer without ever referring to Christian doctrine or practice. The scholiast of the Geneva manuscript of the *Iliad* (thirteenth century) compiled valuable scholarly material from a now lost manuscript or manuscripts. In 1336 George Chrysokokkes, physician and as-

---

[17] Λανθάνον τὸ πολύπουν ἔχουσι τῇ ταχείᾳ συνεκφωνήσει τῶν φωνηέντων καὶ σῴζεται ὁ τροχαϊκὸς ῥυθμός. *Comm. in Il.* 1, 19, 15 – 16 van der Valk.

[18] *Comm. in Il.* 1, 47, 27 – 48, 13 van der Valk.

[19] Cf. H. Hunger, *Hochsprachliche profane Literatur der Byzantiner* 2, 77, n. 102.

[20] St. I. Kourouses, Μανουὴλ Γαβαλᾶς, 168 ff.

tronomer, copied—or had copied—a manuscript of the *Odyssey* with a commentary that seems to have been in part his own work (Cod. Vat. Pal. gr. 7). In a manuscript of the *Iliad* written in 1275–76, there appear scholia by George Pachymeres, polymath and historian of the early Palaeologan period. These examples suffice to show that Homer continued to be studied and interpreted. However, commentaries on the grand scale, like those of Tzetzes and Eustathius, were out of fashion. Interest in the Trojan War remained undiminished among the unscholarly public. The *Troas*, 1,166 political verses in vernacular Greek, survives in only a single manuscript.[21] Constantine Hermoniakos's *Metaphrasis of the Iliad*[22] in 8,799 octosyllabic verses, was composed around 1330 for John Comnenus Angelus Doukas, Despot of Epirus—whose real name was Orsini. I once described it as "possibly the worst poem ever written in the Greek language." This was a rather harsh judgement, as Elizabeth Jeffreys has persuasively argued.[23] Both these poems owe much to Tzetzes' *Homeric Allegories*, as well as to the chronicle of Manasses. But Hermoniakos had at least looked at a text of the *Iliad* accompanied by scholia and had also made use of Euripides' *Hecuba*. There survive also a number of Byzantine prose prefaces to the *Iliad,* which provide in simple form the background to the story of the Trojan War.

Sometime during the fourteenth century—we cannot be more precise—an anonymous poet translated into vernacular Greek the *Roman de Troie* of Benoît de St. Maure.[24] Benoît was a relatively learned poet, a member of the court circle of Henry II of England in the latter half of the twelfth century. He knew no Greek, but he had read the Latin versions of Dictys of Crete and Dares the Phrygian, as well as the *Fables* of Hyginus, the *Ilias Latina* and the *Excidium Troiae*, the *Achilleid* of Statius, and some poems of Ovid. The translation, which in places is better described as an adaptation, introduced into the Greek world motifs that had survived only in the Latin West, though no doubt they went back to Greek sources. It also offered a view of the Trojan War perhaps fresher than that of the Byzantines, who associated it with their own schooldays.

Be that as it may, *The Trojan War* (Πόλεμος τῆς Τρῳάδος) is the longest poem in vernacular Greek surviving from the Middle Ages—14,367 political verses—and it is preserved in at least seven manuscripts. We can

---

[21] First published by Lars Nørgaard and Ole L. Smith, *A Byzantine Iliad: The Text of Par. Suppl. Gr. 926.*

[22] E. Legrand, *Constantin Hermoniacos. La Guerre de Troie.*

[23] E. M. Jeffreys, "Constantine Hermoniakos and Byzantine Education."

[24] Cf. H. G. Beck, *Geschichte der byzantinischen Volksliteratur*, 138–39.

fairly assume that it was relatively widely read or recited. Apart from 150 verses published by Mavrophrydes in 1866 and 100 published by Linos Polites in 1969, the poem is still unpublished. A critical edition by Manolis Papathomopoulos and Elizabeth Jeffreys is almost ready for the press. It will be interesting to study in detail how the bilingual translator handles his Old French original. What kind of filter did the Western material pass through, and what additions, if any, were made from Byzantine sources?

Several questions suggest themselves when one looks at Homer in Byzantium. One is why, for thousands of years, a profoundly Christian society learnt to read with understanding from a poem that was not only couched in an archaic and difficult *Kunstsprache* but was also thoroughly pagan in atmosphere and filled with divine interventions, epiphanies, quarrels between gods, and the like. Would it not have been simpler to begin with some familiar liturgical text, whose language and concepts would be already familiar? Dr. Sysse Engberg has recently drawn our attention to the practice of learning to read from the *Oktoechos* and the Psalms and then going on to the *Apostolos* and the *Anagnostikon*, a practice widespread from the sixteenth century if not earlier.[25] Around 800, George Choiroboskos composed Epimerisms on the Psalms, similar to the Homeric Epimerisms, which were still being used by a teacher in Constantinople in the middle of the tenth century. Incidentally, Gaisford's text of these Epimerisms is far from complete. So the idea of learning to read from Christian texts was not wholly strange to the Byzantines. Yet Homer's *Iliad* and *Odyssey* never lost their place as the school texts par excellence.

Another strategy would have been to Christianize Homer, as Epictetus was Christianized. Systematic allegorical interpretation would have sanitised the venerable pagan poem. Some hesitant steps were taken in that direction, but there was never a Christian Homer as there was an *Ovide moralisé* in the West. Indeed, it would be quite hard for the most single-minded allegoriser to elicit an unambiguous Christian message from the *Iliad*. The *Odyssey* is another matter; it could easily be turned into a kind of *Pilgrim's Progress*. But from antiquity, the *Odyssey* always took second place after the *Iliad*. There are fewer papyri, fewer medieval manuscripts, less extensive commentary, no paraphrase. Established practice was too strong to be radically changed.

The persistence of the *Iliad* as a schoolbook is to be explained in part by the inertia of the educational tradition. It was easier to do what one's predecessors had always done. The necessary teaching aids were available. One was spared the hard work of thinking for oneself. Another factor is surely that the fourth- and fifth-century church fathers belonged to the educated urban upper classes, for whom a familiarity with a limited corpus of Greek literature was not merely a badge of social status but the mark of full cultural development. They all quote Homer in their sermons, though John Chrysostom coyly calls him "a poet of the Greeks" (τὶς παρ' Ἕλλησι ποιητής). More than any other theologian, Basil propounded the view that Christians could profit from the study of pagan literature—though it lacked the authority of the Scriptures—at school and presumably in after-school years. This emerges from many of his great sermons, and in particular from his *Address to Young Men*. The date, occasion, and literary genre of this work have often been discussed inconclusively;[26] and the work is preserved in countless manuscripts—Boulenger knew of more than eighty—from the ninth century to the fifteenth. Its Latin translation by Leonardo Bruni (ca. 1409) was of great influence in encouraging classical studies in the Renaissance.[27]

But Byzantine interest in Homer calls for more than a pedagogical explanation. The Byzantines were well aware that their own culture and their own peculiar identity had two roots—pagan and Christian, or the "outside" (τὰ ἔξωθεν or τὰ θύραθεν) and "our own" (τὰ ἡμέτερα). History and tradition had made Homer the very symbol of a complex and tenacious culture that distinguished the Greek from the barbarian and also from the non-Greek Christian, Orthodox though he might be. It was a commonplace of Byzantine rhetoric, ecclesiastical as well as profane, to quote side by side a tag from Homer and a passage from the Scriptures, most often from the Psalms. It is a kind of shorthand of cultural and ethnic identity, the counterpart of Alexios I's defence of his seizure of church property to pay his army in 1083 by citing precedents of David and Pericles.[28] The importance of Homer to the Byzantines explains the constant use of half-proverbial tags from Homer by learned and unlearned alike, the programme of acculturation of Manuel I's German consort by beginning with Homer, and the learning and passion with which Eustathius expounds the Homeric poems, drawing not only on the accumulated erudition of a millennium and a half but also on sympathetic observation of the life around him and its habits of speech. But this element in Byzantine

---

[26] Most recent and among the most plausible treatments is that by Ann Moffatt, "The Occasion of St. Basil's Address to Young Men."

[27] Cf. C. Vasoli, "Leonardo Bruni," in *Dizionario biografico degli Italiani* 14, 621.

[28] Anna Comnena *Alexiad* 6.3.

culture did not travel easily. Christian doctrine and Christian literature had been translated from Greek into Armenian, Georgian, Syriac, Coptic, or Slavonic, but Homer was never translated until the Renaissance. It was not until 1444 that books 1–16 of the *Iliad* were rendered into Latin by Lorenzo Valla. Manuscripts of the Greek text had come to Italy much earlier. Manuel Chrysoloras almost certainly brought a Homer in his baggage when he came to Florence in 1397 to teach Greek. His pupil Vergerio had a manuscript of the *Odyssey* in 1401, as had another pupil, Palla Strozzi, in 1404.[29] By 1475 the Vatican Library had nine copies of the *Iliad* and four of the *Odyssey*. And it was a Byzantine scholar, born in Athens and educated in Constantinople, Demetrios Chalkokondyles, professor of Greek in Perugia, Padua, Florence, and Milan, and teacher of Politian, Grocyn, Linacre, and Reuchlin, who in 1488 prepared for the press the *editio princeps* of the *Iliad* and *Odyssey*, printed in Milan by another Greek, Antonios Damilas from Crete.

[29] Cf. R. R. Bolgar, *The Classical Heritage and Its Beneficiaries*, 498.

CHAPTER SEVEN

Renaissance Readers of Homer's Ancient Readers

ANTHONY GRAFTON

IN 1599 Johannes Kepler received a curious assignment from his old astronomy teacher in Tübingen, Michael Maestlin. The dean and professor of Greek, Martin Crusius, was preparing a commentary on Homer to prove that the poet had had encyclopedic knowledge of—among other subjects—ethics, economics, politics, and physics. He had interpreted the encounters of Homer's gods as favorable and unfavorable conjunctions of the stars named after them and had asked Maestlin to date them and describe them in modern, astronomically precise terms. Maestlin claimed to find the suggestion reasonable. But he thought that an astrologer rather than an astronomer should do the necessary computation. He therefore turned to his young protégé, who indeed served as provincial astrologer in Graz.[1]

Kepler replied by making fun of the whole enterprise. He urged Maestlin to take on the vast job of finding conjunctions and oppositions to match every divine conversation in Homer. "Why don't you," he asked, "read all of Homer, assign his story the firm chronological place which it still lacks, fix the individual colloquies to their calendar dates, do all the computations, and produce ephemerides for the whole twenty years?"[2] He promised that if Maestlin would work out all these dates and planetary positions, he, Kepler, would happily play the astrologer and interpret the effects of the planetary positions on the events Homer described. Kepler's offer was clearly not meant seriously, and Maestlin did not accept it. And the episode as a whole seems to encapsulate the collision of tradition and modernity—in this case of humanist scholarship and modern science. It seems altogether reasonable that the great astronomer Kepler could see—as an old-fashioned polyhistor like Crusius could not—that Homer was a poet, not a master of the sciences, and that a mathematical and astronomical analysis of his work would be a waste of time.

At least two connected factors have encouraged modern scholars to assume that the most innovative thinkers of the Renaissance rejected the

[1] Johannes Kepler, *Gesammelte Werke*, 13, 30.
[2] J. Kepler, *Gesammelte Werke*, 14, 45.

tradition of allegorical exegesis. In the first place, avant-garde humanists sometimes seemed to make a point of their distaste for allegory. The authors of the *Letters of Obscure Men*, for example, forged a justly famous set of letters in the names of the opponents of Erasmus and Reuchlin, revealing the ignorant way they read too much, not too little, into classical texts. Friar Conrad Dollenkopf writes as follows to Ortwin Gratius:

> I already know by heart all the fables of Ovid in his *Metamorphoses*, and can expound them in four senses: that is, of course, naturally, literally, historically, and spiritually—and that is more than the secular poets [humanists] can do. Just now I asked one of these fellows the origin of "*Mavors*." He offered a conjecture but it was false. So I corrected him and told him that Mavors was derived from "*mares vorans*," being a man-eater—and he was put to confusion. I next demanded of him the allegorical meaning of the Nine Muses. Again he was at fault. Then I told him that the Nine Muses signify the seven choirs of angels. . . . You will see that nowadays these poets only study their art literally, and do not comprehend allegorizing and spiritual expositions: as the Apostle says, "The natural man does not receive the things of the spirit of God."[3]

Even at the start of the Northern Renaissance, allegory seemed a survival of the fusty late-medieval world of the classicizing friars.

By the 1560s the classicizing friars were forgotten, and resort to allegory seemed to some up-to-date scholars not a traditional error but an inexplicable inadvertence: a pointless abdication of the historical sense that knew the difference between Christians and pagans. When Jean Dorat lectured on the *Odyssey* at the Collège Royal, he explained the plot as the story of the individual's search for virtue and read many characters and incidents in still more imaginative ways. Aeolus's sack, for example, he took as a manual of meteorology that Odysseus had used, a *Hitchhiker's Guide to the Aegean*; the incestuous matings of Aeolus's children represented the effects of the zodiacal signs.[4] Dorat's former student Joseph Scaliger reacted with just the sort of evaluation that any charismatic and hardworking teacher must appreciate: "The man's begun to debase himself and to amuse himself by finding the whole Bible in Homer."[5]

Professional humanists were not the only ones to find the relation of

---

[3] Francis Griffin Stokes, ed., *Epistolae obscurorum virorum* 1.28; for the Latin, 73; trans., 343 (adapted).

[4] For a study and samples, see G. Demerson, "Dorat, commentateur d'Homère."

[5] P. Desmaizeaux, ed., *Scaligerana*, 20.

ancient authors to traditional allegories problematic. Rabelais too insisted that Homer could never have had in mind the sophisticated doctrines and lessons that his ancient readers found in him. "Do you honestly believe," he asked readers of *Gargantua*, "that Homer, when he wrote the *Iliad* and the *Odyssey*, had in mind the allegories which have been foisted off on him by Plutarch, Heraclides Ponticus, Eustathius, and Phornutus [Cornutus], and which Politian has purloined from them? If you do believe this you are far indeed from my opinion, which is that Homer could no more have dreamed of anything of the sort than Ovid in his *Metamorphoses* could have been thinking of the Gospel Sacraments."[6] Allegoresis—ancient and medieval, scholastic and Byzantine, moral and physical—appears in such testimonies not as part of the classical tradition but as an obstacle to its recovery.

The humanists' eighteenth-century successors, the founders of modern, professional classical scholarship, found the sirens of allegory even less alluring than the humanists had. They treated it as of merely historical interest, as evidence not about Homer but about his ancient readers. And they insisted that a modern approach to Homer must begin from a rejection of the normal ancient approach to him. It is well known that Johann Martin Chladenius began the modern tradition of writing on hermeneutics with his *Einleitung zur richtigen Auslegung vernünftiger Reden und Schriften* of 1742. He argued, subtly and at Germanic length, that an interpretation must begin from the standpoint of the author and the traditions of the genre within which he worked. A reader who criticized Virgil for the chronological error of making Aeneas meet Dido, for example, was not astute but incompetent. He failed to realize that Virgil had not taken account of precise dates. All he had needed in Dido was a female protagonist for "eine angenehme, obwol Tragische Avanture mit dem Aeneas, dessen Umstände er sich ebenfalls nicht so gantz individuell vorgestellet hat."[7]

It is not so well known that Chladenius began his career as the inventor of modern theories of interpretation by rediscovering and attacking their ancient counterparts. As a young Wittenberg M.A. in 1732, he presided over public disputations by two students on "The excellence and utility of the Greek scholia on the poets." This meant, by the pleasant custom of the time, that Chladenius wrote dissertations, for a fee, which the stu-

---

[6] I borrow the translation from Jean Seznec, *The Survival of the Pagan Gods*, 95, n. 53.

[7] [. . . a pleasant, though tragic adventure with Aeneas, the details of whose situation he in any case did not imagine with such specificity.] Peter Szondi, *Einführung in die literarische Hermeneutik*, 63.

dents had to defend orally in Latin. Many such theses were routine biographies of a single ancient statesman or writer. But Chladenius was far more ambitious. He discussed the Greek scholiasts at length. He rightly insisted that any judgment of ancient scholarship must rest on the evidence of scholia and commentaries, because ancient critics could be seen there, like craftsmen in their shops, practising their trade and shaping the text of Homer. He thus showed that scholia both required and rewarded analysis. But he also showed that they were often composite in nature. Only the presence of originally distinct strata could explain their strangely variegated styles and mutually incompatible arguments. For all their richness, however, they could not serve as a guide to the modern reader of ancient texts:

> As long as the texts of the poets were valued, it was believed that an allegorical meaning underlay them. And in the old days it was the scholiasts' job to uncover this. But they strove less to uncover the actual meaning which the poets wrapped in obscurity than to do something far easier: to make anything at all mean anything else, and to invent multiple meanings for a single myth. As soon as they began to prefer their own ideas to those of the poets, they interpreted everything allegorically. Daniel Heinsius reveals to us how successful they were: "The Greeks deprived texts of all their force, since they removed all their factual content and, snatched up by the empty wind of their allegories, made up everything as they liked."[8]

Modern hermeneutics, in short, grew from soil made fertile by the ashes of ancient hermeneutics, and the one had to be burned before the other could flourish.

No wonder then that the enlightened scholars of the late eighteenth and early nineteenth centuries could not say enough against the ancient and medieval scholia they unearthed and studied with such zeal. The years 1788 to 1833 were golden ones for the modern study of ancient scholar-

---

[8] Johann Martin Chladenius, *De praestantia et usu scholiorum Graecorum diatribe prima*, 29: "Allegoricum enim sensum fabulis subesse, tamdiu creditum est, quamdiu scripta Poetarum in pretio habita fuere. Et olim illum eruere Scholiastarum officium reputatum est. Hi tamen non admodum diu in illo quem Poetae ipsi fabularum tenebris involverunt eruendo laborarunt, quin potius, quod factu multo erat facilius, quidvis ad quodvis transtulerunt, uniusque fabulae multiplicem sensum confinxerunt. Mox etiam, ubi semel suis magis quam Poetae sententiis delectari inciperant, nihil non Allegorice interpretati sunt, quam vero infelici successu, ex Dan. Heinsio discemus, qui de hac re ita loquitur: Graeci, inquit, omnibus scriptis vim suam eripuerunt, cum nihil Pragmaticum in illis relinquunt, sed vento inani Allegoriarum abrepti, omnia pro nutu fingunt."

ship. They saw the publication of the A and B scholia on the *Iliad*, the partial publication of the Li and Townley scholia, and the efforts of giants like Heyne, Wolf, and Lehrs to excavate from this mass of rubble the history of ancient Homeric philology. But they also saw the Greek commentators and scholiasts definitively dismissed as fools, as incompetents who had not so much got hold of the wrong end of the stick as of the wrong stick. Heyne complained that the scholiasts offered only "*inanes . . . argutiae*" [empty sophistries] and "copious explanations of points that were clear in themselves." Reiske described the Demosthenes scholia as typical: "emptier than a nut with no meat, futile, footling, trivial, foolish." Even C. D. Beck, who published as late as 1785 a curious essay arguing that the scholia could sharpen a modern scholar's sense "of elegance and charm," had to admit that the scholiasts said little of interest about the larger structures of ancient literary works and often missed the points of the smaller episodes on which they concentrated.[9] Karl Lehrs, the great specialist on Aristarchus and other Alexandrian textual critics, warned that "not a single word should be believed" in the exegetical scholia—as opposed to the A scholia with their detailed information on ancient textual criticism.[10] Those who despised ancient and medieval interpreters so thoroughly could hardly imagine that they had been primary models for the first modern scholars in the fifteenth and sixteenth centuries.

In fact, however, Renaissance scholarship was far more complex and ambiguous than scholars of an older generation were willing to accept. Francis Bacon, for example, was long considered a purely modern figure, the great prophet of empiricism who met a modern martyr's death when he left his carriage to investigate the possibility of preserving a chicken by stuffing it with snow—and caught pneumonia. But Charles Lemmi, Paolo Rossi, and others have shown that he took the allegorical tradition in mythography as seriously as the lard that he nailed on his windowsill so that his warts would disappear as it rotted. He saw the Homeric and other myths as the remnants of a lost Greek cosmology far more profound than those of Plato and Aristotle and tried to reconstruct it by plagiarizing allegorists like Natalis Comes.[11] Even Rabelais's preface to *Gargantua* has

[9] For a more detailed account, see Anthony Grafton, "*Prolegomena* to Friedrich August Wolf," 111–19; F. A. Wolf, *Prolegomena to Homer [1795]*, 12–14.

[10] See Martin Schmidt, *Die Erklärungen zum Weltbild Homers und zur Kultur der Heroenzeit in den bT-Scholien zur Ilias*, 3–6.

[11] Charles Lemmi, *The Classic Deities in Bacon*; Paolo Rossi, *Francis Bacon: From Magic to Science*, ch. 2.

turned out, on close recent inspection, to be a complex and difficult document, at least as much an invitation to, as a critique of, allegorical reading, and closely related to Erasmian texts on the same theme.[12] And those whose main interests lay in the interpretation of classical texts studied ancient hermeneutics with the same fascination that they brought to the study of ancient literary texts. When Homer reappeared in the West in 1488, the smooth hulls of the epics were already barnacled with ancient parasites that affected their progress: the Herodotean and Plutarchan lives of Homer and Dio's *Oratio* 53. The sixteenth century buried the texts more and more deeply in retrieved ancient interpretation: the short "scholia Didymi" in 1517, Porphyry's *Homeric Questions* and *Cave of the Nymphs* in Greek in 1524, Proclus's defense of Homer in 1534, the Roman edition of Eustathius in 1542–50, and the *Homeric Allegories* of Heraclitus in Greek in 1505 and in Latin in 1544.[13] Equipped with so many polarized lenses to hold between themselves and the text, most Renaissance humanists naturally did not see Homer plain.

Angelo Poliziano, for example, was perhaps the most historically acute and philologically discriminating Western Hellenist of the fifteenth century. His early scholia on the *Iliad* included an elaborate physical allegory of the Homeric gods, drawn from a work by Demetrius Triclinius. He enriched his interpretative arsenal with other equipment as well, including a Neo-Platonic reading of the two Venuses, which enabled him to make sense of the mortal Diomedes' wounding of Aphrodite: "Venus is wounded in the hand because Plato's heavenly Venus, when polluted in the sense of touch, becomes the vulgar [earthly] one."[14] In his mature years as a professor at the Florentine Studio, he stuffed his prose oration in praise of Homer with allegories drawn from the Plutarchan life. Indeed, even the one famous passage in the oration that seems to stand out as non-allegorical—Poliziano's enthusiastic praise of Homer's ability to compose verse extemporaneously, as it were by inspiration—does not reflect precocious insight into oral poetry.[15] Rather, it shows that Poliziano

---

[12] See Terence Cave, *The Cornucopian Text*; E. M. Duval, "Interpretation and the 'Doctrine absconce' of Rabelais' Prologue to *Gargantua*"; G. Defaux, "D'un problème à l'autre: herméneutique de l'*altior sensus* et *captatio lectoris* dans le Prologue de *Gargantua*"; T. Cave, M. Jeanneret, and F. Rigolot, "Sur la prétendue transparence de Rabelais"; G. Defaux, "Sur la prétendue pluralité du Prologue de 'Gargantua.' "

[13] J. Seznec, *The Survival of the Pagan Gods*; D. C. Allen, *Mysteriously Meant*; P. Ford, "Conrad Gesner et le fabuleux manteau."

[14] A. Levine Rubenstein, "The Notes to Poliziano's 'Iliad.' "

[15] Poliziano, *Opera*, 3 (Lyons, 1537), 68: "Extantque adhuc non pauca canente illo excepta

had read not only the Plutarchan but also the Herodotean life of Homer. This quotes several cute epigrams by Homer and devises biographical anecdotes—presumably by back formation—to account for their extemporaneous composition. No wonder that Homer seemed to Poliziano the paradigm of facility as well as the source of all the sciences and arts.

Erasmus was a brilliant textual and historical critic. He saw through the correspondence of Seneca with St. Paul and the corpus of Pseudo-Dionysius the Areopagite. He knew perfectly well that the works of the ancients came from a classical world fundamentally different from his own Christian one, as his polemical dialogue *Ciceronianus* makes plain. Yet in his manual on Latin composition, the *De duplici rerum ac verborum copia*, he used ancient hermeneutics as well as his own joyous command of the resources of Latin to give the intending Latinist ways of filling pages. He discussed figures of thought as well as figures of speech, and one of the most useful of these was the allegorical tradition known from ancient and Byzantine Homeric commentary:

> [Fables] can be related both fully and briefly, if circumstances and propriety allow. But in the case of those that are wholly lacking in credibility, it is well to have a preface, unless we are joking, to the effect that they were composed with good reason by the wisest men of olden time, and that not without reason have they been honored by the general agreement of men for so many ages. Then we will explain what they meant: For example, if one wished to urge that that should not be sought after which is not consistent with one's nature, he would say that the ancient and wise writers perceived this with discernment and expressed it in a most fitting composition, the traditional fable of the Giants whose rash undertakings ended unhappily. Or if one should propose that the avaricious man does not so much have what he has, as what he does not have, he would use the fable of Tantalus with a preface. . . . Moreover, although the allegorical method is not encountered everywhere to the same extent, nevertheless, it is beyond question that in the skillful authors of antiquity, in all the creations of the ancient poets, allegory is found,

poemata, quae prout a quoque bene maleque acceptus fuerat, continuo in eum subito quodam repentinoque instinctu et ferente (ut aiunt) flatu proferebantur, ut facile intelligantur non quasi sub incudem venisse humanae fabricae, sed divino quodam impulsu instinctuque, velut e cortina atque adyto sacris esse excussa praecordiis. . . ." The reference to individuals' treatment of Homer as the proximate cause of his poems points clearly to the Herodotean *Life*.

either historical, as in Hercules' battle with the two-mouthed Achelous; or theological, as in the example of Proteus turning himself into all kinds of shapes, or Pallas born from the brain of Jove; or scientific, as in the fable of Phaethon; or moral, as in the case of those men whom Circe turned into brute animals by a magic potion and her wand. . . . But not to be too tedious, Eustathius, the Homeric commentator will supply any number of interpretations of this kind.[16]

The trained humanist writer, as this passage shows, had to begin by being a trained humanist reader. And to become that, he clearly had to ascend through all the levels of allegory that the ancients had employed in explicating Homer the moralist, scientist, and theologian. No wonder that so many vernacular writers of the sixteenth century incorporated such readings into their own modern epics—or even their novels, in the case of that purported critic of the allegorists, Rabelais.[17]

Throughout the sixteenth and seventeenth centuries, then, Homer the Theologian—like his brothers Homer the Physicist and Homer the Moralist—was a familiar figure in classroom and study. Introductory orations to course after course praised his inspiration and erudition. Genealogists of philosophy, science, and even technology treated him as the fountainhead of learning as well as of poetry. For all the differences of emphasis and intonation that separated a Melanchthon from an Erasmus, or a Scaliger from a Dorat, few Renaissance scholars would have disagreed with the traditional assertions of Homer's profundity, morality, and learning that filled—for example—Chapman's prefaces to his translation: "out of him, according to our most graue and iudicial *Plutarch*, are all Arts deduced, confirmed, or illustrated."[18] Certainly the great French scholar Jean de Sponde would not have done so; after all his Latin prefatory matter, itself steeped in the ancient interpreters, taught Chapman that "So kings hide their treasures & counsels from the vulgar, *ne euilescant* [lest they be vulgarized] (saith our *Spond.*): we haue example sacred enough, that true Poesies humility, pouerty & contempt are badges of diuinity, not uanity."[19] An international consensus recognized Homer as a sage and saw allegoresis as the Ariadne's thread that could lead the reader through

[16] Erasmus, *De utraque verborum ac rerum copia lib. ii*, 2.11 (Amsterdam, 1645), 241–44; *On Copia of Words and Ideas*, D. B. King and H. Rix, trs., 70–71.

[17] See esp. Michael Murrin, *The Allegorical Epic*.

[18] J. E. Spingarn, ed., *Critical Essays of the Seventeenth Century*, 1, 67.

[19] J. E. Spingarn, ed., *Critical Essays*, 1, 68; cf. F. L. Schoell, *Etudes sur l'humanisme continental en Angleterre*, 162–77.

the maze of his poems to the core of truth. If Scaliger mocked Dorat's Homeric allegories, his fellow student Willem Canter—a pioneer in the study of Greek metrics—seized on them and vulgarized them in a famous chapter of his *Novae lectiones*.[20] And Ronsard fervently thanked the Hellenist who had taught him how poets concealed high truths in their verses.

At this point we seem to confront a paradox. Avant-garde humanists both ridiculed and practiced the various forms of allegory when reading Homer. The Renaissance both revived the epics and repressed them; both read them in the light of their original, pagan, historical context and explained them as veiled statements of timeless truths that Christians as well as pagans embraced. But in fact, the paradox is largely artificial. Modern scholars, long apprised of the rich information in the Venice A and B scholia and elsewhere and schooled in the history of ancient scholarship, naturally see allegorical and historical forms of reading as contradictory— as their ancient predecessors in the Alexandrian Museum also did. Until very recently, moreover, they were schooled to side with Aristarchus against the allegorists, whose reasoning was more likely to be smirked at than sympathetically explicated even by specialists.

Renaissance scholars, however, did not enjoy the benefits—or suffer from the limitations—of a modern classical education. They received the ancient allegorists as part of the same classical heritage that included the ancient texts they explicated. And they took them not as innocent misreaders of canonical texts but, for the most part, as scrupulous explicators of inspired classics who used allegory critically and sparingly. This was, after all, the genuine spirit of such ancient allegorists as Porphyry—who explicitly distinguished between unforced allegories, like his own reading of *The Cave of the Nymphs* (36), and forced ones, like the (possibly comic) Christian allegorization of the conflict of Achilles and Hector as that of Christ and the Devil that he mocked in a lost work.[21] No wonder, then, that the ancient allegorists seemed to their Renaissance readers to offer not quaint updatings of unseemly bits of Homer but highly rational judgments about which allegories did and which did not carry conviction. Heraclitus, for example, already reported the ancient suggestion that

[20] P. de Nolhac, *Ronsard et l'humanisme*; Frances A. Yates, *The French Academies of the Sixteenth Century*, ch. 2. For more detailed accounts of the Renaissance's varied reception of ancient Homeric allegoresis, see Noémi Hepp,"Homère en France au xvie siècle"; T. Bleicher, *Homer in der deutschen Literatur (1450–1740)*.

[21] G. Binder, "Eine Polemik des Porphyrios gegen die allegorische Auslegung des Alten Testaments durch die Christen."

Crusius and Maestlin revived in their own language: that Homer's conjunctions of the gods were astronomical. But he did more: He rejected it as fanciful, just as Kepler would—and may well have been the source for Kepler's criticism as well as for Crusius's project (Heraclitus *Quaest. Hom.* 54; cf. Plutarch *De aud. po.*19e). Similarly, Henry Reynolds derived his preference for physical over moral allegories from the Stoic materials preserved by Cicero and others, rather than from a modern consciousness that moral allegoresis did not fit Homer.[22]

An explicitly discriminating allegorist like Palaephatus could win the interest of the most discerning modern rationalists, from Joseph Scaliger in the sixteenth century to Lodewijk Caspar Valckenaer in the eighteenth. Scaliger made ruthless fun of Dorat's theological allegories. But he eagerly accepted and embroidered on Palaephatus's theories that Daedalus's moving statues had had their legs separated and that Scylla had been a fast pirate ship.[23] Valckenaer headed one page of his notes on the ancient *mythographi* with the fundamental and traditional question, *Quid sub fabulis?*—only to give himself the dustiest of answers, *nihil.*[24] Yet he too found in Palaephatus's reductions of rich myths to dry facts the "simplex veritatis . . . sigillum."[25] It was not until the very end of the eighteenth century that F. A. Wolf definitively relegated ancient allegorical readings of Homer to the realm of history. Before his time even the sharpest critics of some forms of allegory—like his own teacher C. G. Heyne—were normally not modern Aristarchuses, opponents of all allegories, but modern Porphyrys, who thought that they themselves knew where to draw the obscure but vital line that the targets of their criticism overstepped.[26] And some of the sharpest early students of ancient allegoresis, like Chladenius, drew their insights from what would now seem unexpected sources—in his case, the preface to Eustathius's commentary on the *Iliad*, which seemed to him a model call for restraint in reading.[27]

---

[22] A. M. Cinquemani, "Henry Reynolds' *Mythomystes* and the Continuity of Ancient Modes of Allegoresis in Seventeenth-Century England."

[23] J. C. Scaliger, *Thesaurus temporum*, 2d ed. (Amsterdam, 1658), *Animadversiones in chronologica Eusebii*, 45, 54; Scaliger took Daedalus's statues as genuine αὐτοκίνητα filled with quicksilver, thus going even farther than Palaephatus did, but in the same direction; on Scylla he liked what Palaephatus had to say.

[24] [What is beneath the myths? . . . Nothing.] Leiden University Library MS BPL 396, fol. 69 recto.

[25] [the plain stamp of truth] Leiden University Library MS BPL 394, fol. 4 verso: "Quod vero Palaephatus Scyllam triremem faciat, minus placet et simplex veritatis quod in aliis capp. elucet sigillum non habet. de figura enim plane silet."

[26] M. Murrin, *The Allegorical Epic.*

[27] J. M. Chladenius, *De praestantia*, 29: "A duobus igitur potissimum Scholiastarum vitiis

In the end, the humanists' reactions to ancient readings of Homer were far too complex to be summed up neatly. Their intellectual project had many strands. They discovered the historical distance that really separated the Christian present from the pagan past. They reasserted the special power, even the autonomy, of classical poetry. But they also compiled meticulous, myth-by-myth compendia of traditional allegories.[28] Their historical situation forced this range of approaches on them. Unlike the Alexandrian scholars, after all, early modern humanists had to win their way gradually and with difficulty to a full knowledge of Greek literature and its history. Unlike the Alexandrians, too, most of them dealt with Homer in a variety of contexts: as a subject to be sold to bored students, as a text to be made safe for the classroom, as a model for imitation by modern vernacular poets, and as a source for historical facts or philosophical doctrines. In many of these situations, it was natural to assume that allegoresis provided a trustworthy as well as useful means for deriving the right sort of sense out of Homer. Yet those who made this assumption when praising or teaching Homer to an audience of laypeople might make quite different ones when writing about textual or interpretative problems for an audience of scholars. Some individuals read their Homers in radically different ways at different times, as the logic of their situations and their own experience of Greek culture changed. And the potential for debate between individuals was considerable.

Sometimes the simplest of all scholarly methods, confrontation with the original sources, led humanists to question or modify ancient Homeric hermeneutics. Pseudo-Plutarch, whom Poliziano ransacked so thoroughly, explained at length that Homer had anticipated the doctrines of the major ancient philosophers. That was why so many of them had quoted or adapted Homeric tags. As Poliziano put it, "Whenever anyone argues about what should be the truth . . . , Homer is cited as an authority, as if it were impossible for anything to be other than as it appeared to Homer."[29] But Poliziano also knew the ancients who had cited Homer, and close examination of their practice sometimes revealed more complex literary filiations than 'Plutarch' would lead one to expect. In *Politics* 1253a, a famous passage, Aristotle described the man without a polis as either more or less than human:

Poetarum interpretes sibi caveant. Primo, ne τὰ ὁμολογουμένως ἱστορούμενα, ut Eustathius appellat, allegorica interpretatione corrumpant. . . ."

[28] See the classic essay by Eugenio Garin, "Le favole antiche."

[29] A. Levine Rubenstein, "The Notes to Poliziano's 'Iliad,' " 213–14, 224: "Quo effectum est ut qui de his rebus disputant cum quid verum esse volunt arguere, homerum testem adducant, quasi impossibile est, eam rem aliter se habere, atque homero visum sit."

—ὥσπερ καὶ ὁ ὑφ᾿ Ὁμήρου λοιδορηθεὶς "ἀφρήτωρ, ἀθέμιστος, ἀνέστιος·" ἅμα γὰρ φύσει τοιοῦτος καὶ πολέμου
ἐπιθυμητής—

—like the "clanless, lawless, hearthless" man reviled by Homer, for
a man who is by nature unsocial is also a "lover of war"—

Poliziano recognized the couplet Aristotle referred to (*Il.* 9.63-64):

ἀφρήτωρ, ἀθέμιστος, ἀνέστιός ἐστιν ἐκεῖνος
ὃς πολέμου ἔραται ἐπιδημίου ὀκρυόεντος.

Clanless, lawless, heartless is he who desires civil war, which chills
the soul.

Seeing also that Aristotle had not read these lines as a precise anticipation
of his own views, he wrote: "But Aristotle cites only one clause from
these verses. And he as it were takes Homer's opinion in reverse. For
Homer says that he who loves war lacks relatives, laws and home, while
Aristotle says that he who lacks relatives, laws, and home loves war and
is therefore a wicked man."[30] Poliziano drew no general conclusions (and
his observation remained unpublished until the late twentieth century).
But his greatest sixteenth-century admirer, Pier Vettori, both repeated
and refined it. He found yet another classical reference to the same tag in
the beginning of Cicero's *Philippic* 13:

Nam nec privatos focos nec publicas leges videtur nec libertatis iura
cara habere, quem discordiae, quem caedes civium, quem bellum
civile delectat.

Now it seems to me that a man who delights in discord, in massacres
of citizens, and in civil war holds dear neither our private hearths nor
our public laws nor the rights of freedom.

And unlike Poliziano, he explained the differences between the original
and Cicero's version in this way: "Cicero follows a different, or rather a
contrary, order. For he translates the poet's third word first, the second
next; as to the first, he did not give an equivalent for it because, I think,
it would not fit Roman customs. Instead of saying ["clanless"] he said

---

[30] A. Poliziano, *Miscellanea centuria secunda*, 95: "Sed eorum versuum tantum apud Aristotelem comma unum ponitur. Accipit autem ille quasi reciproce Homeri sententiam: nam,
cum carere eum cognatis, legibus, laribus Homerus dicat cui bellum sit cordi, contra Aristoteles bellum dicit ei esse cordi, atque ob id ipsum esse improbum hominem, qui cognatis,
legibus, laribus careat. . . ."

"libertatis iura cara non habere" [does not hold dear the rights of free-dom]. And one need not translate everything literally when tags like this are being rendered for inclusion in a speech or another text of that sort."[31]

The ancient biography claimed that the widespread presence of Homeric tags in later texts proved Homer's omniscience. But the modern scholars who compared specific Homeric quotations with the original learned exactly the reverse: that later writers had audiences, goals, and contexts that differed sharply from Homer's. They had found in him not a primeval wisdom that they could employ unchanged, but a lexicon of appealing phrases that they could appropriate and amend to their liking. The most unhistorical of all ancient versions of Homer, when checked against textual reality, could thus lead a Renaissance reader to a high level of historical insight into classical modes of citation and quotation.

Sometimes, too, the humanists found, in the relics of ancient Homeric scholarship, provocative hints that Homeric epic lay entirely outside the normal categories of classical texts. The hints were scanty enough, and the texts they appeared in have often been scathingly criticized as inaccurate by modern philologists. Yet these hints and stories supplied rich materials for the hermeneutical imagination to play with; and that imagination often put them to uses as striking as they are now unexpected.

Consider the *Poetics* of Julius Caesar Scaliger, the first full-scale modern treatment of the field, which appeared in 1561. Scaliger had read Aristotle's *Poetics* and knew that simple, unified poems were superior to complex, episodic ones. He also knew, from *Poetics* 1461, that ancient readers had found a good many flaws in Homer's version of epic: inappropriate adjectives, apparent contradictions, simple absurdities. He ignored Aristotle's caution that Glaucon had exposed such criticisms as captious, resting as they did on wrong assumptions about what the author had had in mind. Instead he took Aristotle's program for a defense of Homer as the basis for an attack. He compiled a long list of defects in the *Iliad* and *Odyssey*, subjecting Homer to a literary mugging that rivals Mark Twain's essay on Fenimore Cooper for both savagery and wit. Homer made the sun, who sees everything, miss the slaughter of his cattle. He made Priam ask the names of Greek heroes who had besieged his city for

---

[31] P. Vettori, *Variarum lectionum libri xxv* (Florence, 1553), 3: "Ordinem tamen diversum sequitur, vel contrarium potius: quod enim tertium est poetae verbum, primis ipse vertit: secundum autem sequentibus. Primum reddere atque exprimere non curavit: quod (ut arbitror) non responderet moribus atque institutis Romanorum: sed pro illo inquit libertatis iura cara non habere. Nec tamen exquisite cuncta interpretari necesse est, cum huiuscemodi loci vertuntur atque in oratione scriptove aliquo simili includuntur."

ten years. He made Odysseus strain to follow a sirens' song that would not have made Scaliger's cook dance. He made Achilles so effeminate that he wept and so poor that he could not afford a slave to brush the flies off Patroclus's body. The two epics were merely an awkward reworking of oral materials already traditional when Homer fused them together: "He was instructed by rustics and little old ladies in Ithaca and Chios and elsewhere in the tales that he inserted into his works."[32] Aristotle thus was made, against his own intentions, to denigrate Homer—and provide the basis for an exaltation of the more tasteful and sophisticated Virgil. And Homer was reduced to the low, but suggestive, position of a primitive.

Other humanists soon found ancient weapons with which to counter this attack. Obertus Giphanius, whose edition of Homer appeared in 1572, turned up in Josephus the argument that the Homeric texts were later than Near Eastern scriptures, and more corrupt as well, because they had originally been preserved orally as songs (*Contra Apionem* 1.2). Giphanius used this information about the transmission of the text to excuse its apparent flaws and incongruities: "Josephus warns us that some vestiges of the earlier contradictions remain in the texts, since some contradictions are found in Homer. One of these is perhaps the error criticized by Scaliger about the sun, who does not see his cattle being devoured even though he sees and hears everything else."[33] One could thus save the poet at the expense of admitting the imperfect state of his work—a step to be taken again and again in centuries to come.

But one could also reflect more systematically about the nature of the Homeric text and the context it sprang from—and by doing so rebut Scaliger's charges as unfair to the texts as well as to their author. Isaac Casaubon agreed with Giphanius that the epics must have undergone radical change in the course of centuries of oral transmission: "If what Josephus says is true, . . . then I do not see how [Homer's poems] could be had in a sufficiently correct form even if we should have the most ancient man-

[32] J. C. Scaliger, *Poetices libri septem* (Lyons, 1561), 11: "Neque vero Homerus ipse tam docuit vel Comoediam vel Tragoediam, quam est edoctus ab agrestibus atque aniculis in Ithaca et Chio et alibi, fabellas, quas operibus intertextas accommodaret." Needless to say, Scaliger showed a very different attitude towards the works—and wisdom—of his ideal epic poet, Virgil.

[33] *Homeri Ilias seu potius omnia eius quae extant opera*, O. Giphanius, ed. (Strassburg, 1572), 1, 15: "Confusionis quoque prioris vestigia quaedam esse reliqua monet Iosephus in Apionem, quod quaedam in Homero reperiantur inter se pugnantia. Quorum ex numero hoc sit fortasse quod taxat Scaliger de Sole, qui boves suos devorari non viderit, cum alia videat et audiat omnia."

uscripts, since they were probably written down quite differently from the way they had been composed by him."[34] But he still thought one could glean enough from other ancient sources about the poems and their author to prove that Scaliger's acerbic commentary was misguided. Scaliger had thought Homer's heroes far too plebeian: "One should not imitate Homer, who calls Achilles swift even when he was cooking."[35] Casaubon, however, found a long description of the daily life and customs of Homeric man in the *Deipnosophistae* of Athenaeus, which he edited. Book 1 of the epitome remarks that "with an eye to the seemly, Homer introduced his heroes feasting on meat alone. Moreover, they prepared it for themselves. For it means no ridicule or shame to see them getting a meal and cooking it. In fact, they practiced self-service from set purpose, and took pride, as Chrysippus says, in the dexterity they possessed in these matters" (1.18b, Loeb). As the appearance of the name Chrysippus suggests, Casaubon saw this passage as a Stoic moral allegory, an effort to make the apparent crudity of the heroes' customs evidence of their philosophical ἀταραξία. Deftly turning this unhistorical effort to explain away Homeric crudities into a historical effort to explain them in the light of the author's and his heroes' social context, he wrote: "I wish this had occurred to that excellent and—in my view—incomparable man who includes among his criticisms of Homer the fact that he represents Achilles carrying out servile tasks. In fact if any criticism is to be admitted here, it lies at the door of the age, not the poet. For poets imitate both true reality and what happens around them, and both the Bible and the ancient history of the pagans show that this is how men lived in those days."[36] The simple life of Homer's heroes thus became a lesson not in moral philosophy but in social history. Homer's primitivism became not a defect but a description—and a defense.

No wonder that Scaliger's, Giphanius's and Casaubon's comments

<hr>

[34] Quoted by F. A. Wolf, *Prolegomena*, ch. 39, n. 42.

[35] J. C. Scaliger, *Poetice*, 118: "Non ut Homerus, qui etiam coquinam procurantem Achillem vocat celerem."

[36] I. Casaubon, *Animadversionum in Athen. Dipnosophistas libri xv* (Lyons, 1621), 43: "Vellem istius venisset in mentem summo illi et iudicio meo incomparabili viro, qui in Homeri criminatione hoc quoque inter alia ei obiicit, quod Achillem inducat servilia saepe munera obeuntem. Enimvero si crimen hic ullum admissum, seculi non poetae crimen est; sunt enim poetae τῶν ὄντων καὶ τῶν γιγνομένων μιμηταί. Ita autem vixisse tum homines et sacrae testantur literae, et vetus τῶν ἔξωθεν historia comprobat." To be sure, Casaubon was not always so severely historical in viewpoint. He took Homer's version of the myth of Tantalus, for example, as a "vestigium . . . fugientis memoriae lapsus protoplasti hominis et expulsionis eius e Paradiso" (ibid., 58).

continued to attract the attention of seventeenth-century debaters over
the merits of the ancients and moderns like Mme Dacier and even of eighteenth-century philologists like Wolf. To a surprising extent, they ad-
umbrated the debating positions of the Neo-Classic age. Defenders of
modernity like Perrault would follow Scaliger's lead and abuse Homer
for his lapses in etiquette and taste, his princesses who did their own laun-
dry and his palaces that had dung piles before them. Defenders of Homer
would emulate Giphanius and Casaubon, arguing that the epics had been
corrupted in transmission and in any event imitated the realities of a simpler and a purer world. Humanist readings of the epic, not his own historical sense, still inspired Richard Bentley's famous effort to set the bard
into his context: "Homer wrote a sequel of Songs and Rhapsodies, to be
sung by himself for small earnings and good cheer, at Festivals and other
days of Merriment."[37] All these positions could be extracted, in the alem-
bics of imaginative readers like Giphanius and Casaubon, from the dried
and tattered remains of ancient response to Homer. From the ancient hermeneutical manuals, formal commentaries, and other scattered materials
mobilized in the sixteenth century, one could frame almost any imaginable interpretation of the canonical but alien text, from shattering critique
to unwavering defense.

Evidently, then, the classical heritage offered its Renaissance readers a
rich palette of interpretative colors, which they applied to Homer with
freedom and abandon. No single formula can do justice to their experience of ancient reactions to the *Iliad* and *Odyssey*. It seems reasonable to
close, accordingly, not with a thesis but with a vignette: a more detailed
study of how one mature Renaissance scholar used, abused, and confused
the many ancient readings of Homer that he studied. Guillaume Budé
came from a high bourgeois family long employed by the French state.
Trained in Roman law at Orléans and helped to study Greek by George
Hermonymus and Janus Lascaris, he won wealth and honor in the service
of Francis I and distinction in the European republic of letters. He pro-
moted the foundation of the lectureships that became the Collège Royal,
and he himself became the greatest Hellenist in Europe. His *Commentarii
linguae Graecae* of 1529 offered the first large-scale guide to Greek prose
usage based on direct observation of the texts.[38] And he produced a

---

[37] Quoted by F. A. Wolf, *Prolegomena*, ch. 27, n. 84.

[38] See in general P. G. Bietenholz and T. B. Deutscher, eds., *Contemporaries of Erasmus*,
vol. 1, article on Guillaume Budé, by M. M. de la Garanderie (with bibliography); an ele-
gant recent account of Budé's version of humanism can be found in T. Hampton, *Writing
from History*, 31–47.

stately series of learned works on the study of ancient culture and institutions, several of which included Homeric excursuses that became famous. His *Annotationes in Pandectas* of 1508, the first example of the distinctively historial approach to Roman law that became known as the *mos gallicus*, exposed Poliziano's plagiarism of pseudo-Plutarch. His *De Asse* of 1515, the first systematic study of ancient coinage, took Athena's restraint of Achilles in *Iliad* 1 as an allegorical statement of the principle that powerful men must be guided by wisdom and learning. And his late, troubled work *De transitu Hellenismi ad Christianismum*, which raised serious questions about the enterprise of Christian humanism, took *moly* as an allegorical representation of wisdom.

Budé's applications of allegoresis were not unusual. But they are uniquely rewarding for our purposes because another, complementary document enables us to see precisely how he arrived at them—and, more importantly still, how he used the ancient sources where he first encountered most of them. In 1949 a sumptuous two-volume copy of the first edition of Homer, published in 1488, was given to Princeton University Library. Local scholars soon discovered a fact known in the eighteenth century, when the book belonged to a private collection in Paris, but since forgotten. The rich Latin and Greek marginalia that adorn its pages are the work of Budé, whose arms an illuminator added to the beginnings of the *Iliad* and *Odyssey*.[39] The material in this book—one of the most striking documents of the entire French Renaissance—enables us to see exactly how Budé read classical texts and ancient interpretations, before his own strong tastes and prejudices had fused them into the finished statements of his books. It provides a vivid glimpse of the study of a Renaissance reader of Homer and his ancient readers.

The text of the first edition, as I have indicated, bore plenty of signposts for the serious reader to use in seeking the core of meaning concealed by the surface of the epics. It came, for example, with pseudo-Plutarch's treatise on *The Life and Writings of Homer*. Budé read this with as much

[39] J. H. Hanford, "An Old Master Restored: The Homeric Commentary of Guillaume Budé at Princeton." I compared the notes with the facsimiles of Budé's handwriting in L. Delaruelle, *Répertoire analytique et chronologique de la correspondance de Guillaume Budé*, and E. A. Lowe and E. K. Rand, *A Sixth-Century Fragment of the Letters of Pliny the Younger*; N. G. Wilson generously guided me in this task. There seems to be no doubt of the authenticity of the notes in Princeton, and it is easy to distinguish Budé's notes from the much scantier ones of another, unidentified annotator. For Budé's working copies of classical texts see the excellent study by V. Juren, "Fra Giovanni Giocondo et le début des études vitruviennes en France," with bibliography.

care as the texts it introduced. 'Plutarch' argues (ch. 92) that the ancient sages had set out their deepest thoughts in poetic form because by doing so they both pleased the learned and baffled the ignorant, who could not despise what they did not understand. Budé marked the passage boldly and applied it frequently to the Homeric text, testing and embellishing 'Plutarch' 's own detailed allegories as he went. At 129, for example, 'Plutarch' explicates Athena's restraint of Achilles as a physical allegory of the bipartite soul and a moral one of the opposition between prudence and anger. At *Iliad* 1.193 Budé referred back to this interpretation in a marginal note. And in *De Asse* he worked a restatement of it into a prominent position in his argument that even aristocrats must study. Here he described the Homeric scene as a "memorabile figmentum ac memoria etiam atque etiam tenendum" [a memorable fiction, unceasingly to be kept in mind]; and he summed up its message in terms that pseudo-Plutarch had not used but would almost certainly have accepted: "Those who lack wisdom and prudence cannot carry out great deeds in war and peace."[40]

Pseudo-Plutarch, however, was far from the only ancient reader who helped Budé penetrate between the lines, and some of the results he drew from his more recondite sources were hardly obvious. In 102 'Plutarch' explains that the battle of the gods in *Iliad* 21 teaches a lesson about natural oppositions. The combat of Athena and Ares, in particular, stands for the conflict of τὸ λογιστικὸν τῷ ἀλογίστῳ, τουτέστι τὸ ἀγαθὸν τῷ κακῷ [the rational against the irrational, which is to say, good against evil]. Budé here offered in the margin, as he often did, a brief summary in Greek: περὶ τῆς τῶν θεῶν παρατάξεως παρὰ τῷ ποιητῇ [about the poet's juxtaposition of the gods in battle], as well as a reference to *Iliad* 21. At the margin of 21.410 he repeated and expanded on 'Plutarch' 's allegoresis:

> Recte autem Mars id est impetus a sapientia vincitur: et iniusta causa a iusta: mars denique ex faemina tantum natus: a pallade ex viro tantum nata et armata. vide Plut supra. . . .

> And rightly is Mars (that is, violent force) defeated by wisdom, and the wrong cause by the right—and Mars, finally, who was born only of a female, by Pallas, born of and armed uniquely by a male. See Plutarch above. . . .

---

[40] Guillaume Budé, *Opera omnia*, 2, 23. For a contrasting treatment, see Erasmus's adage "Festina lente" (*Adagia* II.i.1).

The curious point here is not the general tenor of Budé's note but the specific addition that he makes to 'Plutarch': that the offspring of a male only, Athena, rightly defeated the offspring of a female only, Ares. This is incorrect mythology: Ares was hardly a wise child, but he knew his own father. It does not come from pseudo-Plutarch. And Eustathius— whom Budé cites elsewhere—says correctly that Athena was born of a male alone, ἐξ ἀνδρὸς μόνου, and Ares of a female *as well* [as a male], καὶ ἐκ γυναικός. No manuscript of Eustathius seems to have dropped the καί, and Budé could hardly have misconstrued the passage. Accordingly, he must have used a source as rare as it was wrong or misleading. And in fact the error identifies it precisely. The b scholia observe on this passage: ἔστι γὰρ ἡ μὲν ἐξ ἀνδρὸς μόνου, ὁ δὲ ἐκ γυναικός [She is born from a male only, he from a female]. The exegetical scholia were of course still unpublished, as they would long remain; but apparently Budé had some access to their wealth of curious ideas about Homer's undermeanings— and the politics and culture of his day.[41]

More surprisingly still, Budé also had a source of information about the unique Alexandrian material in Venetus A. He used the obelus, frequently, as a *signe de renvoi*. More revealingly, he used information from the A scholia to reconstruct the Alexandrians' efforts to athetize the inappropriate bits of the *Iliad*. Many scholars knew in general from pseudo-Plutarch that Aristarchus had put Homer's works into order. But from the scholia Budé drew specific facts about this project: for example, that Aristarchus had athetized Paris's challenge to the Greeks:

Quod nec arma habet monomachiae apta: et absurdum est hominem timidissimum omnes simul fortissimos provocasse.

Because he had no weapons fit for a duel, and it is absurd for the most cowardly of men to challenge all the bravest at once.

To be sure, Budé did not consider A necessarily superior to b; in this case, for example, he used the interpretation found in the bT scholia to refute the Alexandrians' criticism:

---

[41] Naturally Renaissance scholars did not view the exegetical scholia with the contempt of their modern successors. See, e.g., C. Hornei's preface to his edition of the T scholia on *Iliad* 9 (Helmstedt, 1620), dedicatory epistle: "Totae enim occupatae fere sunt, non tam in vocum explanatione quam in observationibus et monitis rhetoricis, ethicis, et politicis ex poeta deducendis, quam opt. et tantum non unicam esse interpretandi poetas rationem nemo ignorat nisi et quid sit poetica ignoret."

Aliqui sic interpretantur: προκαλίζετο πάντας ἀρίστους τῶν τρώων, ἀντίβιον μαχέσασθαι τῶν ἀργείων. et recte sic accipiunt [on *Il.* 3.19].

Some interpret this as follows: "He called upon all the bravest" of the Trojans, "to do battle against" the Argives. And they are right to understand it in this way.

Yet from our point of view, the value of Budé's conclusions matters less than the richness of his sources. Whatever his immediate sources—perhaps a manuscript compilation by his friend Lascaris, though not Lascaris's own annotated Homer (BAV Inc. I.50), another copy of the first edition, which swarms with notes that do not match Budé's—they glittered with interpretative gold and pyrites that did not become the public property of scholars until the eighteenth century. Working with manuscript sources alone, Budé tasted every flavor of ancient Homeric criticism, from the most fanciful allegoresis to the most austere textual criticism.

Budé did not limit himself to sources that modern scholarship takes seriously. He read Dio and summarized in his margin the passage in which Dio describes how hard he finds it to decide between those who explicate Homer's gods allegorically and those who condemn them as immoral. He read pseudo-Herodotus as well. This life treats Homer not as an inspired moralist but as a wandering bard. It offers biographical contexts for his compositions, usually by back-formation—a process nowadays much decried. Budé, however, accepted pseudo-Herodotus's method and results. 'Herodotus' explains the name Homer as a reference to the poet's blindness, "since the Cymeans call blind men ὅμηροι. And so the man who was previously called Melesigenes acquired the name Homer (13)."[42] Budé summarized this passage and added a specific reference to "book 8 of the *Odyssey*, where he mentions Demodocus."[43] He thus showed that he had learned from ancient example to read the texts as autobiography as well as philosophy.

Sometimes, too, Budé enriched the tradition of Homeric exegesis with materials originally alien to it. At *Iliad* 20.307–08, for example, he writes:

Poeta hic praesagit Romanum imperium. nam licet antiquior ipse roma fuerit: potuit tamen hoc praescivisse vaticiniis sibyllarum aut aliis oraculis. hunc autem versum καὶ παῖδες παίδων ferunt ho-

---

[42] I use the translation by Mary R. Lefkowitz in her *The Lives of the Greek Poets*.

[43] "Vide odyss. 8ο ubi τοῦ δημοδόκου meminit." On *Od.* 9.63–64 Budé writes δημόδοκος and adds one of his standard *signes de renvoi*, a pointing hand.

merum ab orpheo accepisse, orpheum ab oraculo quodam apollinis. ab homero deinde virg. et nati natorum et qui nos ab il. [*Aeneid* 3.98].

Here the poet gives an intimation of the Roman empire. For although he was himself earlier than Rome, he could nevertheless have had a premonition of this by the prophecies of the Sibyls or of other oracles. They say that Homer got this verse, "and his sons' sons" from Orpheus, and that Orpheus got it from some oracle of Apollo. Then from Homer, Virgil: "And the sons of his sons and those that will be born from them."

Budé could find a reference to a Homeric prophecy of Rome's future in the bT scholia, which also explained that the poet had derived this enlightenment ἐκ τῶν Σιβύλλης χρησμῶν [from the Sibyl's prophecies]. But the remainder of the literary genealogy he offered came not from the Greek but from the Latin scholarly tradition, as represented by Servius on *Aeneid* 3.98: "Sane hic versus Homeri est, quem et ipse de Orpheo sustulit, item Orpheus de oraculo Apollinis Hyperborei." [This verse is clearly from Homer, and he received it from Orpheus, and Orpheus from the oracle of Hyperborean Apollo.] Evidently Budé's ancient world, like that of the *grammaticus urbis Romae*, had room for inspired pagan prophets—at least at the relatively early period, before 1508, when he compiled these notes.

For all the meticulousness that Budé showed as he recorded and combined ancient readings, however, he evidently considered himself bound *nullius in verba*. Juxtaposition of original notes and finished literary texts often shows him adapting or rejecting ideas that he had originally taken down with literal accuracy. In the margin of his working copy of the *Odyssey*, for example, he explains the marvellous plant *moly* exactly as Eustathius had, as a gift of the god Hermes:

Ἔστι δὲ θεόσδοτον ἀγαθόν. ἀλληγορεῖται δὲ πρὸς τὴν παιδείαν. ὁ Ἑρμῆς ἐκφαίνει ταῖς λογικαῖς μεθόδοις. . . . (cf. Eustathius on *Od.* 10.306)

And it is a god-given good. Allegorically, it designates education. Hermes reveals [it] by rational procedures. . . .

But when he returned to the passage in the late *De transitu*, his assumptions about the validity of pagan culture—and the inspiration and morality of pagan poets—had shifted. He therefore interpreted the same text in quite a different sense. The greatest scholars, he said, had held that by the

name *moly* Homer had referred to wisdom: "This man, the most clever
of mortals, thought wisdom so powerful that it could restore the characters of men which had degenerated into brute and animal-like or bovine
states to themselves and to humanity."[44] But he himself refuted this traditional view as the inadequate one of mere pagans: "If that can be said of
Greek philosophy, which is really an invention of mortals, how much
more appropriately can we attribute it to the divine teachings? Among
the great differences between Homer's *moly* and ours is this: His is drawn
from the earth and human inventiveness, ours from the wells of celestial
wisdom."[45] In this finished account, Budé ignores the central point he had
taken from the more optimistic Eustathius in his original note: Homer
too portrayed *moly* as a divine gift, not a human invention. In fact, this
text would seem to make a more plausible basis for Christian allegoresis
than—for example—the passage between Achilles and Athena in *Iliad* 1,
which Budé did allegorize as a younger man. Evidently he felt entirely
able to modify his hermeneutical sources when they did not meet his
needs or fit his prejudices of the moment.

In the end, Budé had no doubt that he, not the ancient allegorists, was
in charge. In the earliest of his substantial discussions of Homer, that in
the *Annotationes in Pandectas*, he offered no allegoresis even though he
wished to forge a defense of the study of poets, which his fellow lawyers
had disparaged, and allegory and the defense of poetry went naturally
together. He made fun of Poliziano for plagiarizing pseudo-Plutarch's
demonstration that Homer contained all knowledge. And he offered his
own, quite individual account of the Plutarchan life. Here he said nothing
at all about Homer the Encyclopedist. Instead he quoted a single passage
that he had already marked in his working copy, 216, where Plutarch
describes Homer as the master of painters as well as poets, because of his
ability to represent every sort of animal from lions to pigs, and to compare them appropriately to men.[46] Did Budé's emphasis on Homer the
Painter represent a rejection of Poliziano's Homer the Philosopher?

[44] G. Budé, *De transitu Hellenismi ad Christianismum*, 179–80: "Sub nomine autem molyos
herbae Homerus philosophiae doctrinam significasse symbolice creditur a doctissimis.
Cuius vim eam esse (ut volunt) arbitratus est ille vir mortalium ingeniosissimus eamque
facultatem, mores ut hominum degeneres et efferatos aut veterinarios factos atque pecu-
arios, sibi tandem illa naturaeque humanae restitueret."

[45] G. Budé, *De transitu*, 180: "Id quod si de Hellenica philosophia dictum est, quae mortalium revera inventum fuit, quanto nos congruentius id tribuere divinae disciplinae potui-
mus? Inter moly enim nostrum atque illud Homericum cum plurimum, tum hoc refert,
quod illud e puteis sapientiae coelestis, hoc e terra effoditur humanisque inventis."

[46] G. Budé, *Opera*, 3, 212. In his copy of Homer, Budé writes ὅμηρος ζωγραφίας δι-
δάσκαλος and ἡ ποιητικὴ ζωγραφία λαλοῦσα by ps.-Plutarch 216.

Certainly one collateral piece of evidence suggests as much. Budé's copy of one of the most systematic of all Renaissance allegorical commentaries, Landino's *Disputationes Camaldulenses* (Florence, n.d.), is preserved in the Bibliothèque Nationale (Rés. Z 1059). Its margins summarize Landino's explication of Virgil point by point, with single words, phrases, and occasional pointing hands—all normally signs of interest and often of assent. But sometimes summary yields to dissent—and even contradiction. Landino explains that Mary does her work with the mind alone, which is immortal and incorruptible; Martha does hers with the senses, which men share with animals. That is why Mary is told that she has chosen "the best part [*optimam partem*] which shall not be taken away from her." Budé's marginal note reads, "graece non optimam sed bonam legitur. quare tu falso argumentaris"—"In the Greek text the reading is 'good,' not 'best.' Therefore your deduction is false [sig. c iii verso]." Elsewhere he questions Landino's etymological explanation of the name Gerion as *terrae litem*: "but there is an eternal struggle of the earth, that is, the body against the spirit." Budé in this case preferred a less instructive but more accurate etymology: "Cum hoc sensu pugnat orthographia. geryones enim scribitur γηρυόνης—" "The spelling conflicts with this interpretation, since Geryon is spelled γηρυόνης [in Greek, from γηρύω, 'sing'] [sig. h. verso]." Even Landino's allegories, in short, elicited a range of responses from Budé; no wonder that he did not simply accept the far more richly varied Homeric readings that he encountered in treatises, scholia, and commentaries.

One striking feature of Budé's response to Homer's ancient readers, then, is its flexibility. Another is its immediacy. Like many of the great sixteenth-century humanists, Budé won more respect than affection. His rather chilly formality emerges well from the famous remark that he made to the servant who came to tell him, at his wife's request, that their house was on fire, "Kindly inform your mistress that domestic matters are her affair." Yet his shifting and intimate responses to Homer's exegetes show a more flexible and responsive personality than the anecdote leads one to expect. So do those of his marginal notes to pseudo-Plutarch and Homer, which take the form not of Greek phrases or obeli but of skillful caricatures of the faces of gloomy scholars.[47] And so, more interestingly still, do some of the curious sparks that the ancient readers struck from Budé's imagination as he worked through them. In chapter 30 of pseudo-Herodotus, Homer meets women sacrificing to a goddess. The

[47] Budé's copy of Vitruvius (Paris BN Rés. V.318) also bears many splendid illustrations by him.

priestess, annoyed, says "Man, get away from our rites." Homer asks which god she is sacrificing to. When told it is the protectress of children, he utters an extemporaneous prayer in verse: "Hear me, as I pray, Protectress of Children, grant that this woman reject love and sex with young men, but let her delight in old men with grey brows whose strength has been blighted, but whose hearts still feel desire."[48] Beside these verses Budé has entered not a summary but an expression of strong interest: a pointing hand and the words σημειώσαι ταῦτα τὰ ἔπη [note these verses]. The ancient anecdote evidently echoed his hopes—or fears?—about his own much younger wife, whom he married at the then ripe age of thirty-seven.

This fresh and serious response to a text that now seems comic should, I think, serve as a lesson. Budé did not need Paul Veyne to teach him to listen when the Greeks told stories about their heroes and traditions, however foolish an individual witness might seem. He knew that all branches of the ancient scholarly tradition had to be studied before any of them was cut off. He read Homer's ancient readers with the care, the attention, and the willingness to argue that he brought to any other ancient text. And he found in them the same rewards and excitements that he found in the epics they dealt with. His approach, which most of his contemporaries shared, demands attention and respect. I wonder if it is merely a historian's ignorance that leads me to suspect that it might repay imitation as well.

[48] The translation is that of M. R. Lefkowitz, *The Lives of the Greek Poets*, 151.

* Contributors *

ROBERT BROWNING is Professor Emeritus of the University of London and a Fellow of the British Academy. His books include *Justinian and Theodora*; *The Emperor Julian*; *Byzantium and Bulgaria*; *Studies on Byzantine History, Literature and Education*; *History, Language, and Literature in the Byzantine World*; and *Medieval and Modern Greek*; and he is editor of *The Greek World: Classical, Byzantine and Modern*.

ANTHONY GRAFTON is Professor of History at Princeton University. He is author of *Joseph Scaliger, A Study in the History of Classical Scholarship, 1: Textual Criticism and Exegesis*, as well as numerous articles on the Renaissance humanists. He is also co-translator of F. A. Wolf's *Prolegomena to Homer*, and co-editor of *The Uses of Greek and Latin: Historical Essays*.

JOHN J. KEANEY, a co-editor of this volume, is Professor of Classics at Princeton University. He is the author of numerous articles on classical philology, manuscript tradition, and textual criticism, with particular emphasis on Aristotle and Theophrastus. He is the author of the forthcoming *The Composition of Aristotle's* Athenaion Politeia: *Observation and Explanation* and a new edition of the *Lexeis* of Harpocration.

ROBERT LAMBERTON, a co-editor of this volume, is Assistant Professor of Classics at Princeton University. He is author of *Homer the Theologian* and *Hesiod*, and translator of *Porphyry on the Cave of the Nymphs*. He is currently working on Plutarch and problems of ancient hermeneutics.

A. A. LONG is Professor of Classics at the University of California, Berkeley. His books include *Language and Thought in Sophocles, Hellenistic Philosophy*, and (with D. N. Sedley) *The Hellenistic Philosophers*, and he is editor of *Problems in Stoicism*.

JAMES I. PORTER is Assistant Professor of Classics at the University of Michigan, Ann Arbor. He is author of *The Material Sublime. Towards a Reconstruction of Materialist Critical Discourse and Aesthetics in Antiquity* (diss. Berkeley, 1986), which he is currently revising, and of articles on Philodemus and Hellenistic poetics.

N. J. RICHARDSON is a Fellow and Tutor of Merton College, Oxford. Aside from his annotated edition of *The Homeric Hymn to Demeter*, he has written several articles on the interpretation of the *Iliad* and *Odyssey* in antiquity, including "Homeric Professors in the Age of the Sophists."

CHARLES SEGAL is Professor of Classics at Harvard University. Among his most recent books are *Pindar's Mythmaking*; *Orpheus, the Myth of the Poet*; and *Lucretius on Death and Anxiety*. His numerous articles span the range of classical literature.

* Bibliography *

NOTE: The following bibliography includes those books and articles to which reference is made in the text, but does not include complete bibliographical information on editions of classical and Byzantine authors, with the exception of those editions cited repeatedly or for the comments of their editors. In these instances, the edition will be found under the name of the editor. In general, works published before 1700 are not listed here (unless as reprints), and relevant bibliographical information for such works will be found ad loc. in the notes.

Allen, D. C. *Mysteriously Meant: The Rediscovery of Pagan Symbolism and Allegorical Interpretation in the Renaissance.* Baltimore: Johns Hopkins Univ. Press, 1970.

[Anon., ed.] "Der orphische Papyrus von Derveni," *Zeitschrift für Papyrologie und Epigraphik* 47 (1982): 1–12 (in a new pagination sequence following p. 300).

Austin, Norman. *Archery at the Dark of the Moon: Poetic Problems in Homer's Odyssey.* Berkeley: Univ. of California Press, 1975.

Ax, Wolfram. "Aristarch und die 'Grammatik,' " *Glotta* 60 (1982): 96–109.

Bachelard, Gaston. *La Poétique de l'espace.* 2d ed. Paris: Presses Universitaires de France, 1957.

Bachmann, Wilhelm. *Die ästhetischen Anschauungen Aristarchs in der Exegese und Kritik der homerischen Gedichte.* 2 vols. Nuremberg: Programm des Alten Gymnasiums, 1902–04.

Barthes, Roland. *The Pleasure of the Text.* Richard Miller, tr. New York: Hill & Wang, 1975.

Beck, Hans-Georg. *Geschichte der byzantinischen Volksliteratur.* Vol. 3 of Part 2 of the *Byzantinisches Handbuch,* itself the 12th section of the *Handbuch der Altertumswissenschaft* (Iwan von Müller, ed., succeeded by Walter Otto and Hermann Bengtson). Munich: Beck, 1971.

Benjamin, Walter. *Illuminationen: Ausgewählte Schriften.* Frankfurt: Suhrkamp, 1977.

Berger, Hugo. *Geschichte der wissenschaftlichen Erdkunde der Griechen.* Leipzig: Veit, 1903.

Bergren, Anne. "Helen's 'Good Drug': *Odyssey* iv, 1–305," 201–14 in S. Kresic, ed., *Contemporary Literary Hermeneutics and Interpretation of Classical Texts.* Ottawa: Univ. of Ottawa Press, 1981.

Bertolini, Francesco, "Dal folclore all'epica: esempi di trasformazione e adattamento," 131–52 in D. Lanza and O. Longo, eds., *Il meraviglioso e il verosimile tra antichità e medioevo.* Biblioteca dell' "Archivum Romanicum," ser. I, 221. Florence: Olschki, 1989.

———. "Odisseo aedo, Omero carpentiere: *Odissea* 17.384–85," *Lexis* 2 (1988): 145–64.

Bietenholz, P. G., and T. B. Deutscher, eds. *Contemporaries of Erasmus: A Bio-*

graphical Register of the Renaissance and Reformation. 3 vols. Toronto: Univ. of Toronto Press, 1985–87.

Binder, G. "Eine Polemik des Porphyrios gegen die allegorische Auslegung des Alten Testaments durch die Christen," Zeitschrift für Papyrologie und Epigraphik 3 (1968): 81–95.

Blank, David L. "Remarks on Nicanor, the Stoics, and the Ancient Theory of Punctuation," Glotta 61 (1983): 48–67.

Bleicher, T. Homer in der deutschen Literatur (1450–1740). Zur Rezeption der Antike und zur Poëtologie der Neuzeit. Stuttgart: Metzler, 1972.

Bolgar, R. R. The Classical Heritage and Its Beneficiaries. Cambridge: Cambridge Univ. Press, 1954.

Brendel, Otto J. Symbolism of the Sphere: A Contribution to the History of Earlier Greek Philosophy. Maria W. Brendel, tr. Leiden: Brill, 1977.

Browning, Robert. "Homer in Byzantium," Viator 6 (1975): 15–33.

Budé, Guillaume. De transitu Hellenismi ad Christianismum (1535). M. Lebel, ed. and tr. Centre d'études de la Renaissance de l'Université de Sherbrooke. Sherbrooke, Quebec: Ed. Paulines, 1973.

———. Opera omnia [1557]. 4 vol. Rpt. Farnborough: Gregg International, 1966.

Buffière, Félix. Les Mythes d'Homère et la pensée grecque. Paris: Les Belles Lettres, 1956.

———, ed. Héraclite: Allégories d'Homère. Paris: Les Belles Lettres (Budé), 1962.

Bühler, Winfried. Beiträge zur Erklärung der Schrift vom Erhabenen. Göttingen: Vandenhoeck & Ruprecht, 1964.

Carroll, M. Aristotle's Poetics ch. xxv in the Light of the Homeric Scholia. Diss. Johns Hopkins, 1895.

Cave, Terence. The Cornucopian Text: Problems of Writing in the French Renaissance. Oxford: Oxford Univ. Press, 1979.

———. Recognitions: A Study in Poetics. Oxford: Oxford Univ. Press, 1988.

———, M. Jeanneret and F. Rigolot. "Sur la prétendue transparence de Rabelais," Revue d'histoire littéraire de la France 86 (1986): 709–16.

Chladenius, Johann Martin. De praestantia et usu scholiorum Graecorum diatribe prima. Wittenberg: Eichsfeld, 1732.

———. Einleitung zur richtigen Auslegung vernünftiger Reden und Schriften [1742]. Facsimile rpt. Instrumenta Philosophica, Series Hermeneutica, 5. Düsseldorf: Stern, 1969.

Cinquemani, A. M. "Henry Reynolds' Mythomystes and the Continuity of Ancient Modes of Allegoresis in Seventeenth-Century England," Publications of the Modern Language Association 85 (1970): 1041–49.

Clarke, Howard. Homer's Readers: A Historical Introduction to the Iliad and the Odyssey. Newark: Univ. of Delaware Press, 1981.

Collart, Paul. "Les Papyrus de l'Iliade [1]," Revue de Philologie 6 (1932): 315–49; [2] Revue de Philologie 7 (1933): 33–61.

Coulter, James A. *The Literary Microcosm: Theories of Interpretation of the Later Neo-platonists.* Columbia Studies in the Classical Tradition, 2. Leiden: Brill, 1976.

Dachs, Hans. *Die λύσις ἐκ τοῦ προσώπου. Ein exegetischer und kritischer Grundsatz Aristarchs und seine Neuanwendung auf Ilias und Odyssee.* Diss. Erlangen, 1913.

Dawson, D. *Allegorical Readers and Cultural Revision in Ancient Alexandria.* Berkeley: Univ. of California Press, forthcoming.

Defaux, G. "D'un problème à l'autre: herméneutique de l'*altior sensus* et *captatio lectoris* dans le Prologue de *Gargantua*," *Revue d'histoire littéraire de la France* 85 (1985): 195–216.

————. "Sur la prétendue pluralité du Prologue de 'Gargantua,' " *Revue d'histoire littéraire de la France* 86 (1986): 716–22.

De Lacy, Phillip. "Stoic Views of Poetry," *American Journal of Philology* 69 (1948): 241–71.

Delaruelle, L. *Répertoire analytique et chronologique de la correspondance de Guillaume Budé.* Toulouse and Paris: Champion, 1907.

Demerson, G. "Dorat, commentateur d'Homère," 223–34 in *Etudes seiziémistes offertes à V.-L. Saulnier.* Geneva: Droz, 1980.

Desmaizeaux, P. *Scaligerana.* Amsterdam: Covens and Mortier, 1740.

Diels, Hermann. *Doxographi graeci.* 4th ed. 1879. Rpt. Berlin: De Gruyter, 1965.

Dillon, John M., ed. *Iamblichi Chalcidensis in Platonis dialogos commentariorum fragmenta.* Philosophia antiqua, 23. Leiden: Brill, 1973.

Duckworth, George E. *Foreshadowing and Suspense in the Epics of Homer, Apollonius, and Vergil.* Princeton: Princeton Univ. Press, 1933.

————. "ΠΡΟΑΝΑΦΩΝΗΣΙΣ in the Scholia to Homer," *American Journal of Philology* 52 (1931): 320–38.

Duval, E. M. "Interpretation and the 'Doctrine absconce' of Rabelais' Prologue to *Gargantua*," *Etudes rabelaisiennes* 18 (1985): 195–216.

Dyck, A. R., ed. *Epimerismi Homerici, I: Epimerismos continens qui ad Iliadis librum A pertinent.* Sammlung griechischer und lateinischer Grammatiker, 5.1. Berlin: De Gruyter, 1983.

Engberg, Sysse. "Greek Literacy and Liturgical Books," *Epsilon* 2 (1988): 31–41.

Erasmus, Desiderius. *On Copia of Words and Ideas.* D. B. King and H. Rix, trs. Milwaukee: Marquette Univ. Press, 1963.

Erbse, Hartmut. *Beiträge zum Verständnis der Odyssee.* Berlin: De Gruyter, 1972.

————. *Beiträge zur Überlieferung der Ilias-Scholien.* Zetemata, 24. Munich: Beck, 1960.

————. "Über Aristarchs Iliasausgaben," *Hermes* 87 (1959): 275–303.

————. "Zur normativen Grammatik der Alexandriner," *Glotta* 58 (1980): 236–58.

————, ed. *Scholia Graeca in Homeri Iliadem (scholia vetera).* 7 vols. Berlin: De Gruyter, 1969–88.

Farron, S. G. "The Odyssey as Anti-Aristocratic Statement," *Studies in Antiquity* 1 (1979–80): 50–101.

Finsler, Georg. *Homer in der Neuzeit von Dante bis Goethe.* 1912. Rpt. Hildesheim: Georg Olms, 1973.

Ford, P. "Conrad Gesner et le fabuleux manteau," *Bibliothèque d'Humanisme et Renaissance* 47 (1985): 305–20.

Frede, Michael. "Chaeremon der Stoiker," ANRW 2.36.3 (1989): 2067–2103.

———. "The Origins of Traditional Grammar," 338–59 in his *Essays in Ancient Philosophy.* Minneapolis and Oxford: Univ. of Minnesota Press and Oxford Univ. Press, 1987.

———. "Principles of Stoic Grammar," 301–37 in his *Essays in Ancient Philosophy.* Minneapolis and Oxford: Univ. of Minnesota Press and Oxford Univ. Press, 1987.

Frontisi-Ducroux, Françoise. *La Cithare d'Achille.* Rome: Ed. dell'Ateneo, 1986.

Frye, Northrop. *The Anatomy of Criticism: Four Essays.* 1957. Rpt. New York: Athenaeum, 1967.

Furley, David. *The Greek Cosmologists, 1: The Formation of the Atomic Theory and Its Earliest Critics,* Cambridge: Cambridge Univ. Press, 1987.

Gaisford, T. *Georgii Choerobosci Dictata in Theodosii Canones, necnon Epimerismi in Psalmos.* Oxford: 1842.

Gallavotti, Carlo. "Tracce della Poetica di Aristotele negli scolii omerici," *Maia* 21 (1969): 203–14.

Garbrah, Kweka A. "The Scholia on the Ending of the Odyssey," *Würzburger Jahrbücher für die Altertumswissenschaft* NF 3 (1977): 7–16.

Garin, Eugenio. "Le favole antiche," 63–84 in his *Medioevo e Rinascimento.* Rome and Bari: Laterza, 1973.

Gisinger, F. "Oikumene (1)." P-W 17, 2123–74.

Goldhill, Simon. "Reading Differences: The *Odyssey* and Juxtaposition," *Ramus* 17 (1988): 1–31.

Grafton, Anthony. "*Prolegomena* to Friedrich August Wolf," *Journal of the Warburg and Courtauld Institutes* 44 (1981): 101–29.

Grivec, F., and F. Tomšič. *Constantius et Methodius Thessalonicenses: Fontes.* Radovi staroslavenskog Instituta, Knjiga 4. Zagreb: Palaeoslavic Institute, 1960.

Groningen, B. A. van. "ΕΚΔΟΣΙΣ," *Mnemosyne* 16 (1963): 1–17.

Grube, G. M. A. *The Greek and Roman Critics.* Toronto: Univ. of Toronto Press, 1965.

Gudeman, A. "Κριτικός." P-W 11, 1912–15.

———. "Λύσεις." P-W 13, 2511–29.

Hahm, D. E. *The Origins of Stoic Cosmology.* Columbus: Ohio State Univ. Press, 1977.

Halliwell, Stephen. *Aristotle's Poetics.* Chapel Hill and London: Univ. of North Carolina Press and Duckworth, 1986.

Hampton, Timothy. *Writing from History: The Rhetoric of Exemplarity in Renaissance Literature.* Ithaca: Cornell Univ. Press, 1990.

Hanford, J. H. "An Old Master Restored: The Homeric Commentary of Guillaume Budé at Princeton," *Princeton University Library Chronicle* 18 (1956), 1–10.

Hardie, Philip R. "*Imago Mundi*: Cosmological and Ideological Aspects of the Shield of Achilles," *Journal of Hellenic Studies* 105 (1985): 11–31.

————. *Virgil's Aeneid: Cosmos and Imperium*. Oxford: Oxford Univ. Press, 1986.

Havelock, Eric A. *The Literate Revolution in Greece and Its Cultural Consequences*. Princeton: Princeton Univ. Press, 1982.

————. *Preface to Plato*. Cambridge: Harvard Univ. Press, 1963.

Heath, Malcolm. *Unity in Greek Poetics*. Oxford: Oxford Univ. Press, 1989.

Helck, Johannes. *De Cratetis Mallotae studiis criticis, quae ad Iliadem spectant*. Diss. Leipzig, 1905.

————. *De Cratetis Mallotae studiis criticis, quae ad Odysseam spectant*. Dresden: Programm des Gymnasiums zum heiligen Kreuz, 1914.

Henrichs, Albert. "Die Kritik der stoischen Theologie im PHerc. 1428," *Cronache Ercolanesi* 4 (1974): 5–32.

————. "Philosophy, the Handmaiden of Theology," *Greek, Roman and Byzantine Studies* 9 (1968): 437–50.

Hepp, Noémi. "Homère en France au xvie siècle," *Atti della Accademia delle Scienze di Torino, Classe di scienze morali, storiche e filologiche* 96 (1962): 389–508.

————. *Homère en France au xviie siècle*. Bibliothèque française et romane (Strasbourg), Etudes Littéraires, 18. Paris: Klincksieck, 1968.

Herington, C. J. *Poetry into Drama: Early Tragedy and the Greek Poetic Tradition*. Sather Classical Lectures, 49. Berkeley: Univ. of California Press, 1985.

Hermann, Godfried, ed. *Draconis Stratonicensis liber de metris poeticis et Io. Tzetzae exegesis in Homeri Iliadem*. Leipzig: Weigel, 1812.

Hilgruber, Michael. "Dion Chrysostomos 36 (53) und die Homerauslegung Zenons," *Museum Helveticum* 46 (1989): 15–24.

Hintenlang, H. *Untersuchungen zu den Homer-Aporien des Aristoteles*. Diss. Heidelberg, 1961.

Howes, G. E. "Homeric Quotations in Plato and Aristotle," *Harvard Studies in Classical Philology* 6 (1895): 153–237.

Hunger, Herbert. *Hochsprachliche profane Litaratur der Byzantiner*. Part 5 of the *Byzantinisches Handbuch*, itself the 12th section of the *Handbuch der Altertumswissenschaft* (Iwan von Müller, ed., succeeded by Walter Otto and Hermann Bengtson). 2 vols. Munich: Beck, 1978.

Innes, D. C. "Gigantomachy and Natural Philosophy," *Classical Quarterly* 29 (1979): 165–71.

Janko, Richard. *Homer, Hesiod and the Hymns: Diachronic Development in Epic Diction*. Cambridge: Cambridge Univ. Press, 1982.

————, tr. *Aristotle*, Poetics I *with the* Tractatus Coislinianus; *A Hypothetical Reconstruction of* Poetics II; *The Fragments of the* On Poets. Indianapolis: Hackett, 1987.

Jeffreys, E. M. "Constantine Hermoniakos and Byzantine Education," Δωδώνη 4 (1975): 81–109, rpt. in E. M. Jeffreys and M. J. Jeffreys, eds., *Popular Literature in Late Byzantium*. London: Variorum, 1983.

Jensen, Christian, ed. *Philodemus über die Gedichte, fünftes Buch*. Berlin: Weidmann, 1923.

Juren, V. "Fra Giovanni Giocondo et le début des études vitruviennes en France," *Rinascimento*, ser. II, 14 (1974): 101–15.

Kapsomenos, S. G. "The Orphic Papyrus Roll of Thessalonica," *Bulletin of the American Society of Papyrologists* 2 (1964): 3–14 [discussion: 15–31].

Kassel, Rudolf. "Antimachos in der Vita Chisiana des Dionysios Periegetes," 69–76 in C. Schäublin, ed., *Catalepton. Festschrift für Bernhard Wyss zum 80. Geburtstag*. Basel: Seminar für klassische Philologie der Universität, 1985.

Kazhdan, A., and S. Franklin. *Studies in Byzantine Literature of the Eleventh and Twelfth Centuries*. Cambridge-Paris: Cambridge Univ. Press and Ed. de la Maison des Sciences de l'Homme, 1984.

Kepler, Johannes. *Gesammelte Werke*. Munich: Beck, 1937.

Kidd, I. G. *Posidonius II: The Commentary*. Cambridge: Cambridge Univ. Press, 1988.

Kindstrand, Jan Fredrik. *Homer in der zweiten Sophistik*. Acta Universitatis Upsaliensis; Studia Graeca Upsaliensia, 7. Uppsala: Univ. of Uppsala, 1973.

———, ed. *Isaac Porphyrogenitus, Praefatio in Homerum*. Uppsala and Stockholm: Almqvist and Wiksell, 1979.

———, ed. *[Plutarchus] De Homero*. Leipzig: Teubner, 1990.

Kourouses, St. I. Μανουὴλ Γαβαλᾶς. Athens: Myrtides, 1972.

Kroll, W. "Krates (16)." P-W 11, 1634–41.

Labarbe, Jules. *L'Homère de Platon*. Bibliothèque de la Faculté de Philosophie et Lettres de l'Université de Liège, fasc. 117. Liège: Faculté de Philosophie et Lettres, 1949.

Lamberton, Robert. *Homer the Theologian, Neoplatonist Allegorical Reading and the Growth of the Epic Tradition*. The Transformation of the Classical Heritage, 9. Berkeley: Univ. of California Press, 1986.

———. [review of Malcolm Heath, *Unity in Greek Poetics*]. *Ancient Philosophy* 11, 2 (1991), forthcoming.

———, tr. *Porphyry on the Cave of the Nymphs*. Barrytown, NY: Station Hill Press, 1983.

Lang, K., ed. *Cornuti theologiae graecae compendium*. Leipzig: Teubner, 1881.

Laurenti, R. "L'iponoia di Antistene," *Rivista critica di Storia della Filosofia* 17 (1962): 123–32.

Leaf, Walter, ed. *The Iliad*. 2 vols. London: Macmillan, 1886–88.

Lefkowitz, Mary R. *The Lives of the Greek Poets*. Baltimore: Johns Hopkins Univ. Press, 1981.

Legrand, E. *Constantin Hermoniacos, La Guerre de Troie*. 1890. Rpt. Athens: B. N. Gregoriades, 1974.

Lehrs, K. *De Aristarchi studiis homericis*. 2d ed. Leipzig: Hirzel, 1865.

———, ed. *Herodiani scripta tria emendatiora*. Königsberg: Samter, 1848.

Lemmi, Charles. *The Classic Deities in Bacon. A Study in Mythological Symbolism*. Baltimore: Johns Hopkins Univ. Press, 1933.

Levine Rubenstein, A. "The Notes to Poliziano's 'Iliad,' " *Italia Medioevale e Umanistica* 25 (1982): 205–39.

Lloyd, G. E. R. *Magic, Reason, and Experience: Studies in the Origin and Development of Greek Science*. Cambridge: Cambridge Univ. Press, 1979.

Lolos, A. *Der unbekannte Teil der Ilias-Exegese des Johannes Tztezes (A97–609)*. Königstein: Heim, 1981.

Long, A. A. "Stoa and Sceptical Academy. Origins and Growth of a Tradition," *Liverpool Classical Monthly* 5.8 (1980): 161–74.

———, and D. N. Sedley. *The Hellenistic Philosophers*. 2 vols. Cambridge: Cambridge Univ. Press, 1987.

Lord, George deF. *Homeric Renaissance: The Odyssey of George Chapman*. New Haven: Yale Univ. Press, 1956.

Lowe, E. A., and E. K. Rand. *A Sixth-Century Fragment of the Letters of Pliny the Younger: A Study of Six Leaves of an Uncial Manuscript Preserved in the Pierpont Morgan Library, New York*. Washington: Carnegie Institute, 1922.

Lucas, D. W., ed. *Aristotle. Poetics*. Oxford: Oxford Univ. Press, 1968.

Ludwich, Arthur. *Aristarchs homerische Textkritik nach den Fragmenten des Didymos dargestellt und beurtheilt*. 2 vols. Leipzig: Teubner, 1884–85.

Maass, Ernst, ed. *Commentariorum in Aratum Reliquiae*. Berlin: Weidmann, 1958.

Markus, Ralph A. "St. Augustine on Signs," *Phronesis* 2 (1957): 60–83.

McNamee, Kathleen. "Aristarchus and 'Everyman's' Homer," *Greek, Roman, and Byzantine Studies* 22 (1981): 247–55.

Meijering, Roos. *Literary and Rhetorical Theories in Greek Scholia*. Groningen: Forsten, 1987.

Mette, Hans Joachim. "Krates von Pergamon 1953–83," *Lustrum* 26 (1984): 95–104.

———. *Parateresis: Untersuchungen zur Sprachtheorie des Krates von Pergamon*. Halle: Niemeyer, 1952.

———. *Sphairopoiia: Untersuchungen zur Kosmologie des Krates von Pergamon*. Munich: Beck, 1936.

Moffatt, Ann. "The Occasion of St. Basil's Address to Young Men," *Antichthon* 6 (1972): 74–86.

Monsacré, Hélène. *Les Larmes d'Achille. Le héros, la femme, et la souffrance dans la poésie d'Homère*. Paris: Albin-Michel, 1984.

Morris, Ian. "The Use and Abuse of Homer," *Classical Antiquity* 5 (1986): 81–138.

Morrison, James V. *Homeric Misdirections: False Predictions in the Iliad*. Diss. Univ. of Michigan, 1988.

Most, Glenn W. "Cornutus and Stoic Allegoresis: A Preliminary Report," *ANRW* 2.36.3 (1989): 2014–65.

Müller, Konrad. "Allegorische Dichtererklärung," P-W Supplementband 4, 16–22.

Murnaghan, Sheila. *Disguise and Recognition in the Odyssey*. Princeton: Princeton Univ. Press, 1987.

Murrin, Michael. *The Allegorical Epic: Essays in Its Rise and Decline*. Chicago: Univ. of Chicago Press, 1980.

Nagy, Gregory. *Pindar's Homer. The Lyric Possession of an Epic Past*. The Mary Flexner Lectures, Bryn Mawr College, 1982. Baltimore: Johns Hopkins Univ. Press, 1990.

Nardelli, M. L., ed. *Due trattati filodemei "Sulla poetica." Ricerche sui papiri ercolanesi*, vol. 4. Naples: Giannini, 1983.

Newton, Rick M. "Odysseus and Hephaestus in the *Odyssey*," *Classical Journal* 83 (1987): 12–20.

Nickau, Klaus. *Untersuchungen zur textkritischen Methode des Zenodotos von Ephesos*. Berlin: De Gruyter, 1977.

Nolhac, P. de. *Ronsard et l'humanisme*. Paris: Champion, 1921.

Nørgaard, Lars and Ole L. Smith. *A Byzantine Iliad: The Text of Par. Supp. Gr. 926*. Copenhagen: Museum Tusculanum, 1975.

Olson, S. Douglas. "*Odyssey* 8: Guile, Force and the Subversive Poetics of Desire," *Arethusa* 22 (1989): 135–45.

Ong, Walter J. *Orality and Literacy. The Technologizing of the Word*. London: Methuen, 1982.

Pease, Arthur Stanley, ed. *Ciceronis De Natura Deorum*. 2 vols. Cambridge: Harvard Univ. Press, 1955–58.

Petersen, Christian, ed. *Phaedri Epicuraei, vulgo Anonymi Herculanensis, De natura deorum fragmenta*. Hamburg: Programm des akademischen Gymnasiums, 1833.

Pfeiffer, Rudolf. *History of Classical Scholarship From the Beginnings to the End of the Hellenistic Age*. Oxford: Oxford Univ. Press, 1968.

———. *History of Classical Scholarship From 1300 to 1850*. Oxford: Oxford Univ. Press, 1976.

———. "*Philologia Perennis*." Festrede. Munich: Bayerische Akademie der Wissenschaften, 1961.

Poliziano, Angelo. *Miscellanea centuria secunda*. V. Branca and M. Pastore Stocchi, eds. (ed. minor) Florence: Olschki, 1978.

Porter, James I. "Content and Form in Philodemus: The History of an Evasion," forthcoming.

———. "Philodemus on Material Difference," *Cronache Ercolanesi* 19 (1989), 149–78.

Pötscher, Walter. "Das Selbstverständnis des Dichters in der Homerischen Poesie," *Literaturwissenschaftliches Jahrbuch* NF 27 (1986): 9–22.

Poulet, Georges. *Metamorphoses du cercle*. Paris: Plon, 1961.

Pucci, Piero. *Hesiod and the Language of Poetry*. Baltimore: Johns Hopkins Univ. Press, 1977.

————. *Odysseus Polutropos: Intertextual Readings in the Odyssey and the Iliad.* Cornell Studies in Classical Philology, 46. Ithaca: Cornell Univ. Press, 1987.

————. "The Song of the Sirens," *Arethusa* 12 (1979): 121–32.

Puelma, Mario. "Der Dichter und die Wahrheit in der griechischen Poetik von Homer bis Aristoteles," *Museum Helveticum* 46 (1989): 65–100.

Quilligan, Maureen. *The Language of Allegory: Defining the Genre.* Ithaca: Cornell Univ. Press, 1979.

Raaflaub, Kurt. "Die Anfänge des politischen Denkens bei den Griechen," 189–271 in *Pipers Handbuch der politischen Ideen*, I. Fetscher and H. Münkler, eds., vol. 1. Munich and Zurich: Piper, 1988.

Rahner, Hugo. *Griechische Mythen in christlicher Deutung.* Zurich: Rhein-Verlag, 1945.

Reinhardt, Carl. *De Graecorum theologia capita duo.* Berlin: Weidmann, 1910.

Richardson, N. J. "The Contest of Homer and Hesiod and Alkidamas' *Mouseion*," *Classical Quarterly* 31 (1981): 1–10.

————. "Homeric Professors in the Age of the Sophists," *Proceedings of the Cambridge Philological Society* 21 (1975): 65–81.

————. "Literary Criticism in the Exegetical Scholia to the *Iliad*: A Sketch," *Classical Quarterly* 30 (1980): 265–87.

————. "Recognition Scenes in the *Odyssey* and Ancient Literary Criticism," *Papers of the Liverpool Latin Seminar* 4 (1983): 219–35.

Römer, Adolph. *Aristarchs Athetesen in der Homerkritik.* Leipzig: Teubner, 1912.

————. *"Die Homercitate und die Homerischen Fragen des Aristoteles,"* *Sitzungsberichte der königlichen bayerischen Akademie der Wissenschaften* 1884, 264–314.

————. *Die Homerexegese Aristarchs in ihren Grundzügen,* E. Belzner, ed. Paderborn: Schöningh, 1924.

Rose, Valentinus, ed. *Aristoteles psuedepigraphus.* Leipzig: Teubner, 1863.

————, ed. *Aristotelis qui ferebantur librorum fragmenta.* Leipzig: Teubner, 1886.

Rosenmeyer, Thomas G. *DEINA TA POLLA. A Classicist's Checklist of Twenty Literary-Critical Positions.* Arethusa Monographs, 12. Buffalo: State Univ. of New York Press, 1988.

————. "Design and Execution in Aristotle, *Poetics* ch. xxv," *California Studies in Classical Antiquity* 6 (1973): 231–52.

Rossi, Paolo. *Francis Bacon: From Magic to Science.* S. Rabinovich, tr. Chicago: Univ. of Chicago Press, 1968.

Russell, D. A. *Criticism in Antiquity.* Berkeley: Univ. of California Press, 1981.

————, ed. *'Longinus' On the Sublime.* Oxford: Oxford Univ. Press, 1964.

————, and M. Winterbottom, eds. *Ancient Literary Criticism. The Principal Texts in New Translations.* Oxford: Oxford Univ. Press, 1972.

Rusten, Jeffrey S. "Interim Notes on the Papyrus from Derveni," *Harvard Studies in Classical Philology* 89 (1985): 121–40.

Saïd, Suzanne. "Les crimes des prétendants, la maison d'Ulysse et les festins de l'Odyssée," 9–49 in S. Saïd et al., *Etudes de littérature ancienne*. Paris: Presses de l'Ecole normale supérieure, 1979.

Sbordone, Francesco, ed. *Philodemi de poematis. Ricerche sui papiri ercolanesi*, vol. 2. Naples: Giannini, 1976.

Schadewaldt, Wolfgang. *Von Homers Welt und Werk*. 4th ed. Stuttgart: K. F. Koehler, 1965.

Schäublin, Christoph. "Homerum ex Homero," *Museum Helveticum* 34 (1977): 221–27.

Schenkeveld, D. M. "Strabo on Homer," *Mnemosyne* 29 (1976): 52–64.

Schibli, Hermann S. *Pherekydes of Syros*. Oxford: Oxford Univ. Press, 1990.

Schlachter, Alois. *Der Globus. Seine Entstehung und Verwendung in der Antike*, F. Gisinger, ed. Στοιχεῖα, Studien zur Geschichte des antiken Weltbildes und der griechischen Wissenschaften, 8. Leipzig: Teubner, 1927.

Schlunk, Robin R. *The Homeric Scholia and the Aeneid. A Study of the Influence of Ancient Literary Criticism on Vergil*. Ann Arbor: The Univ. of Michigan Press, 1974.

Schmidt, Martin. *Die Erklärungen zum Weltbild Homers und zur Kultur der Heroenzeit in den bT-Scholien zur Ilias*. Zetemata, 62. Munich: Beck, 1976.

Schoell, Frank L. *Etudes sur l'humanisme continental en Angleterre*. Paris: Champion, 1926.

Schrader, Hermann, ed. *Porphyrii Quaestionum Homericarum ad Iliadem pertinentium reliquias*. 2 fasc. Leipzig: Teubner, 1880–82.

———, ed. *Porphyrii Quaestionum Homericarum ad Odysseam pertinentium reliquias*. Leipzig: Teubner, 1890.

Scully, Stephen. "The Bard as the Custodian of Homeric Society: *Odyssey* 3.263–72," *Quaderni Urbinati di Cultura Classica* 37 (= NS 8) (1981): 67–83.

Segal, Charles. "Andromache's Anagnorisis: Formulaic Artistry in *Iliad* 22.437–76," *Harvard Studies in Classical Philology* 75 (1971): 33–57.

———. "*Kleos* and Its Ironies in the *Odyssey*," *L'Antiquité Classique* 52 (1983): 22–47.

———. *Pindar's Mythmaking: The Fourth Pythian Ode*. Princeton: Princeton Univ. Press, 1986.

———. "Ritual and Commemoration in Early Greek Poetry and Tragedy," *Oral Tradition* 4 (1989): 330–59.

———. "Theater, Ritual, and Commemoration in Euripides' *Hippolytus*," *Ramus* 17 (1988): 52–74.

Seznec, Jean. *The Survival of the Pagan Gods. The Mythological Tradition and Its Place in Renaissance Humanism and Art*. B. F. Sessions, tr. New York: Harper, 1953.

Sheppard, Anne D. R. *Studies on the 5th and 6th Essays of Proclus' Commentary on the Republic*. Hypomnemata, 61. Göttingen: Vandenhoeck and Ruprecht, 1980.

Simonsuuri, Kirsti. *Homer's Original Genius: Eighteenth-Century Notions of the Early Greek Epic*. Cambridge: Cambridge Univ. Press, 1979.

Snodgrass, Anthony. *Archaic Greece: The Age of Experiment*. Berkeley: Univ. of California Press, 1980.

———. *The Dark Age of Greece: An Archaeological Survey of the Eleventh to the Eighth Centuries B.C.* Edinburgh: Univ. of Edinburgh Press, 1971.

Solmsen, Friedrich. "Beyond the Heavens," *Museum Helveticum* 33 (1976): 24–32.

Spengel, Leonard, ed. *Rhetores graeci*. 3 vols. Leipzig: Teubner, 1853–56.

Spingarn, J. E., ed. *Critical Essays of the Seventeenth Century*. 3 vols. Oxford: Oxford Univ. Press, 1908–09.

Stanford, W. B. *Enemies of Poetry*. London: Routledge and Kegan Paul, 1980.

Steinmetz, Peter. "Allegorische Deutung und allegorische Dichtung in der alten Stoa," *Rheinisches Museum* 129 (1986): 18–30.

Stewart, Andrew F. "Narration and Illusion in the Hellenistic Baroque," in Peter Holliday, ed., *Narrative and Event in Ancient Art*. Cambridge: Cambridge Univ. Press, 1992.

Stewart, Douglas. *The Disguised Guest. Rank, Role and Identity in the Odyssey*. Lewisburg, Pa.: Bucknell Univ. Press, 1976.

Stokes, Francis Griffin, ed. *Epistolae obscurorum virorum*. London: Chatto & Windus, 1909.

Svenbro, Jesper. *La Parole et le marbre, Aux origines de la poétique grecque*. Diss. Lund, 1976.

Szondi, Peter. *Einführung in die literarische Hermeneutik*, J. Bollack and H. Stierlin, eds. Frankfurt: Suhrkamp, 1975.

Tate, J. "The Beginnings of Grek Allegory," *Classical Review* 41 (1927): 214–15.

———. "Cornutus and the Poets," *Classical Quarterly* 23 (1929): 41–45.

———. "On the History of Allegorism," *Classical Quarterly* 28 (1934): 105–14.

———. "Plato and Allegorical Interpretation [1]," *Classical Quarterly* 23 (1929): 142–54; [2], *Classical Quarterly* 24 (1930): 1–10.

Thalmann, William G. *Conventions of Form and Thought in Early Greek Poetry*. Baltimore: Johns Hopkins Univ. Press, 1984.

Theseus, Nicolaos. Ὁμήρου Ἰλιὰς μετὰ παλαιᾶς παραφράσεως ἐξ ἰδιοχείρου τοῦ Θεοδώρου Γαζῆ. Florence: Nicolaos Carlis, 1811.

Tigerstedt, E. N. *The Decline and Fall of the Neoplatonic Interpretation of Homer*. Commentationes Humanarum Litterarum, 52. Helsinki: Societas Scientiarum Fennica, 1954.

Trendelenberg, Adolf. *Grammaticorum Graecorum de arte tragica iudiciorum reliquiae*. Diss. Bonn, 1867.

Uhden, Richard. "Die Weltkarte des Martianus Capella," *Mnemosyne* 3 (1936): 97–124.

Usener, Hermann, ed. *Epicurea* [1887]. Rpt. Studia philologica, 3. Rome: Bretschneider, 1963.

Valk, Marchinus van der. *Researches on the Text and Scholia of the Iliad*. 2 vols. Leiden: Brill, 1963–64.

Valk, Marchinus Van der, ed. *Eustathius, Commentarii ad Homeri Iliadem pertinentes ad fidem codicis Laurentiani editi.* Leiden: Brill, 1971–87.

Vasoli, C. "Leonardo Bruni," 618–33 in vol. 14 of *Dizionario biografico degli Italiani.* Rome: Instituto della Enciclopedia Italiana, 1972.

Vernant, J.-P. "Figures féminines de la mort en Grèce," 131–52 in his *L'Individu, la mort, l'amour.* Paris: Gallimard, 1989.

Vicaire, Paul. *Platon, critique littéraire.* Etudes et Commentaires, 34. Paris: Klincksieck, 1960.

Wachsmuth, Curt. *De Cratete Mallota disputavit adiectis euis reliquis.* Leipzig: Teubner, 1860.

Wachsmuth, R. *De Aristotelis studiis Homericis capita selecta.* Diss. inaug. Berlin, 1863.

Walsh, George. *The Varieties of Enchantment: Early Greek Views of the Nature and Function of Poetry.* Chapel Hill: Univ. of North Carolina Press, 1984.

Walz, Christian, ed. *Rhetores Graeci.* 9 vols. in 10. Stuttgart: Cotta, 1832–36.

Wehrli, Fritz. *Zur Geschichte der allegorischen Deutung Homers im Altertum.* Diss. inaug. Basel. Borna-Leipzig: R. Noske, 1928.

Weinstock, S. "Die Platonische Homerkritik und seine Nachwirkung," *Philologus* 82 (1926–27): 121–53.

West, M. L. *The Orphic Poems.* Oxford: Oxford Univ. Press, 1983.

West, Stephanie. *The Ptolemaic Papyri of Homer.* Papyrologica Coloniensia, 3. Cologne: Westdeutscher Verlag, 1967.

Whitman, Cedric H. "Hera's Anvils," *Harvard Studies in Classical Philology* 74 (1970): 37–42.

Wolf, F. A. *Prolegomena to Homer [1795].* A. Grafton, G. W. Most, and J. E. G. Zetzel, trs. Princeton: Princeton Univ. Press, 1985.

Wyatt, William F., Jr. "The Intermezzo in Odyssey 11 and the Poets Homer and Odysseus," *Studi Micenei ed Egeo-Anatolici* 27 (1989): 235–53.

Yates, Frances. A. *The French Academies of the Sixteenth Century.* London: Routledge, 1947.

Zumthor, Paul. *La Poésie et la voix dans la civilisation médiévale.* Collège de France: Essais et Conférences. Paris: Presses Universitaires de France, 1984.

* Index *